A Paris Symphony

Musical Life in 19th Century France

A personal view by

Shlomo Hed

A PARIS SYMPHONY

Musical Life in
19th Century France

A personal view by

SHLOMO HED

SAMUEL WACHTMAN'S SONS   DEKEL PUBLISHING HOUSE

A Paris Symphony - *Musical Life in 19th Century France*

Shlomo Hed

Copyright © 2013

Dekel Publishing House
www.dekelpublishing.com

North American rights by
Samuel Wachtman's Sons, Inc.
ISBN 978-1-888820-56-0

Chief editor:	Hugo N. Gerstl
Language editing:	Katie Roman

Cover image
Paris © Mrusty, Dreamstime.com

Cover design and typesetting by

DESIGN PEAKS®

For information contact:

Dekel Publishing House	**Samuel Wachtman's Sons, Inc.**
P.O. Box 45094	2460 Garden Road, Suite C
Tel Aviv 61450, Israel	Monterey, CA 93940, U.S.A.
Tel: +972 3506-3235	Tel: 831 649-0669
Fax: +972 3506-7332	Fax: 831 649-8007
Email: info@dekelpublishing.com	Email: samuelwachtman@gmail.com

TO ADA

Ada radiated light and nobility. Her humanism and integrity were equaled only by her boundless empathy for everyone who surrounded her. During the days we worked together in the Music Department of the Israel Broadcasting Authority we collaborated on several projects. The most ambitious and the most rewarding of them was the series *Dod le Madame Bizet* in 1985. And that was the primer for this book, which is, naturally, dedicated to her.

Ada Brodsky died on April 12, 2011.

In loving memory.

Shlomo Hed

TABLE OF CONTENTS

GENESIS

This is a book for music lovers. In order to write it I had to witness several people die in improbable circumstances. Alkan, Bizet, César Franck, and Chausson all passed away following unusual mishaps.

But I have also had the privilege to resuscitate an obscure banker from the slush pile of history and rescue him from the greedy claws of oblivion.

The miniseries *Heine's Legacy*, which I produced in the framework of my weekly program *The Art of the Lied*, was broadcast in December 1984. Ada Brodsky's help in supplying outstanding translations for the poems had been, as usual, invaluable. In the wake of that program, Brodsky asked me to cooperate with her on a program she was considering on the subject of Heine in Paris.

Ada Brodsky was born in Frankfurt-on-the-Oder (the one in the east, not the larger and much more famous Frankfurt-am-Main). She was fourteen when she arrived in Israel and it took her no time to gain a masterly command of the Hebrew language. Her many-faceted creative activities bore the imprint of the cultural background on which she had been reared: the poetry of Goethe and Schiller and the musical world of Bach and Beethoven. During the years she worked for the radio she produced many biographical programs on the lives and works of the great composers.

Then she decided to dedicate herself mainly to literary work. She published several books of Hebrew translations, mainly in the field of the art song. But her achievements in this field were crowned by her triumphant monograph on the poet Rainer-Maria Rilke.

After an exchange of views, the project expanded into a series dealing with the Grand Opéra and cultural life in Paris during the first half of the nineteenth century. I came up with the idea that instead of our usual approach of relating facts and reading letters, we should use an imaginary diary written by some hypothetical eyewitness, a puppet we could create according to our needs.

We started reading everything we could find surrounding this topic and we sat for days in the National Library of Israel at the Hebrew University, taking notes and gathering material, until one day, by some fluke, I stumbled upon a remarkable person, a retired stockbroker whose sister had married the composer Fromental Halévy. This person, called Jacob Hippolyte Rodrigues-Henriques, was born in 1812 and died at the ripe old age of eighty-six in 1898. This was way beyond the scope we had originally intended to give to our series but there was one important thing that tipped the scales in favor of making him our puppet: he was also an amateur composer. And indeed we made him the hub of our program, as he would be the one who could sketch a reliable description of the cultural atmosphere in nineteenth-century Paris. Brodsky would write most of the text and coach the many speakers and actors who would participate in the recordings, while I would do most of the research and take charge of the musical illustrations for the programs.

And this brought us to Paris, Brodsky and me, in order to do some sleuthing and take a trip of a century and a half into the past.

In Paris we visited many of the places that played such an important role in the musical life of the nineteenth century. We went to the Palais Garnier (Opéra National de Paris), the Salle Favart (Opéra-Comique) and Offenbach's Bouffes-Parisiens. We attended the Conservatoire and the Salle Pleyel.

But I think that the most memorable visits we made were to the school on the rue des Blancs-Manteaux, that elementary school where Charles Alkan's father had taught solfeggio and rudiments of grammar and arithmetic to children living in the Marais, and to the places where most of the people we would talk about in our series were buried, the Montmartre and the Père Lachaise cemeteries.

In the Montmartre Cemetery we found the graves of Hector Berlioz, Fromental Halévy, Pauline Viardot, Charles Valentin Alkan, and several other dear and important personalities. But at the tombs of Offenbach and Heine we made special stops to collect ourselves.

In the Père Lachaise Cemetery we found the graves of Chopin, Bizet, Daudet, Delacroix, Auber, Rossini, and Bellini. In the Jewish plot of this cemetery we found the vault of the Rodrigues-Henriques family; and some fifty meters from there, in the non-Jewish part, there was another vault marked with the name Rodrigues-Henriques—and it was conspicuously topped with a cross!

We spent days without end at the Bibliothèque nationale de France (it was still situated on the rue de Richelieu) gathering important material. But when we visited the library of the Conservatoire we were in for a big surprise. We were shown several sheets of music written by Jacob Hippolyte Rodrigues and I actually held in my hands a huge manuscript score of his opera *David Rizzio*. We were also told that the Prix Rodrigues still existed but the amount of the prize had not changed since it was founded and was still (at the time of our visit) 1,500 francs, which was a ridiculously paltry sum. But during the first half of the nineteenth century that was a substantial pile of money.

Back in Israel we feverishly started recording the series of twenty-six programs called *Dod le Madame Bizet* (Madame Bizet's uncle), which was broadcast starting mid-summer 1985.

This is an imaginary diary kept by Hippolyte Rodrigues. The facts and dates relating to the works and lives of the composers and other people in this book are, as far as I have been able to ascertain, accurate. The involvement of the characters with Hippolyte Rodrigues is, in most cases, pure fiction (except for his ties with the Halévy family, which are a historical fact).

Over twenty years elapsed before I decided it was time to reshuffle all that material and try to present it to the English-speaking public. Here it is. If you enjoy reading it half as much as I have enjoyed writing it, this will amply justify all the work I have put into it.

Shlomo Hed
Jerusalem
July 2013

INTRODUCTION

My original diary was, of course, written chronologically. But here I have tried to edit it in such a way as to have every part of it center about a well-defined topic, mostly an exceptional personality. This is why some events will be reported more than once (for instance the happenings in Baden-Baden at the time of the premiere of *Béatrice et Bénédict* appear both in connection with Bizet getting entangled in a fight, and when I write about Berlioz's last years).

I also very often, in complete disregard for grammatical consistency, mix past tense and present tense. This, I feel, portrays the difference between the evaluation of an impression left in the moment and an impression as seen through the distance of time, and the copying of entire passages, almost word for word, from my original sources.

The political and social changes that have occurred in the (more or less) seventy years covered by this diary have had a deep influence on our everyday life, on our consciousness of the world, and on our general outlook on life and its ultimate goal.

I would like to suggest a conclusion summing up the creative urges that have driven our nineteenth century toward the twentieth century that will soon be dawning upon the next generation. This is pure conjecture and only a matter of wildly guessing at future events (though my guesses are, of course, based on actual trends). I have a deeply rooted feeling that our culture is rushing headlong toward an impasse. I feel that some artists are going to suggest new ways of expression; some of them will certainly turn back to the past for inspiration and others will be as revolutionary in their outlook as to be ungraspable at first, thus driving their converts to clash with society. But, naturally, I won't be here to witness this. What a pity…it will undoubtedly be enthralling.

Jacob Hippolyte Rodrigues

Paris, September 5, 1892

1

Prelude to Act 1

To present the facts in the right perspective I want to point out my ties with the Halévy family and through them to Bizet. I grasp this occasion to give a brief review of my family's history.

According to the tradition passed from mouth to ear, generation after generation, my forefathers left the Holy Land in 133 AD after the Bar-Kokhba revolt and emigrated to Portugal, then to Spain. In 1495 the family fled the horrors of the Inquisition and found refuge in Bordeaux, on the beautiful Garonne River, in southwestern France. My father, Isaac Henriques-Rodrigues, inherited the thriving family banking firm that was the cornerstone of the fortune I made when I entered the sanctuary of Mammon, la Bourse, the Paris stock exchange. My mother, Esther (née Gradis), came from a family whose trade was shipbuilding. Their contribution to the expanding and strengthening of the French fleet in the eighteenth century was such that King Louis XVI bestowed upon them a title of nobility. The implementation of this was made impossible when my forefather found out that he would have to swear allegiance on the Holy Bible, "their" Bible, containing the New Testament, and that, of course, was out of the question.

I was born in Bordeaux on August 5, 1812 (one year to the day after Ambroise Thomas!), the eighth of my parents' nine children, and despite having become a Parisian I still look upon that city as my homeland. Anytime I need a vacation, or whenever there is work to be done for which I need seclusion and introspection, I either go back to Bordeaux, to the ancient family house in town, or to the Château de Fromont, the beautiful mansion I acquired in Champrosay, in the midst of the soft hills some twenty kilometers south of Paris.

My father decided to leave Bordeaux in 1819, when I was seven, because he was convinced that Paris was a much better place to give his children a modern education, without prejudice to the Jewish upbringing and learning of Hebrew that I had started in the small synagogue of Bordeaux, and was to follow now in the capital.

Paris had been out of bounds for Jews for centuries, and only some five hundred of them lived there illegally until the Revolution. But when Napoleon granted the Jews civil rights and equality, they started swarming into the city, not only from all corners of France but from Germany and even from distant Poland and Russia.

My eldest sister, Eugénie Esther Rebecca, had left home a few years prior to our leaving Bordeaux. She was sixteen when I was born, and she married the Jewish Genoese merchant Joseph Eugène Foa in 1814, when I was only two years old. Foa left her soon after the birth of their second son, and she struggled hard to raise her family. She came to live with us on the rue de Montholon for a short while. She became quite famous as a writer, under her married name, Eugénie Foa, and under the pseudonym of Maria Fitz-Clarence. In the late thirties she came under the influence of the Abbé Ratisbonne and converted to

Catholicism; since then, and until her death in 1856, our relations had become quite icy.

One year after we settled in Paris, in 1820, my sister Hannah Léonie was born.

In such a large family, in our new surroundings, I had rather a lot of time to myself and spent most of it in the company of my classmates, mainly young Jewish boys my own age. Our school, a private institution situated on the rue des Blancs-Manteaux, opposite the Église Saint-Gervais, was run by M. Morhange. His eldest son, one year my junior, was to become the famous composer and pianist Charles Alkan, and our lifelong friendship dates from those school days when we ran and played on the grounds of the small park opposite the schoolhouse.

In 1826 my father died; that is when my mother decided to move to the big apartment on the rue de Montholon, to the same building where two of my uncles, Henri and Édouard Rodrigues, already lived with their numerous family members. Édouard's son, Olinde, was the foremost disciple of Saint-Simon, and with him one of the founders of socialism. After having received, together with Prosper Enfantin, Saint-Simon's last instructions, my cousin Olinde established the newspaper *Le Producteur* and started the political movement that grew into a sect with followers all over France.

In the same building also lived the two Pereira brothers, the financial wizards who amassed one of the greatest fortunes in the Second Empire. The elder brother, Émile, married one of Olinde's sisters. He soon became a staunch follower of the Saint-Simonians and under his brother-in-law's influence he grew more and more convinced of man's rule over nature and its treasures. Under the guidance of the revered teacher he foresaw a vast network of railways reaching the far end of the world that would bring civilization to every forsaken corner—nay, that would help transform the remotest spots on earth into animated and lively centers! In this dream thousands of factories would sprout like mushrooms from the earth, and people from all social strata would work in them, side by side, in an outburst of brotherly joy and creativity, and would join forces in forwarding progress and guaranteeing the prosperity of their country; this would indeed be a decisive step toward man's redemption and salvation.

Émile Pereira and his younger brother Isaac found a mighty ally on their way to achieving their dreams in Napoleon III, when he became emperor of France. This was the man who in 1844 published an essay on the abolition of poverty, called "L'Extinction du paupérisme," and the support he gave the Saint-Simonians' cause, and the Pereira brothers more specifically, was to assure their way to success.

Since my father's death in 1826 my mother managed the family business with the help of a professional staff that my father had the foresight to install as a management committee. But, as a matter of fact, I was expected to take over when I would, as was hoped, get my law degree. Sure enough, on my twenty-first birthday, the three of us—my mother, my youngest sister, and I—went south to Bordeaux where a solemn meeting of the management committee was held at which I was installed as executive head of the banking firm Les fils d'A. Rodrigues. As a neighbor of the Pereira brothers I wasted no time learning from them the art of making wise investments. In spite of my natural inclinations drawing me toward art and research, I was caught in the turmoil of my business activities. Those were the days when we all believed salvation was at hand and a new and better world was in the making. I became a tiny wheel in the gigantic mechanism of success and failure, profit and loss, the real size of which I was at that time unable to fathom. So, armed with the know-how I had acquired from the Pereira brothers and the financial backing of the respected family banking enterprise, I became one of the familiar faces at the Paris stock exchange, and, quickly enough, a very wealthy man—a pillar of society. In fact, more due to luck than wisdom or insight, I gathered substantial capital. This made it possible for me at the ripe old age of forty-three, after twenty-two years in the service of Mammon, to relinquish the family business to the hands of a management committee, just as my father had done thirty years before, until my son Edgar could take the reins. I could now devote all my time to the two fields that I had always seen as my calling: music and theology. Looking back on things now, and knowing what happened after the stock market boom, I got out of the game two years or so before things began to go sour. But this, of course, is just more proof that my friends are right in calling me Happy Hippo.

I am a God-fearing man, and I have come closer to religion as I've grown in age and wisdom. Still, I am a staunch believer in luck—so much so that I am firmly convinced that luck is an inherited trait, a strain that has run in my mother's family for as long as we can remember. Yes, I know, people say this is sheer fantasy and superstition, but the signs are too obvious, from generation to generation, to be ignored. We have a Hebrew word for it in the family: *hashgahah*. Literally translated, it means "monitoring," or "supervising"—but in practice we use it to refer to Providence. So while praising God with every new day given to me, I also add a silent prayer and thank *hashgahah* for my good fortune. It is my belief that it is this same Providence that guided my mother when, after becoming a widow, she came to live in this building, where both the Pereira brothers and the Halévy family had their homes, a fact that would play such a dominant role in molding my character, in guiding me in my preferences, and in paving the way to my future.

Our building on the rue de Montholon was situated only a few minutes from the great synagogue on the rue de la Victoire and from the opera house on the rue Le Peletier; it was also the residence of the Halévy family. The brothers Fromental and Léon had lived there with their sisters Flore and Mélanie since the death of their father (who died the same year as mine, 1826), the erudite and God-fearing Élie Halévy, one of the pillars of the Parisian Jewish congregation.

Élie Halévy took great care when bringing up his children not to infuse his own erudition in their education, so as not to hinder their smooth integration into French society. Whatever he consciously and knowingly withheld from his children was denied his children's children by a natural process. So when his granddaughter Geneviève, Bizet's widow, was asked if she had considered conversion to Christianity, she answered, "I have too little religion to convert it into another one."

Fromental Halévy, who was to become both my teacher and my brother-in-law, was an outstanding musician. He won the Prix de Rome at the age of twenty, in 1819, with his cantata "Herminie," after twice succeeding only in getting the second prize at age seventeen and then eighteen. While still himself a student he was hired to teach his fellow students solfeggio at the Conservatoire. Shortly after his return from Italy he was appointed professor of harmony and accompaniment, and sometime later he was put in charge of the class of counterpoint and fugue. But this could not satisfy the ever-active Halévy. Besides teaching and composing (he would set to music almost any text that was put to him, not bothering too much about its literary merits), he also felt a need to participate in the actual performance of music. That is why he acted as *maestro al cembalo* at the Italian Opera for three years, until he was engaged as *chef du chant*, a coveted and respected position at the Opéra.

I remember perfectly well every corner of the little room he called his studio, where he would work relentlessly for hours, until late at night, piling up manuscript paper in neat stacks on the wooden shelves behind his writing table, next to the upright piano of which he was so proud. On this piano, manufactured by the elder Roller, he followed my progress in the art of deciphering musical scores. I was, naturally, very proud of those visits and grateful for the time my famous neighbor so lavishly granted me. From time to time, as good neighbors should, all the Halévy family would reciprocate and come to visit us. At those times we would have a big meal, all of us gathered around the big oak table in our dining room. That is how the ties between our two families tightened slowly but steadily.

When in 1837 Fromental Halévy was offered a luxurious apartment at the Opéra and moved there with his brother and his two sisters, we continued to cultivate the friendship that had grown over eleven years of good neighborly relations. So no one was really surprised when on a beautiful spring day, on April 24, 1842, the chief rabbi of Paris united Fromental Halévy and my sister Léonie Rodrigues in the holy bonds of matrimony in accordance with ancestral Jewish rites. Halévy was still a shy bachelor at the age of forty-three, and Léonie was a beautiful budding flower at twenty-two.

And since we are dealing in matrimonial affairs, I should also mention the fact that two other unions where cemented between residents of our big building on the rue de Montholon. In the same building there also lived the well-known architect Hippolyte Lebas, who earned national recognition after he built the Notre-Dame-de-Lorette Church. Léon Halévy married Lebas's daughter, and their son Ludovic became one of the foremost librettists in France. And as I related earlier, Émile Pereira married my cousin Suzanne Rodrigues, Olinde's sister.

My brother-in-law Fromental Halévy was a soft-hearted man; he never could turn down a plea for help, be it well-founded or not. A striking example is his attitude toward young and penniless students and his tutoring of Jacques Offenbach, whom he encouraged and helped while teaching him the art of composition without remuneration of any kind. But not all those who craved help were as worthy as Offenbach. Halévy was always surrounded by a swarm of naggers and bores that wasted his time and took advantage of his generosity. His composition courses at the Conservatoire, which I had the privilege to attend for a while as the senior student in the class, were constantly interrupted by similar supplicants—a singer who would have his voice appraised, a composer eager to submit his output to benevolent criticism, an instrumentalist looking for work, a librettist without connections. With all and every one of them Halévy would sit down and talk in the middle of his course while his frustrated pupils would start teaching each other whatever they thought they had grasped from the strands of information their teacher had managed to communicate. They did so whenever their teacher failed to appear altogether, which was quite a frequent occurrence due to his social and professional obligations. He was so overburdened that he utterly lost control over his daily schedule; he had to cope with meetings at the Institut, rehearsals at the theater, auditions of every kind, social calls and receptions, and in addition thereto, the ever-present urge to write more and more operas in the eternal and futile hope of somehow matching the success of *La juive*.

He was so busy that at some time in his life he just gave up fighting to keep up with his schedule, and with some kind of acceptance of his fate, he let the unavoidable pass over him without showing too much concern, with a kind of lethargy, almost laziness, that became proverbial in Paris. This also became his teaching method. Once, before I myself joined his composition class, a young acquaintance of mine complained to me that he stumbled on his counterpoint studies. Halévy was very surprised when I reported this fact to him.

"What is he talking about?" he asked. "What does he know about the subject? As a matter of fact, he never studied counterpoint!"

"What do you mean?" I insisted. "If he is a student in your composition class, he is supposed to have gone through a course covering the basics, isn't he?"

"Rubbish," answered Halévy. "I never make this a condition for joining my class. I'm not dealing with children. All my students have reached the age when a man should know whatever it is he needs to reach his goal. I'm always willing to listen to anyone. I check and make corrections in the works they submit to me: overture, symphony, waltz, or song. When the famous Louis Antoine Jullien was a pupil of mine he refused to do the exercises I had assigned, and insisted on bringing me dances and quadrilles instead; I simply corrected those and we both were happy with this compromise! This is for me a matter of conscience: never thwart your pupil's wishes."

Halévy had a knack for languages and had an almost religious veneration for any kind of dictionary. He was also a very talented orator and his rhetorical abilities helped him toward being elected, in 1854, to the coveted post of secretary for life of the Academy of Fine Arts, at the Institut of France, one of the highest honors in French public life.

His curiosity was boundless; everything interested him, enthralled him, and filled him with a momentary sorrow that he did not choose one specific field to be the center of his activities. When he read about history, he wished he had become an historian; reading a book on military strategy, he on the spot regretted not being a general; a geology textbook would leave him daydreaming about the bliss of being a geologist; and reading an exposé on politics, he would most seriously wonder if it was not high time he put all his musical activities behind him and start a new life immersed in state affairs.

Like all the notables of the Parisian Jewish community, he was a staunch French patriot and France's greatness and prosperity were his foremost priorities. The military adventures of Napoleon III, harshly criticized in enlightened circles, filled him with naive admiration and fervor. At times he would indulge in daydreaming, seeing himself riding a white horse, heading the mighty army fighting the foe, holding in his hand the banner of freedom.

My sister Léonie, I'm sorry to say, in spite of her being a wonderful person, never could cope with the task of bringing some order into my brother-in-law's hectic life and overburdened schedule. She was a lively and sparkling woman; she loved entertaining and having guests all over the house, treating them lavishly to the best that was available. She had also inherited from our mother a keen interest in the arts, and was something of a sculptress herself. But her main interests lay in collecting all kinds of *objets d'art*, miniatures, paintings, figurines and antiques. She would spend more money than she could afford on her hobby. The Halévy home looked like a picture gallery that doubled as an antique warehouse. It was impossible to take a step in the crowded little rooms without stumbling on a terracotta figurine, or a fine porcelain vase, or encountering a Louis XIV writing desk, or a Louis XV upholstered chair.

Eugène Delacroix, a regular visitor (and later to become a neighbor and friend of mine, when I would purchase, jointly with Fromental and Léonie Halévy, the summer residence at Château de Fromont), doesn't mince words when he describes in his memoirs the way of life in my sister's household:

> Mme Halévy has converted the house into a junk heap. The heating is stifling. Mme Halévy has cluttered the place up with pots, pans, and old pieces of furniture. This madness one day will bring her to the poorhouse! Fromental has changed and aged; he looks like a man who, unwittingly, has been made an accomplice in a crime. How can he do any serious work in the middle of this pandemonium? Add to this the fact that his new post at the Académie takes much of his time and removes him further and further away from the serenity and tranquility he needs for his creative work. I will always consider it a riddle and a wonder, how those people, constantly pressed by debts on one hand, and on the other hand full of obligations brought upon them by their excessive coquetry, can keep a smiling face, burdened by all their troubles.

Fourteen months after their marriage, the Halévy couple was blessed with the arrival of a daughter, Julie Esther Anna. She was one of those fascinating creatures fated for a premature death, the signs of which could be found in her golden sweetness, akin to the semi-brightness of a sunset. She emanated both a physical and moral beauty. She was also, not surprisingly, a gifted musician and a wonderful pianist. At an early age she and her cousin Ludovic (the son of her father's brother Léon Halévy) pledged their hearts to each other. The blooming of this puppy love into a mutually true and deeply rooted feeling brought about the decision of the two young people to marry, in spite of the difficulties they knew they would have to overcome due to the fact that they were first cousins. But as fate would have it, that was not to be. Ludovic, who in some distant future would write the bulk of the libretto for

Carmen, would need years to overcome the sudden loss of his beloved Esther.

The second daughter of Léonie and Fromental Halévy, Marie Geneviève Raphaëlle, was born six years after Esther, in 1849. She was the exact opposite of her sister, both in her looks and in her moods, and she stormed Esther's clear tranquility like a summer hurricane. A short time after Geneviève's birth, Léonie suffered the first attack of the nervous illness that from then onward would necessitate her internment in a sanatorium at more or less regular intervals. After each treatment she would come home and resume her normal daily routine. She would then forget, or seem to forget, all things related to her illness. Those were the circumstances that drove Esther into taking upon herself the burden of her young sister's upbringing and education. She was also the only person who knew how to calm Geneviève and talk her into reasonable behavior.

The Halévy family stayed in Nice during Fromental's final illness. From there Geneviève, who was thirteen at the time, sent me a steady stream of letters, all of them starting with the greeting "Dear and beloved Uncle Hippo," in which she described the tedious life in "exile" and her yearning for the city she loved so much, Paris. "There is only one city in the world where one can live, and that is Paris!" she wrote. Those letters were written with so much imagination, in such a perfect style, with so much assurance and poise that all of us were sure she would become a writer.

I wish I had only half of her talent for writing, and then maybe the books I wrote would have met with some public acclaim. But nevertheless, I wrote those books, while Geneviève, to my great sorrow, squandered her inborn gifts and never even tried to realize the potential her family had seen in her.

I have always professed that genius is not enough; in addition, you need a good cultural background on which to build, and also a certain amount of sweat and toil.

2

THE CONSERVATOIRE

When my niece, Geneviève—she was thirteen at the time—wrote in a letter from Nice that Paris was the only city in the world worth living in, she was not far from the truth. Anyhow, for a French musician, there is no alternative. Even highly gifted musicians from other nations are drawn to Paris as if by a magnet: Meyerbeer, Chopin, Cherubini, Rossini, and Offenbach, to name only a few, have made it their permanent home. Others like Gluck, Spontini, Liszt, Verdi, Wagner, and Donizetti have lived in Paris for lengthy periods, some with more, some with less success. Not every Frenchman agrees with the well-known saying "*La France, c'est Paris.*"

In Bordeaux, my hometown, for instance, the general consensus is that Bordeaux—and only Bordeaux—truly represents and embodies the spirit of France. But even in Bordeaux, everyone accepts the fact that the musical center of France is Paris. No active musician can stray far from the capital. You need to meet theater directors and convince them to stage your works; you need to meet poets to write your libretti;

conductors who will play your symphonies; not to mention the need to rub shoulders with other musicians to stay in the frontline of public attention. All those you will meet only in Paris. If, in order to earn your living, you have to take quarters in another city, you are sunk. This will be the proof that you are an utter failure, or, at the very best, a second-rate pretender.

No active musician can venture to leave the city for any length of time. Naturally, sometimes to ease stress and to lessen some of the daily burden, you have to take a vacation. Gounod, for instance, whenever he felt the pressure becoming insufferable, ran away to one of his cities of refuge, London or Rome. My brother-in-law Fromental Halévy needed a well-deserved rest and looked for peace and quiet in Nice. But the musician who needs to find work in the provinces to earn his bread must forget all his dreams of fame and success. If you need to find an impresario, a singer, or a choreographer, there is only one place where you can find him: in his box at the Opéra-Comique. The muses' dwelling place is Paris!

I still remember the days when you could, in a single afternoon, meet Rossini strolling on the boulevard des Italiens, Verdi in the Tuileries Garden, Liszt on the rue de la Chaussée d'Antin, and Wagner near the Salle Favart. And to crown the evening, you could greet the ailing Heine trying to overcome excruciating pain in his bed (which he called his mattress tomb) on the rue d'Amsterdam, or visit Chopin, who was fighting his illness in his apartment at Place Vendôme. As for your French colleagues, needless to say they're all available, living just around the corner. And whether you like it or not, you will meet them all the time, at the Opéra, at the theater, in the café, in the salons, on the boulevards, and in the park.

The strategic centers of those activities are situated mainly at the Institut, at the Académie (our famed opera house), at the Théâtre

Italien, at the Opéra-Comique, and in the peerless greenhouse, the Conservatoire.

I personally have very fond and nostalgic memories of this great institution. I love that ridiculous inner courtyard with its unbelievable mixture of eerie sounds produced by countless singers, flautists, percussionists, violinists, and pianists all practicing their scales at the same time, sending their streams of notes in a polyphonic cacophony into the air. That is where I spent quite a large part of my youth, and it was to me like a second home.

When I was a student at the Conservatoire we were never taught about the way our institution came into being. Being afflicted by nature with an insatiable curiosity, I set out to learn about it.

The origins of the Conservatoire de Paris can be traced back to the creation of the Royal School of Singing by decree of Louis XIV on June 28, 1669. But its true beginning should be attributed to the nomination of the composer Gossec as the head of the institution in 1784. In 1793, it merged with the school for musicians of the National Guard, and was renamed the Institut national de musique. It was headed by Bernard Sarrette, the conductor of this military fanfare. Two years later, the National Convention established during the Revolution renamed it the Conservatoire national de musique. The first 350 pupils began their studies there in October 1796. In March 1800, Napoleon decided on a complete reshuffling of the organization of the school. Sarrette remained as director, but five "Inspectors of Tuition" were given authority over the teaching program: Gossec, Méhul, Cherubini (all three composers of international renown), Lesueur, and Monsigny (the latter two respected composers had a solid local reputation).

Cherubini was a very stern and obstinate man. Shortly after he was appointed in 1822 as sole director of the Conservatoire, he issued new rules to strengthen discipline and to impose his views in the field of moral behavior. Here is a story Berlioz told me. I can recall it almost verbatim:

> In order to prevent members of the opposite sex from intermingling without being supervised by one of the teachers, Cherubini decided that from that point on male students would enter the school through the gates in the Faubourg Poissonière, while the old entrance—on the rue Bergère, situated at the other end of the building—would be permitted to members of the fairer sex only. A few days after this new arrangement came into force, I went to the library, innocently entering the building as usual from the rue Bergère, unaware of the fact that I was committing a major crime. I had almost arrived at the door to the library, when suddenly one of the servants blocked my way, like a vindictive Cerberus, and ordered me to retrace my steps, go out where I had come in, make a circuit of the building, and reenter it through the proper gate. The absurdity of the request was such that I burst into laughter and just went on my way, ignoring his gesticulations.
>
> A few minutes later, as I was already entirely engrossed in the score of Alceste and had forgotten everything about the incident, our director came into the library, followed by the keeper of feminine modesty who had tried to stop me from entering the institution. Cherubini's face was even paler than usual, his eyes glowed with a malevolent light, and his mounting rage hampered his speech in such a manner that he actually stuttered when said to me, "So you are the man who dares violate my orders and come in through the door that I forbade you to use."
>
> I answered that I was sorry, that I had not heard of the new regulations, and that in the future I would comply with the rules of the house.
>
> "I'm not talking about the future! And what are you doing here?"

"As you can see for yourself, sir, I'm studying Gluck's scores."

"What do you need Gluck's scores for? And who gave you permission to enter the library?"

I, too, was slowly losing my temper and I answered in an angry tone, "I need no permission to enter the library. It is open to the public from ten to three, and it seems to me that I'm within the time limits. I come here to study what, in my opinion, is the greatest dramatic music ever written. I'm perfectly within my rights."

"Rights? You have no rights at all! I forbid you to come here!"

"And I shall return whenever I need to, and whenever I please!"

"What is your name, your name?"

"My name is of no concern to you and I won't tell you what is. You may someday hear it, but as for today, I will keep it to myself."

"Catch him! Catch him and throw him in jail!" Cherubini shouted to the servant.

Then, to everyone's surprise and profound amusement, they started running around the big table, trying to catch me, knocking down some chairs along the way. There was much turmoil, but I had no trouble escaping. With a great guffaw, I shouted to then, as I slammed the door behind me, "I won't tell you my name, and I will be back in the library whenever it suits me."

I'm quite sure that Cherubini never forgot that incident. Still, he had no reservations when, in 1839, Berlioz was nominated as *conservateur* in that same library. And ten years after Cherubini's death, Berlioz became head of that same library. This was the beginning of his lifelong struggle for assertiveness. He remained head librarian to the day of his death three years ago.[1]

---

1   This page from my diary was written in 1872 (J.H.R.).

While I agree with Berlioz that Cherubini was not an easygoing man, neither was Berlioz. But whatever he demanded from others, he demanded of himself foremost. Thanks to my brother-in-law Fromental Halévy, who was a pupil and an unconditional admirer of Cherubini, I was able to establish a personal acquaintance with the man. I came to know him in those hours when he would shed his outer armor and reveal his true personality. I discovered a sensitive man who worked relentlessly under the sharp eye of universal criticism, aiming at improving his own work as well as the environment in which he lived.

Cherubini died in his eighty-second year—a ripe old age! Going home after the funeral, Halévy opened his heart to me and said,

> He was very proud of his age, because in his eyes this symbolized authority. And in the same way he gave old age its due, so old age paid back with full respect to his mental abilities, to the sharpness of his judgment, to the lucidity of his wisdom. I know that underneath there was always a constant current of anxiety, a dread of the loss of his grip on his intellectual abilities. He was unwilling to compromise, and his motto was "All or nothing." Shortly after his eighty-first birthday, last September, he confided to me that he felt he was growing old. This made me immensely sad, because I knew exactly what he meant; and I was right. That was six months ago. How I loved that man!

Some thirty years have passed since his demise, and in that short time Cherubini's operas, like most of his works, have been forgotten. Only the two requiem masses are still performed from time to time.

I hear that in Germany Mendelssohn is still a staunch advocate of Cherubini's music and includes it in his concert programs on many occasions. Even Beethoven himself showed great respect for this man who was ten years his senior. When Cherubini visited Vienna, Beethoven was eager to show him the score of the *Missa solemnis* and hear his opinion of it. I think it is also worthwhile to mention the close relationship between Cherubini's *Les deux journées* and Beethoven's only opera, *Fidelio*. Both are "rescue operas" written on the librettos by Jean Nicolas Bouilly.

Thinking of Cherubini's legacy leaves me brooding. I'm not talking about his music, which, to my taste, is like yesterday's soup brought to a lukewarm temperature before being served again. But I really admire the changes he brought to the Conservatoire in the forty-two years of his tenure. New classes were built; the façade of the building on the rue Faubourg Poissonière was entirely rejuvenated; the curriculum was enlarged and a whole series of new instruments were taught side by side with the traditional ones. His most important achievement was probably the transformation of the library into a real national musical archive. Not only did he manage to assemble a huge collection of old instruments, but even more important, he obtained musical manuscripts from all over Europe. He also managed to get a commitment from the government that one copy of every book and publication on a musical subject and every musical score published in France would automatically find its way to the Conservatoire's library. (By law, two copies of everything published in France must be furnished to the state authorities. From that point on, if it had any relation to music, one copy would automatically find its way to the library.) Even Berlioz could not deny that the fact that Gluck's complete works, which he loved so dearly, were now available at the library and their availability was entirely Cherubini's achievement. The creation of the Société des concerts du Conservatoire was also Cherubini's doing. From that point forward, the Parisian public was able to become acquainted with the masterpieces of orchestral music, foremost of which were Beethoven's symphonies. That was a revolutionary change—keep in mind that in Paris the words "music" and "opera" are, for all practical purposes, synonymous.

Saint-Saëns remembers fondly the days when, while still a toddler, his mother took him there to listen to music. He told me that the sound of the symphony orchestra opened an entirely new world for his understanding of the power of musical expression, a world that had hitherto been confined to the piano and the human voice. From that time to the present day he has become a permanent visitor, and even as a student, when he could not spare the money to buy tickets, he always went to those concerts and, with the aid of a sympathetic usher, he was permitted to steal into the concert hall and enjoy the music.

As I said, I'm not a great admirer of Cherubini's music, though I know that many musicians of his generation have praised his work.

I think this might be because I am a romantic at heart, whilst he was a protagonist of conservative classicism. Now that I think of it, it is probably the same disdain my friend Delacroix holds for Cherubini's friend Ingres and his paintings. I can see all the qualities, the know-how, and the huge effort invested in those works, but they simply do not awaken any emotional reaction in me—only placid consideration.

At the beginning of February 1842, barely five weeks before his death, Cherubini was replaced at the helm of this institution by Auber, who headed it until his death in 1871. Since then Ambroise Thomas has been in charge.

Auber was appointed director at the Conservatoire on the specific recommendation of Louis-Philippe, king of France. For sixty years this man waged a heroic struggle against his innate aversion to hard work. He managed to write some sixty operas (most of them to librettos by Eugène Scribe) that were staged at the Opéra-Comique, without the composer ever being present at the performances. He once candidly admitted, "If I had been forced somehow to witness the performance of one of my works, I would have been unable to write a single note of music ever after that."

He had made it a habit to work at night, and to compensate for the lack of sleep, he took short naps during the interminable meetings he had to sit in on to fulfill his duties as director of the Conservatoire, as a composer, and as a member of the Institut de France.

Aside from music, he had two great passions: women and horses. He once declared, "I was passionately in love with music when I had just met it, when we became lovers. When it became my mistress, I still had the highest regard for our relationship. But when I officially became married to music my feelings toward it definitely cooled down!" Rossini described Auber as "a great musician who wrote little music."

In 1830, Auber came to the forefront of international politics with his opera *La muette de Portici*. The work fomented revolutionary sentiments and patriotic outbursts. It was a direct factor leading to the independence of Belgium. After the performance of the opera on August 25 at the Théâtre de la Monnaie in Brussels, the audience took to the streets singing the duet "Amour sacré de la patrie," kindling the uprising that led to the separation from the Kingdom of the Netherlands.

Auber died last year during the unrest of the Parisian Commune. This is how Fromental Halévy's nephew Ludovic described the funeral service:

Saturday, July 15, 1871

The funeral service for Auber in the Trinity Church. A very big crowd; many beautiful women. The full corps de ballet of the Opéra, and all the female pupils from the Conservatoire. The orchestra and the choirs gave a peerless performance. From the place where we were seated in the church, we could hear this wonderful concert though being unable to see anything of the ceremony itself; no view of the priests or of the coffin. We had to pinch ourselves in order to remember that we were in a church and not in the theater.

On my leaving the place with the crowd I found myself behind one of the sacristans; he was talking with an elderly lady and said to her,

> It's incredible how overburdened we are lately. We have to perform all our duties simultaneously: marriages, baptisms, burials. That should come as a surprise to no one: who wanted to get married during the war or during the Commune? True enough, people did not stop dying during that time, but no one in his right mind wanted to be buried under the rule of the Commune, and in the meantime we stored them all in our cellars. This man, whose coffin we are following now, has been with us for over two months, and there are still some waiting for burial that preceded him here.

Auber was over eighty-eight when he passed away. As I heard him say, "I am *not* eighty-eight. I am four times twenty-two!" Cherubini died when he was almost eighty-two. Let us all hope that Ambroise Thomas, who is now sixty years old and has been appointed the next head of the Conservatoire, will also last into his eighties (at least) and we will have a nice chain of directorships that will bring us to the threshold of twentieth century.

Ambroise Thomas was born on August 5, 1811, one year to the day before I was born; but he was born in Metz in Lorraine, while I was born under the sunny skies of Bordeaux in the south. It is premature to voice an opinion on what the Conservatoire will look like under Thomas's leadership, as one year has hardly elapsed since he took the reins. I will certainly come back to judge his achievements in a few years.

One of the annual highlights in the life of the graduate students at the Conservatoire is the preparations and turmoil surrounding the Prix de Rome.

This is a competitive examination, held every year at the Académie des beaux-arts, in the fields of painting, sculpture, engraving, architecture, and music. Its aim is to try to choose the most talented pupils, those who will have the best chance of becoming real artists, and foster them for the five first years of their budding careers. The winners are granted an annual income of three thousand francs for a period of five years. The first two of those years are to be spent at the Villa Medici, that stronghold of the French Academy in Rome. The third year is to be spent traveling in Germany in order to gather and accumulate artistic impressions that could ultimately enrich the cultural baggage of the young laureates.

All the walls of the Villa Medici in Rome are decorated with portraits of former laureates of the Prix de Rome and every year several new ones are added. Most of the names are unknown to me; have you ever heard of Bouteiller, Riffaut, Barbereau, Maillart, or Gastinel? But next to these forgotten heroes who failed to fulfill the hopes invested in them there are such great names as Halévy, Berlioz, Thomas, Gounod, Bizet, and Massenet, which shine proudly and bear witness to the greatness of our French culture.

All of them were guests of the French government and residents at the Villa Medici. There is justice and investment, wisdom and generosity in awarding this gift. It is like an installment to those youngsters during this crucial period of their lives, the time when they cease being students and begin their arduous road toward being full-fledged artists and, if luck and talent permit, fame.

This stipend affords them a few years to blossom without the daily pressure of the struggle for economic survival, in the wonderful setting of a foreign but friendly environment and meeting in a cultural center that is not France.

The prize was founded in 1803 and the first winner in the field of music was some forgotten musician called Androt. The candidates register at the office of the Institut and are then called to go through a preliminary examination, whose purpose is to choose the six most promising students. The choice is made by a committee consisting of the six composers who are members of the Institut and an additional three other composers. The competition takes place in June, but the final decision is normally handed down in October when the cantata by the winner is performed. The six candidates who reach the final stage of the competition are confined, each one in a small, separate room, with a piano. They have twenty-one days to compose a cantata on a given text, for one or two singers with full orchestral accompaniment.

They are forbidden to leave the premises until they hand over the finished composition. They are all locked in their boxes, whose doors are opened every day at eleven in the morning and six in the evening when they meet to take their meals together. When all the finished scores are in possession of the committee, the jury meets again, this time with the addition of two other members of the Institut—either a painter and a sculptor or an architect and an engraver, in whatever combination is convenient (even two members who practice the same craft). They listen to the cantatas performed by one or two singers, as the case may be, with a piano accompaniment.

After that hearing, the voting takes place. But this is only the first stage, as the full body of the Académie has to ratify the findings of the jury. This normally takes place one week later, with thirty to thirty-five permanent members of the Académie casting their votes. This plenary session can either accept or overrule the verdict of the original jury. That is how committees whose majority members, though deemed to be artists themselves but are not musicians, make binding decisions on the future of young composers. Even laureates like Berlioz, Bizet, and Massenet, when I asked them about this absurdity, have complained about this procedure, and consider themselves to have been lucky, either with the composition of the jury or with the poor quality of the work of their fellow competitors. Still, somehow the system seems to work. In any case I can visualize no other way to implement this wonderful grant.

1892

Who is it that said, "There is good music, there is bad music, and there is music written by Ambroise Thomas"? That sentence is well-known, but no one was willing to assume paternity of it. So for a long time I just assumed that the origin of this saying was some jealous colleague, some frustrated student, or some impatient critic who did not know exactly what to write for his column. But during a recent chat I had with Emmanuel Chabrier, he confessed that he had coined this saying. And knowing Chabrier's boisterous character has taken off much of the edge of this saying. In my opinion, Thomas is first of all an efficient director, energetic and endowed with ideas and initiative. As for his two masterpieces, *Mignon* and *Hamlet,* they will always remain a fair contribution to the string of successful French operas written in the last fifty years.

Perhaps Robert Schumann was right when he wrote about Thomas's Trio for Violin, Cello, and Pianoforte, "This trio is neither heavy nor light; it's not classical, and it's not romantic; it's not deep, nor is it shallow. But it is always friendly to the ear and nice to listen to. And here and there you can find some really good musical invention in it."

From the beginning of his tenure Thomas was able to get a sizeable increase in the budget allocated to the Institut by the government. This enabled him to increase the staff's salaries and to enlarge the number of students that the Conservatoire could accept; more important, he was able to stick to the rule that no tuition fees were to be paid and made it possible to help needy students by giving them financial support to meet their living expenses. He also introduced solfeggio and music history as compulsory subjects for all students.

Thomas was well liked as a man, even by those who found his output old fashioned, but many of his enemies criticized his outspoken conservatism. They blamed the composer of *Mignon* for his harshness toward unruly young students like Chausson, d'Indy, Charpentier, and Duparc. He was accused of meeting the outspoken rebellious attitude of Achille Debussy, one of the younger pupils, with stern repression and hostility. When Ernest Guiraud died in May this year, Saint-Saëns encouraged his friend Gabriel Fauré to seek the nomination for the vacant professorship at the Conservatoire. Thomas blocked the appointment saying, "Fauré? Never! If he is appointed I resign."

Thomas, like many others, held the misconception that the name "Conservatoire" means "the place to keep and safeguard old traditions," and that the director's duty is to make sure those traditions are respected and shielded from corruption. As far as I know, we have inherited the name from those Italian institutions called *conservatorio*, where deserted, orphaned, or illegitimate children were kept (*conservati*) until they were old enough to fend for themselves. Some say that Thomas's main claim to fame is to have been the composition teacher of Massenet, that shameless opportunist whose outspoken success permitted him to achieve the goals Thomas himself has been unable to reach.

So I can only sum up the facts: Since César Franck's death almost two years ago, there has been no one in the teaching body with a shred of broadmindedness, and Franck was a freakish case. So this formidable institution and its head are still among the most reactionary institutions in our "progressive" society. How can I explain the multitude of talents thriving within its walls and that each year join the ranks of those who mold our modern and forward-looking French musical culture?

3

ROME

October 31, 1875

I have just come home now after the memorial concert to Georges Bizet with which the Colonne Orchestra opened the season this year, and my head is spinning; is it possible that five months have already elapsed since he passed away?

In the matter of *Carmen* there seems to be no new developments; it's only thanks to Mme Galli-Marié's stubbornness that they are going to have one or two more performances of the opera, and after that they'll break up the team for good.

I always wondered at the Olympian serenity with which Bizet seems to have accepted the failure of some of his works. However, this time it was different; too many disappointments had piled up in quick succession, and he was shaken and tired. He desperately needed a sign of success, of recognition, of support and encouragement that would restore his self-confidence, not only as a creative artist, but also as a man. For him *Carmen* really was the last-ditch battle—he had invested the last ounces of energy he could summon in that work. But when his hopes and expectations were shattered, he was unable to take the blow, and he collapsed. He was only thirty-six years old!

At the concert I sat next to my niece Geneviève, the composer's young widow. Aloof and silent she was, and so beautiful with her eyes like two deep black ponds. I never managed to solve the riddle of those eyes; even way back at the time of her childhood, when I became the protector of the wretched and wild orphan after she lost her beloved father, even then I was unable to penetrate the secret world behind those two big, glowing eyes. Somehow I'm quite sure that Bizet also found it hard to read those eyes, and that this hastened his downfall; this constant confrontation with the whimsical and unstable personality of his wife left him puzzled and frustrated. While he himself was yearning so desperately for sympathy, support, and understanding, he found himself squandering his precious mental faculties in trying to assist and give guidance to his capricious wife, whose mind wandered so often in the twilight between lucidity and insanity. Finally he did the only sensible thing—he cut himself away. But it was too late; both Geneviève and *Carmen*, who were the two loves of his life, had let him down. And this was to cost him his life.

In the first part of the concert the orchestra played Beethoven's Seventh Symphony, the "Dance of the Blessed Spirits" from Gluck's *Orpheus and Eurydice,* and Saint-Saëns's Fourth Concerto for Piano and Orchestra. After the intermission we heard an elegy composed especially for this memorial by Massenet, followed by a poem written by Louis Gallet and recited by Mme Galli-Marié, while the orchestra played the adagietto from *L'Arlésienne* as a musical background. This music always stirs a tumultuous wave of thoughts, reminiscences, and feelings in me, and while sitting there I suddenly realized that in spite of my being the author of nearly twenty books, and the composer of many piano pieces and songs and a three-act opera, despite these accomplishments, my sole claim to immortal fame is the fact that Bizet dedicated this music, *L'Arlésienne*, to me!

If my name be ever remembered by future generations it will be due to the fact that I extended help and support to this genius, Bizet, in his dark hours of need.

As I said, I have just come home from the memorial concert, and my heart is heavy with nostalgia.

Notwithstanding my natural love and attachment to my own children, I have slowly come to realize that I had a real fatherly love for Georges Bizet and that his death is for me like the loss of a very dear and cherished son.

It was my friend Charles Valentin Alkan who first pointed out Bizet to me. Alkan (whose name at that time was still Morhange) was accompanist in the solfeggio class of Croharé in which the eleven-year-old Bizet distinguished himself. Bizet was about the age of my eldest son Edgar, still a mere child. I vividly remember those fiery and limpid blue eyes set midway between the peach-like cheeks under an unruly mane of fair, wavy hair crowning a high forehead. When I first saw him I had a strange feeling, a kind of mild shock, as if I had suddenly found a long-lost relative. I clearly recall a surge of warmth engulfing me, and I instinctively knew that in some mysterious way the paths of our lives would cross in a decisive manner. And on the spot I made the decision that I would watch, though this might be from some distance, the blooming of this child and take some kind of responsibility for the future of this new foster son.

Only much later did I find out that his uncle, his mother's brother, was François Delsarte, a respected singing teacher and a well-known Catholic activist.

Bizet joined the composition class of Fromental Halévy in 1853 when he was fifteen, after having studied piano with Marmontel and attending Benoit's organ class.

On his first attempt to win the coveted Prix de Rome in 1856, he only succeeded in getting second place. The following year I again eagerly awaited the final decision of the jury. This time my hopes and wishes were fulfilled; Bizet won.

So in the last days of 1857, Bizet crossed the snowy Alps on his way to sunny Rome.

My only visit to Italy had been in January 1836, twenty years before Bizet. My wife Mathilde and I were newlyweds, and we spent a marvelous honeymoon visiting, among other cities, Florence, Venice, Rome, and Naples. And we didn't have enough eyes or ears to take in all the wealth of cultural treasures that cropped up at every corner. But when young Bizet arrived in Rome in 1858, reaping the fruits of his victory at the Prix de Rome, the state of music in Italy had sunk to such a low level that it had become synonymous with mediocrity. This country, which in the past had been a paradise and dreamland for every young musician, had let its great musical tradition deteriorate to such an extent that the really creative and great talents that are left there have been compelled to seek this place, Paris, the soil in which to sow the seeds of their genius, so as to enable them to benefit from the conditions that will bring their gifts to full maturity. Thus, even amongst the members of the Académie, who are renowned for shunning any kind of change, voices were heard questioning whether Rome in the fifties was still the right place to develop the talent and personality of those promising young musicians who had won the Prix de Rome. But the regulations, strong and sanctified by more than five decades of practice, stood firmly against all those halfhearted efforts aimed at bringing change. The keepers of the sacred flame—and they made up the majority of the executive committee—argued against those timid skeptics that Rome was, and still is, the Eternal City, the cradle of our ancestral and universal culture, and notwithstanding the actual state of matters, it must remain an inexhaustible source of inspiration to every artist, be he a sculptor, an engraver, a musician, a playwright, or a painter.

If young Georges Bizet ever felt any gratitude toward the Académie and its members, it was due mainly to their well-known conservatism, this being the main factor that opened for him the gates to the enchanted world of his beloved Italy. To this conservatism he owed the fact that he was given this golden opportunity to stroll in the shadow of the big oaks, on the elegant avenue leading to the gates of the Villa Medici. In this gigantic house, which had been his home for so many months, he reviewed the portraits of hundreds of his colleagues, former Prix de Rome winners, hanging on the walls of the big entrance hall. To reach his room, perched like an eagle's nest and overlooking the whole city ("the highest room in Rome," he used to call it), he had to climb the big spiral staircase to the top of the tower in the right wing.

This was the city in which he spent three formative years, those years during which he passed from adolescence to manhood.

Rossini, who had taken the gifted youngster under his patronage, gave him wise advice on the eve of his departure:

> Go to Rome and discover there the source of melody that flows only under the blue skies of Italy. But go there with no prejudice. Make no comparisons. Try to benefit from the good you hear as well as from the bad. Listen to everything with open ears and without

taking a stand. And above all, avoid criticizing or voicing hastily made opinions. Pretend to be tolerant, or better yet, try to be tolerant wherever you can.

In his first letter from Rome, Bizet gave a detailed description of his life as a resident of the Villa Medici. He radiated happiness in this ideal surrounding. He told about the fellow laureates there, most of them nice youngsters whose company he enjoyed. He wrote about the atmosphere, reminding one of a luxurious boarding school, with the usual childish pranks at the newcomers' expense. Although the veterans naturally acted with some kind of condescension, they always happily shared their acquired experience of the city and its customs. It seems that M. Schnetz, the director, had taken Bizet under his wing and given him preferential treatment, and this seems to have aroused some jealousy.

This M. Schnetz, a painter, was like part of the landscape of the villa, and, indeed, of Rome. He appeared to have contacts everywhere there, in the upper strata of society as well as in the dubious world of bandits and smugglers. Those connections were unbelievably beneficial to all the villa's residents, as no one in Rome dared to harm any of them in any way.

Viewing Bizet's short life in hindsight, I venture to say that the days of his sojourn at the Villa Medici in Rome where the happiest years of his life. He was far from the suffocating love of a sickly and demanding mother, and free from the worries of earning a living. He was leading a quasi-communal life among a bunch of friends and colleagues who had more or less the same goals and desires. And the scenery was a city and a country that grew dearer to him every day. This was a real paradise of youth, and it seems as though it had been created especially for this gay youngster, sparkling with life and eagerly looking for opportunities to relish the true taste of pleasure.

This happy bunch, living on one of the finest panoramic hills of Rome, in a Renaissance dwelling the design and decoration of which were in part due to Michelangelo, lived a scot-free and unrestrained life, with boundless leisure and nothing to thwart their initiatives. Their only obligation was to send home, to the Académie in Paris, the famous *envoi*. Every Prix de Rome laureate was expected to submit, once a year, a new work, to prove to those who had sent him that he was not wasting their money. Young Bizet regarded this yearly task with the utmost seriousness; despite all the social temptations in which he indulged with the frenzy and pleasure of an avowed heartbreaker, he constantly brooded on this subject and was hard put to make up his mind about this obligation. And between balls, suppers, excursions in town and around it, shows at the theater, and nights of lovemaking, there was the omnipresent struggle of his inner self with the doubts and questions that would henceforth be his faithful companions until his last day, the questions and doubts about his way and his future as a creative artist.

On the other hand, judging from one of his letters home, we can appraise the progress and maturing of his critical faculties:

Something great happened to me; until now I have been swaying between Mozart and Beethoven, between Rossini and Meyerbeer. Now I know whom I worship. There are two kinds of geniuses: the natural and impulsive genius and the elaborate and intellectual genius. I won't say that I have no regard for the second kind, but the first one draws my heart toward it with such mighty strength that there is no way to resist it. Yes, I have the courage to prefer Raphael to Michelangelo, Mozart to Beethoven, and Rossini to Meyerbeer. When I look at the Last Judgment, when I hear the Eroica or the last act of Les Huguenots, I am amazed and excited, and I don't have enough eyes, ears, or brains to admire them. But when I look at La belle jardinière, when I hear Le nozze di Figaro or the second act of Guillaume Tell,

I am bathed in a feeling of complete well-being and of boundless bliss. There is an interesting fact: When the sirocco blows here, I can't touch the scores of Don Giovanni, of Le nozze, or of Cosi fan tutte; Mozart's music touches me so deeply that I am literally taken ill. There are also Rossini pieces that have the same effect on me. Strangely enough, Beethoven or Meyerbeer never work on me with that kind of intensity. As for Haydn, he simply puts me to sleep!

I suppose I am entitled to some measure of indulgence for the emotion with which I cite here the first work that occupied young Bizet in Rome; this work is linked directly with me. The story in a nutshell is this: being a wealthy man, I had chosen to give a tangible form to what I call "the double loyalty" in my spiritual life, music and theology. Under the auspices of the Académie des beaux-arts, I established a fund to grant a yearly prize of 1,500 francs for a musical work based on a religious subject. Being biased in favor of the talented younger generation, I added a clause in the regulations limiting the age of the participants to thirty. And to ensure that the quality of the music would be adequate, only Prix de Rome laureates could submit their entries to this competition.

In spite of not being, by nature, overly vain or craving of fame, I must admit that the fact that this prize bears my name fills me with pride and satisfaction.

I feel that a few explanatory sentences are needed here and I'll try to be brief. Due to the comparative research I did between Jewish sources and documents from early Christendom, I came to far-reaching conclusions as to what these two religions have in common. In 1867 I compiled a memorandum for the minister of education in the government of Napoleon III, where I drew the basic lines for a future religion, in the bosom of which the sons of all three monotheistic faiths might find common ground for their belief. Hence my willingness to also encourage works written for performance in church, in spite of my strict adherence to Judaism. After all, in my imagination, I invoked pictures, like a mirage, of the day when churches, synagogues, and mosques would all become temples of worship common to all believers in one God.

From the start I knew that Bizet's decision to compete for the Prix Rodrigues during his first year in Rome was motivated by pecuniary considerations and did not draw its inspiration from religious sources or sentiments. Since then I have heard him declare quite often (maybe as a protest against his uncle François Delsarte's outspoken Catholicism) that he considers himself to be a staunch atheist. But notwithstanding my having no illusions as to his motives, I relished the thought that I might contribute, be it even in a small way, to the well-being of this youngster for whom I had developed such deep affection, and who I prayed would succeed in his undertakings.

In Bizet's letters from Rome to his parents, letters that his father graciously put at my disposal as a basis for preparing biographical notes on his deceased son, I found several allusions to the work meant for the competition. The first one is from February 1858.

> I started working today on a Te Deum for soloists and orchestra, for the Rodrigues competition. If I win the prize, I will ask Father to invest the money for me; I'll need only a very small sum to finance a trip to the Alps, but for the time being those are "Spanish Castles,"[2] or to be more precise, a "Swiss Castle." [He was in the throngs of

---

2   The French saying "*bâtir des châteaux en Espagne*" means planning, in a flight of fancy, an ephemeral future that lacks even a remote chance of being realized.

doubts about his creativity, an experience totally new to him.] This is arduous work, practically hard labor. In my entire life I have never felt so weary. I am chained down to my work like a slave. Even when I was confined to bed with one of my annoying chronic throat inflammations, burning with fever, I went on writing. I somehow fear that as a direct consequence, my music sounds somewhat hectic. If only I was sure that there is some value in what I do. I have completely lost all ability to judge.

Had events taken the course he wished they had taken—and the way I had hoped they would—our friendship would have started at this early stage, instead of being delayed for eight more years, to the days of his engagement to my niece Geneviève Halévy. But his hopes (and likewise mine) were shattered. The Académie voted in favor of Adrien Barthe, the laureate of the 1854 Prix de Rome.

Barthe had made good use of his being in Paris to launch a vigorous public relations campaign. I was bitterly disappointed by this choice because, from the start, I had this inexplicable soft spot for Bizet. The young composer did his utmost and with a commendable dose of courage to overcome his spite and to minimize the importance of what this could have meant to him.

But to me it seems that the blow was much more vicious than he himself would acknowledge. Something of his candid self-assurance was gnawed at its roots. For the first time in his life he had tasted the bitterness of defeat. From now on his soul-searching would become more and more frequent and his doubts would become more distressing.

Traditionally the musician laureates of the Prix de Rome were expected to spend the third and final year of their scholarship in

Germany, the center of contemporary music. Gounod was very much in favor of upholding this rule. But Bizet, who was feeling so good in Rome, under the warm Italian sun, was unwilling to leave the Villa Medici. He succeeded in getting M. Schnetz's unconditional support and, after exchanging a hectic correspondence with the Institut in Paris, was allowed to spend a third year in his beloved Italy.

During those three years I had no contact with Bizet, but my social activities brought about a closer acquaintance with Gounod, a bond that grew into a lasting friendship. From what he told me, week after week, I was able to put together a kind of mosaic of Bizet's life in Rome from which emerged quite clearly the picture of a tremendously gifted youngster groping through a labyrinth of different ways and possibilities, while craving a man of stature and competence to lean upon. But who could possibly provide this much needed stimulus? The old painter, Victor Schnetz? The director of the French Academy in Rome, notwithstanding the fact that he was a complete ignoramus in music, was better fit to serve as a mentor in the field of physical indulgence than as a guide to spiritual achievements. He viewed his own work with a kind of elementary contempt. Once a year he would hold an exhibition of his paintings at the Villa Medici; he would welcome the onlookers with the whimsical warning, "Dear friends, please remember that I loathe frankness!"

By far more apt to fill the role of a spiritual leader was Charles Gounod, Conservatoire graduate and colleague. Gounod, in spite of being in faraway Paris, was well aware of his mission and showered his young friend with letters oozing love, warmth, and magnanimity.

♪ ♪ ♪ ♪ ♪ ♪ ♪

At the Théâtre Lyrique they were rehearsing Gounod's new opera *Faust*. Marie Caroline Carvalho, wife of the theater's director, was to sing the role of Marguerite and the title role was to be sung by Hector Gruyer. But at an advanced stage of the rehearsals, Carvalho and Gounod suddenly decided that the tenor was unable to render the part properly and they gave the role to Joseph Barbot, who had only three weeks to learn the part.

Hector Gruyer and Bizet were close friends; their friendship started when the singer studied his trade with Bizet's father. The *Faust* incident naturally caused a rift between Gounod and Bizet. "My opinion of him as an artist hasn't changed," Bizet wrote to his mother, "but this is once more proof that a great artist is not necessarily an honorable man."

This temporary estrangement left Bizet with no one to turn to for advice and encouragement at that crucial stage of his development as a creative artist. It left him no option but to adopt a method of trial and error. His notes are overflowing with enthusiasm and grandiose projects that never came to anything. First and foremost was the opera *Parisina*, on an Italian libretto by Felice Romani, which had already been set to music by Donizetti. I really don't think he actually wrote any music to this, but he must have been quite preoccupied by it, as he repeatedly brought it up in his letters and conversations.

The many stimuli engendered by contact with so many cultural treasures brought forth one idea after another, each one of them abandoned when a new one fired up his imagination. His first visit to Cape Circe suggested the idea of an ode symphony based on *The Odyssey*. This he planned to become a gigantic work comprising four symphonic movements and five or six segments sung by soloists and choir. But Homer's classicism was soon replaced by a frenzied infatuation with German Romanticism. After the reading of E. T.A. Hoffmann's *Le tonnelier de Nuremberg* he started planning a three-act opera, his fancy being caught especially by the singing tournament. Then it was the turn of Voltaire and Shakespeare, having been enthralled by *Candide*, *Hamlet*, and *Macbeth*. Those were set aside by Cervantes. "For quite a while I have nursed the idea of composing a tragic-comic-heroic opera centered on *Don Quixote*," he wrote home. "Don't you think it is a great idea?"

But in the next letter he wrote, "The newspaper reports that Gounod has started work on a new opera, *Don Quixote*. Quite obviously this removes me from the stage."

Two symphonies that he had started sketching found their way into the hearth. His third symphonic endeavor was to ripen slowly in the back of his mind for eight years.

His natural inclination toward dramatic art drew him to *Esmeralda*, which Victor Hugo had recently adapted from his *Notre-Dame de Paris*. But this too came to nothing. And why not Molière? Back to the opéra bouffe; he started rhyming a libretto based on *L'Amour peintre*.

But he soon had to turn his attention back to the *envoi*.

Traditionally, the first *envoi* from Rome was to be a religious work. I have already mentioned Bizet's attitude toward religion—probably as a reaction to his uncle's militant Catholicism he had become virulently anti-religious. Answering his mother's letter in which she raised the question of his spiritual salvation, he asked her in no uncertain terms to stop nagging him on this subject. And when the matter of the *envoi* was raised by M. Schnetz, he almost lost his temper:

> They want a religious work? All right; I'll give them true religion, but not Christian...pagan! Horace's Carmen saeculare is waiting for the right music to enliven it. Its literary and poetic value is tenfold greater than that of the Roman Catholic mass. As a matter of fact I feel myself closer to paganism than to Christianity. I enjoy reading the work of the classics while in the holy scriptures I find only ego-tism, bigotry, intolerance, and a total lack of good taste.

As was to be expected, the *Carmen saeculare* never went beyond the planning stage. This was as far as Bizet would go toward meeting the

Académie's regulations about the composition of a mass or a work of religious character.

His first *envoi* would be the two-act opera buffa *Don Procopio*. While roaming the streets of Rome, he had stumbled on this Italian farce by Carlo Cambiaggio in a little bookstore. This libretto would have delighted Donizetti and, as Bizet himself told me, the music too was rather in the Donizetti vein. Surprisingly the Académie raised no objection about getting an Italian opera buffa instead of the expected *musica sacra*. There was unanimous praise for eight of the twelve scenes. To my great sorrow, the score has been lost and, in spite of my repeated searches in the archives of the Institut, I have been unable to trace it.[3]

For his second *envoi* he asked a third-rate writer, Louis Delâtre, to select and translate a suitable extract from Camões's *Lusiad*. This would provide the backbone of an ode symphony called *Vasco da Gama*. The text provided by Delâtre proved to be completely unsuitable. Disgusted and disheartened, Bizet shunned the work completely. But a few months later, in dire need of a subject for his second *envoi*, he came to the conclusion that Vasco da Gama was a worthy topic, and that maybe the wretched effort of Delâtre might still come in handy.

He got down to the job of revising the text completely and soon started writing the music simultaneously with the words. He finished the ode symphony in no time and was very happy with the result. On receiving the work, the Académie in Paris gave it a very favorable reception, and this gave young Bizet's self-confidence a welcome and much-needed boost.

3 Editor's note: The original manuscript score of the opera was found in 1894 among Daniel Auber's papers. The opera has since been successfully staged.

Female companionship was always an easy thing for Bizet to acquire. But this was no surrogate for the spiritual partnership for which he so desperately yearned. The tumultuous relationship he had with Seff, the beautiful Roman girl with whom he had spent most of his nights during his last year in the Villa Medici, had nothing whatsoever in common with a great love affair.

This is why the overflowing reservoirs of unexploited emotions had to be directed toward another worthy goal: friendship. He was in dire need of a friend, a kindred spirit with whom he could share his daily experiences. This is a natural inclination at this stage of life when youngsters are on the threshold of manhood. Given his unwillingness to turn to Gounod, he also needed some kind of artistic guidance and encouragement.

Already during the trip that brought the four Prix de Rome laureates for 1857 from Paris to Rome, Bizet had started a lasting friendship with the young architect Joseph Heym. It was with Heym that Bizet made his first excursion out of the city, to the hills surrounding Rome. There he gathered his first impressions of the rural landscapes of Italy, the friendly and hospitable population, the colorful customs and public holidays. During this trip, in the early summer of 1858, he also discovered, while visiting churches and monasteries, the dilapidated and pathetic condition of Italian organs.

Bizet had hoped that the 1858 Prix de Rome recipient for music, imminently expected to arrive in Rome, would add the much-needed dimension of a kindred intellect to the comradeship with Heym and that the three of them could form some kind of youthful alliance. This is the kind of relationship youngsters yearn for at this stage of their lives. But when, early in 1859, the laureate Samuel David made his appearance at the Villa Medici, Bizet at once understood that he would have to look elsewhere for a true and loyal friend.

Jules Didier took the place Bizet had hoped David would take in his affection. He was the painter laureate of 1857, the same year Heym and Bizet had won the Prix de Rome. Didier had a dog that would accompany him everywhere. With Didier and his dog, Bizet roamed the streets of the city extensively and was almost frightened on finding out to what extent he had begun to think of it as "home."

Didier and his dog were also his companions on a two-month trip to the south of Italy. The beauty of the scenery, the historical reminders all around, the happiness in friendship, all those things almost made him forget about the military expedition Napoleon III was waging in northern Italy in an attempt to evict the Austrians from Italy and unify the dismembered country. He was enough of a patriot to call his dog (a poor wandering thing he had found in the streets and adopted without a second thought) Magenta, after the town in Lombardy near which Napoleon III inflicted a crushing defeat on the Austrians, on June 4, 1859.

Bizet had to wait until January 1860 to finally find the true friend he had been seeking for so long. Yes, the friendship with Ernest Guiraud was to be a lasting and solid relationship. It was to last until Bizet's death, and even beyond. When *Carmen* was staged in Vienna in October 1875, a mere three months after the composer's death, the original spoken dialogue was replaced by the recitatives that Guiraud had composed. In 1877, I was in Vienna and naturally went to see this production. My heart was bleeding thinking of Bizet who had been unable to witness the triumphant reception the Austrian capital was giving to his brainchild; he was robbed of the recognition, the laurels, and the glory that the Parisian public should have showered on him. But nothing could lessen the intense pleasure and the aesthetic euphoria with which this experience rewarded me. So it is with immense gratitude that I acknowledge here the magnificent work Guiraud did on those recitatives, with an almost religious respect for his late friend's music, weaving them into the fabric of the whole work and enabling the flow of music and drama to unfold without any hint of disturbance. I think that in the same manner that Mozart's genius permeated the work of the anonymous Süssmayer when he completed his master's unfinished Requiem, the spirit of Bizet soared over Guiraud as he wove his recitatives into the weft of his friend's *Carmen*.

Guiraud was one year older than Bizet. He was born, in June 1837, in New Orleans, to a musical French family. He entered the Conservatoire at sixteen when his family came back to France. (At that time Bizet was already a veteran in the institution, having started his formal education there when he was ten). The two lads were on good terms from the start, but their true friendship was cemented in Rome. Guiraud won his Prix de Rome two years after Bizet with his cantata "Bajazet et le joueur de flûte."

Bizet's last trip in Italy, in which he would discover such pearls as Perugia, Assisi, Rimini, Verona, Padua, and Venice, would be made in the company of this easygoing youngster, Ernest Guiraud, whose friendship he would enjoy to his last day. But now the time had come to cross the Alps again—this time in the opposite direction.

4

GIACOMO MEYERBEER

December 1831

Lately all the talk in Paris is about this new production at the Opéra. All my friends say I must go see *Robert le diable*, which is by this German composer Giacomo Meyerbeer who has been living here in Paris these past five years. He came here from Italy when Rossini invited him to mount a production of his Italian opera *Il crociato in Egitto* at the Théâtre Italien, which has been, so I was told, a smashing success both in Venice (where it premiered) and at His Majesty's Theatre in London shortly thereafter. The role of Armando—which was written for the famous castrato Velluti and sung by him in Venice and in London—was sung here in Paris by Giuditta Pasta. I saw it some three years ago[4] and was quite favorably impressed. I had planned to go to see *Robert le diable* when the weather improved, because it has been bitterly cold in Paris lately and heavy snowfall has made walking in the

---

4   I was sixteen at the time.

streets a heroic expedition. But my friend Charles Morhange, who is a very gifted pianist and a promising student at the Conservatoire, insists that I go as soon as possible. In his opinion this is a masterpiece in the general manner of Auber's *Masaniello* and Rossini's *Guillaume Tell*, but even more strongly emphasizing the innovations of these two operas. Morhange also told me that M. Meyerbeer is a coreligionist of ours, and that he met him last week at the Friday evening service oat the rue de Nazareth synagogue.

Morhange was absolutely right: there is a new era dawning on us in the world of opera. It seems that *Masaniello* and *Guillaume Tell* have been the precursors of this trend, but *Robert le Diable* will no doubt remain the cornerstone of what we shall expect from the new era and its rich promises.

On the following Shabbat I went with Morhange to the synagogue, and sure enough, M. Meyerbeer was there. He wore a conservative, well-tailored light gray suit and had a very simple prayer shawl without the fancy ornaments some people like to show off with nowadays. He must be in his late thirties, quite a young age for a composer who, as far as I know, has already left his imprint on the history of music. He has an intelligent face, with an aquiline nose and a high brow under a wealth of well-groomed black hair. When Morhange introduced me after the service and said I had a keen interest in music, he turned his full attention to both of us, and notwithstanding our youth, he asked our opinion, not only on the production of *Robert le diable*, but on various other cultural topics as well. He showed a special interest in how the younger generation in France reacted to the modern tendencies in literature after the turmoil of Victor Hugo's *Hernani*.

Thus began our close acquaintanceship, I dare say a friendship, which lasted until Meyerbeer's death.

The almighty ruler of the Grand Opéra, the emperor of theater and the champion of success, appeared as helpless and frightened as a little schoolboy whenever the time approached to begin rehearsals on a new work. How, every time anew, Meyerbeer flinched from meeting face-to-face with the menacing and overpowering presence of a new production. How would all those people who are endowing the work with bones and flesh—the performing artists, the men behind the scenes, even ushers—how would they receive his newborn brainchild? What would be their reaction? Would they show enthusiasm for their roles, or would they be cool, aloof, and indifferent, or even worse, hostile?

"Experience has taught me that people don't fancy my music on first hearing it," he told me once. "But still I am very upset. When I played my new work for the singers it left them utterly unaffected. Not one of them complimented me. Don't you think it's a bad omen?"

His immediate reaction to the "bad omen" would be a radical revision of the entire work, a correction here, a change there—and maybe the whole mess would be completely revised. Even if this carried with it some amount of unavoidable unpleasantness, one had to accept it: the payment of fines, the antagonizing of people. What can you do? It's all part of the routine. If it has to be done, it will be done.

One critic sheds a tear on behalf of Eugène Scribe:

All my sympathy goes to M. Scribe, Meyerbeer's faithful librettist.

Everything has already been agreed to, down to the last detail: a duet here, a trio there, here a romance, and a sextet will follow. For the ending a big choral ensemble. M. Scribe goes home happy and satisfied. He sits down at his desk and, as expected, produces his verses. Then he polishes them to the last rhyme. Content after a job well done, he sits down to have a well-earned supper. In the middle of the meal a letter from M. Meyerbeer suddenly spoils the pleasant atmosphere. He lies down and tries to get some much-needed sleep; a new letter from M. Meyerbeer shatters his beneficent slumber while a host of demons dance around his bed to the tune of unearthly sounds that won't abate until daybreak.

In the summer of 1854, a few months after the premiere of Meyerbeer's *L'étoile du nord*, I was invited to supper at Pauline Viardot's. Meyerbeer was the topic of the conversation from the hors d'oeuvre to the dessert. Next to me at the table sat the German writer Heinrich Laube, whose tenure as director of the Vienna Hofburg Theater was a resounding success. There was a moment of awkwardness when Laube unexpectedly mentioned the fact that Meyerbeer was Jewish. But I soon was able to relax as he broached the subject with such tact and perceptiveness that I soon felt free to add my own remarks to the conversation. Here is, to the best of my recollection, what he said:

I was sitting in my hotel room, engrossed in a book, when a knock on the door brought me back to reality. A smallish man, soberly but very correctly dressed, his head slightly bent forward and sidewise, asked if I was Herr Laube. When I responded that I was, he switched to German: Heine had told him I was coming, but as the poet was out of town, he had decided to venture on his own and trouble me with his visit. His manners were refined to excess (this in spite of his having no plans for a new premiere in the foresee-able future, nor having any intention to return to Germany). There was only a well-calculated provision for an eventual future need. After a lengthy conversation and a second meeting at the Hôtel de Paris (Heine was present this time), I can now evaluate him pretty well. He is a wise man, and very diligent. He is strict to the point of pedantry when it comes to his art and its accessibility. (I sometimes think that the words "strict" and "pedantic" were coined with him in mind.) He is adamant as to the unshakable opinion that an opera must be thrilling from the dramatic point of view, and impressive from the theatrical one.

He studied the theater like a playwright, and chose the most talented French librettist, Eugène Scribe, to furnish him with plots and texts.

He is a wealthy man and uses his assets—this too on a very strict basis—to forward his artistic aims and deeds. In this field he never bargains. His time too he hands out lavishly. The artistic form must be worked through with purpose, to perfection, even though this might mean making changes, corrections, and new starts.

What does he think of life, and of his life, so full of worries in spite of his wealth? I am not sure I know the answer to this. He is a rational man. He has very definite opinions on every matter. Moreover, he is Jewish, and as a Jew he certainly has doubts as to whether the eman-cipation will last. This was the main reason for him to put his trust in the French. According to him, the French don't act with suspicion toward Jews; as far as they are concerned a Jew is just another man. His interest in all the facets of liberalism is derived from this belief.

It is merely that he chooses to be cautious, to stay confined to his hideout and to ask questions instead of formulating opinions. So the question is: Who is he? What is he? He is an artist, and a very talented artist. What is his nature, and where are his sources? His origin, his upbringing, the religious ceremonies of his forebears, all those are easily recognizable at the focus of his operas. The synagogue with its heartrending chanting is heard clearly and loudly any time the plot goes somewhat deeper and penetrates the underground strata. The orchestral accompaniment of Bertram in Robert le diable, the personage of Marcel and the entire fourth act or Les Huguenots, the psalmodies of the Anabaptists in Le prophète, all the aforesaid originate in the synagogue. And, you will ask, what about the much-advertised Protestantism that has been hailed and praised? There is no contradiction here. The core of the Lutheran creed is the Holy Scriptures, and those are, to the best on my knowledge, of Jewish origin.

Rossini called him to Paris to stage Il crociato in Egitto at the Théâtre Italien. In Paris he suddenly realized what his true goal should be. It came to him in a flash:

> I wish to create an operatic drama rooted in the history of mankind. It should deal with drives, desires, dreams, and actions of people and of crowds, in a universal language capable of penetrating every ear and reaching every heart. I will have no rest until I realize this dream and make it a tangible musical and theatrical reality.

Meyerbeer's acquaintances agree that in the character of Fidès in *Le prophète* he aimed at portraying his mother, Mme Malka Liebmann Meyer Wulff, whom everyone called Amalia.

Like her husband, Jacob Herz Beer, the composer's father, she came from a wealthy family. Her father was supplier to the Prussian army and had been granted the concession for the Prussian lottery. The family was of direct descent from the venerated Rabbi Moses Isserles and other famous rabbis. Amalia's parents ensured that their daughter would get the broadest possible education, inculcating in her a deep love of art, literature, and music, together with a rigorous observance of Jewish traditions. She managed, with a mixture of good taste and grace, the cultural salon she kept at their spacious house near the Tiergarten. Artists, writers, scientists, and political figures from the entire country would flock to this salon, just as they would meet twenty years later in the Mendelssohn household. She was a good-natured person and had special views on the subject of charity. Heinrich Heine relates that on days when she was not able to extend help to someone in need, she would face a sleepless night.

She proudly raised four sons to manhood: Jacob, the musician; Wilhelm, the astronomer; Heinrich, the adventurer; and Michael, the poet. Her father, Liebmann Meyer Wulff, had an unequivocal preference for his firstborn grandson, whom he called "my little music maker." He bequeathed all his sizeable fortune to him on one condition—that he would adopt his name, which was not too draconian a condition considering the yearly income of 300,000 francs that came with it.

In the beginning young Jacob bore both patronymics with a hyphen between them, but after a while he decided to drop the separation and emerged as the famous Meyerbeer whose name is printed in giant letters on theater posters all over the world. I had the honor and pleasure of meeting Mme Amalia Beer when she came to Paris in rather unhappy circumstances; her youngest son, the poet Michael Beer, died in the prime of life, and she decided to look for solace with her eldest son. To bring some comfort to his mother's bleeding heart, Meyerbeer composed the incidental music to one of his late brother's plays and to several of his graceful poems.

It was very easy to have Mme Beer reminisce about her elder son. It was a way for her to escape from her grief. I was astonished to find that she called her son by the name of Giacomo, the name he had adopted at the age of twenty-five while in Italy, and not Jacob, the name she had bestowed on him when he was born. I presume it was done on his specific demand.

Mme Beer spoke of her eldest son:

I still remember so vividly his first public concert as a pianist. He was only nine years old and he played Mozart's Piano Concerto in D Minor. He was so handsome: white shirt with a broad collar, blue jacket with shining brass buttons, and his yellow leather breeches in the English style. His gentle face was set in a dedicated and energetic look. He was so deeply involved in this inspired music that he completely forgot where he was. An admiring listener offered him a hymn of praise, the first of so many such odes he was to gather over the years:

> Bravely battling with wondrous fingers,
> On Zephyr's wings
> Not yet a youth, yet amongst Masters,
> You pluck the golden strings!
> Rocking our hearts in bliss and joy
> And lo, riding the winds of storm
> Shake the foundations to new form.
> Enchanted Muse such Art enjoy
> A kiss most noble in sweetest breath
> Crowning your brow with laurel wreath!

He was aware that he did not aspire to a career as a virtuoso. He yearned to be a composer, like Mozart, like Haydn, like Beethoven. We put his musical development in the hands of the finest teacher in town, Karl Friedrich Zelter, director of the Singakademie and in later years he would become Felix Mendelssohn's mentor. But the clumsy teaching methods and the uncouth manners of the one-time mason were foreign to the refined youth's nature, which required him to be treated at all times with kid gloves. From Zelter he went over to Anselm Weber, the conductor of the Royal Kapelle. On Weber's recommendation he started studying with the famous Abbé Vogler in Darmstadt. This was where he met and befriended Carl Maria von Weber, who was also a pupil of Vogler's. The firm bonds of friendship and mutual respect between the two youngsters lasted until Weber's untimely death, and even beyond it. With unending patience my son Giacomo toiled on the scattered sketches of Die drei Pintos, the opera Weber had planned and worked on intermittently after finishing Der Freischütz. His relinquishing work on the score after having labored so hard on it was due not to a break of loyalty, but on the contrary, because he respected Weber's memory too much to proceed. I have tried to explain this to his widow, but I'm afraid I was unable to convince her.

As a result of his studies with Vogler, who concentrated mainly on counterpoint and on fugue writing in the strictest style, my son composed a number of operas. But those didn't come close to pleasing the public's taste. They were deemed too heavy and serious, and overly intellectual, as seemed fit for a follower of the over-strict Vogler.

My Giacomo tried his luck in Vienna. There he met Beethoven and was even called to serve him in beating the tympani, together with young Hummel, in several performances of the famous Battle Symphony.[5]

---

5   When she talked to me the good Mme Beer didn't know that the bohemian musician Johann Wenzel Tomášek had published in his memoirs a rather unflattering account of her son's meeting with Beethoven. According to Tomášek the great composer said: "I was not at all satisfied with him. He never beat properly and always came in too late. I had no option but to sharply rebuke him. Ah! Ah!—This really angered him. Nothing will come of him; he doesn't have the guts to beat on time!" (J.H.R.).

In Vienna he also got to know M. Salieri, who advised him to go to Italy in order to get better acquainted with the proper technique in writing for the human voice. Giacomo was grateful for the advice and went off to Venice. He arrived there in the midst of the carnival festivities, and as it happens, also in the midst of the commotion around Rossini's Tancredi.

So what did my Giacomo do while the whole city was dancing and celebrating?

He gathered all the Rossini scores he could get his hands on and started studying and studying, until all the "professional secrets" were secrets no more and he had understood and properly assimilated them.

He immediately started writing Italian operas himself. And what success he attained! His Emma di Resburgo and his Il crociato in Egitto chased even Rossini's own operas from the stages of his very homeland.

My son's German friends, and foremost Weber, were very angry at him, at his turning his back on the German muses and "prostituting his talent." He tried to exonerate himself by explaining that it was the fascinating charm of Italy that had conquered him, and he had written those works not for the sake of cheap success, but out of genuine feeling. In a letter he sent to me shortly after he left Italy for Paris he wrote:

> The gentle gusts of wind and the cooing nightingale loosened my tongue. I was drawn into this enchanted world, and all the scholarly formulas suddenly seemed to evaporate from my mind. After living for one year in Italy I felt Italian in all things: I spoke Italian, I thought Italian, and I felt Italian. The glory of nature, the overpowering art, the gay and happy living and the pleasures of love metamorphosed my whole being; I didn't try to imitate Rossini—I had to write the way I did, because my entire being drove me to it.

And Mme Beer went on with her reminiscences:

Yet the reprimands and vexations of his German friends made their
influence felt. He always knew that Italy was a passing phase and
not the final destination. He was not Rossini, neither by his inner
nature nor by his fundamental talent. In the Italian opera manner he
did not express his inner self. It has suddenly dawned upon me that
he simply might have run out of melodies.

May 6, 1864

I just came home from the solemn funeral ceremony in memory of
Giacomo Meyerbeer held at the Gare du Nord. From there the body
was taken to Berlin in a special train.

Meyerbeer had, in his testament, very specifically asked to be buried
next to the grave of his beloved mother, in the Jewish cemetery of
Schönhauser Allee in Berlin, the city where he had first seen the light
of day. His wife, Minna, and his three daughters, Bianca, Cornélie,
and Cécile, were there, crying their hearts out. A delegation of notables
from different institutions in Paris accompanied the composer on his
final journey. His actual death had occurred on May 2, but Meyerbeer,
who was haunted by the fright of a false death, had specifically given
instructions for a wake to be held over his body for four days and four
nights. Little bells attached to his hands and feet would permit the
watchers to perceive the slightest movement just in case. It seems that
the melodramatic atmosphere ever present in my late friend's operas
had left a tangible imprint on his everyday behavior in real life.

At one o'clock, under the soft rays of a spring sun, the cortege started on its way from the deceased's home at 2, avenue Montaigne, to the distant railway station. Three military orchestras, with a muted accompaniment of drums, played marches from the works of the late composer. In front of the funeral wagon harnessed to six black horses walked Ullman and Isidore, the chief rabbis; the Prussian ambassador; Auber, the elderly director of the Conservatoire; Fresne, the director of the Opéra; Count Bacocci, the general manager of the theaters; and a delegation from the Académie française. The family walked behind the hearse, and after them came ministers of state, notables of the community, officials from the synagogue, and representatives of cultural and artistic institutions of the capital. Behind those came innumerable rows of coaches and thousands of mourners moving slowly on the lengthy course that took them through the Champs-Élysées, the Place de la Concorde, and the boulevards of Paris, which were heavily packed with onlookers.

After two hours, the procession arrived at the main hall of the railway station whose walls had been covered with black cloth. The casket was placed on a sumptuous platform adorned with silver candelabras in which white candles burned. In the background stood the wagon, also strewn with black and decorated with white funeral flowers. The chorus and orchestra of the Opéra performed the prayers from *Le prophète* and from *Dinora*.

Six obituaries were read, including those written by Berlioz and Gautier. The last speaker was Emile Olivier, who represented the opposition in the legislative assembly. Olivier's wife is Liszt's daughter Blandine, Cosima von Bülow's sister. Cosima von Bülow, as it is well-known, has left her husband and lives in sin with Richard Wagner. The unusual family bonds of the orator with the main and most venomous slanderer of the deceased brought to the solemn speech an unintended sense of irony. Olivier read:

This funeral celebration would never be complete if we didn't add to the voices of art, brotherhood, and religion the voice of the entire French nation, which is indebted to the deceased for so many hours of excitement and enthusiasm. Let us bless with a thankful heart those chosen by God who—while we are wrestling with the daily worries and struggles of life—beget, thanks to the genius of their talent, those hymns of hope and comfort that lift us upward into sun-bathed fields.

These delightful melodies are the true arbiters between nations; with their pure sounds they manage to reunite whatever jealousy and caprice have divided. They teach the people, in a language common to all nations, that we were all born to the same mother.

This is how this son of harmony blessed Germany and managed to bind ties of love between two sister nations: the fatherland of Mozart, Beethoven and Meyerbeer, and that of Hérold, Auber, and Halévy.

On hearing this glorious list read by the friend and relative of the author of *The Jews in Music* a cynical thought came to my mind: "Jewish musicians of the world, unite!"

When I came back from the ceremony I was tired and sad. I loved the man who had passed away, and I knew him inside and out. All the glory and the pomp—the sounds, the wreaths, the candles, the eulogies—all those things could not make me forget the barren truth: the exalted Giacomo Meyerbeer, the composer of works like *Robert le Diable, Les Huguenots*, and *Le Prophète,* which form the backbone of modern opera, was after all himself a tragic personage. He was a tormented, frightened, and insecure man to his last day. Was it Berlioz who coined the witticism, "Meyerbeer will be immortal as long as he lives"? The trouble is that Meyerbeer was aware of it, and the terrible thing is that he was willing to ratify this saying with his very own signature.

He once said to me,

At an age when people have normally reached maturity, the very years when the potentials, the character, the achievements of a person are supposed to be definitely formed and defined, I am still overcome by doubt. I feel like a helpless pupil, wondering whether the course I have chosen is the right one; if the penchant I have followed was really my calling; whether I truly deserve the standing I have achieved. And the inner voices reaching me, loudly crying out "No!" are so numerous, thunderous, and deadly that my life has become one big destructive question mark; I'm asking myself whether my whole life has, in fact, been a huge mistake.

He has been accused of being a charlatan, a fraud; but a charlatan is never haunted by the doubts and agonizing birth pangs that accompanied the creation of each of his works. It always took him years to complete an opera, and this tells more about the man than all the eulogies and appraisals that have been published or pronounced these last few days. The writing of The African was a real torture—it tormented him for almost half his lifetime, and in the end he was recalled to join his forebears while still rehearsing the work, as he usually left the score (which will have to be cut by half anyway) open to many last-moment decisions. Unfortunately, those questions will have to be answered by the people he empowered to execute his artistic legacy, though I hesitate to feel confident about their capacity to make the right decisions.

Naturally he was not busy writing solely operas; he composed songs, cantatas, choral music, marches, and a host of other pieces commissioned for special events all over the country.

His appointment as *Generalmusikdirector* to the King of Prussia, though it occupied him for only a few months every year, was also a burden both on his time and on his creative faculties. As were all the thousand and one minutiae he had to cope with: the supervising of performances of his works all over Europe; meetings and discussions with theater managers, librettists, translators, stage directors, choreographers, and set designers; the unending cajoling of famous singers and the scouting for (and training of) new talent; involvement in the family business and helping his brother, the astronomer, run the sugar factory; the constant need to promote himself by establishing new social acquaintances, by playing host or taking part in social events; keeping up to date by reading new scores and listening to his colleagues' new operas on a regular basis; having to consider hundreds of pleas for help every month, some asking for money, others for recommendations, still others for sponsorship; and the reading of critical reviews about his personality, his output, and his works in the German, French, Italian, and English press. And in addition to all these, he waged an eternal struggle with his devastating toothaches; he fought to ease his intestinal pains by taking health baths at sea health resorts or at fashionable spas; he battled the daily torment of worrying over his wife's consumption; and he took zealous care to guide the education of his daughters in accordance with the rules and customs in which he had been reared by his own parents. He was ever unable to draw a distinction between big and small, or between the essential and the accessory; to him everything was large, everything was essential.

Here are a few lines I copied from his diary:

Rehearsals with the quartet. Answer for Scribe. With Schlesinger about the contract. With Lacombe on the tuning of the organ. —Distribution of prizes at the Conservatoire. —Two tickets for Heine for tomorrow's ballet. —Cancel the ball at the Opéra. —Taglioni's accompanist should not take this fast a tempo. —With Lavorne about the clarinet and the horn. —To erase the drums from the "dispute choir." —With Nourrit on the duet in act 4. —Dinner with Hiller. —Rothschild. —Georges Sand. —Sordinos for the horns. —The canon in the duet has to be shortened. —With Deschamps about the changes in the third act.

—Tympani in F-sharp or C-sharp? —Caution the singers about the coming of the journalists. —Make a date to supervise the casting of the bells. —Write to Bianca for her birthday, and to mother for Bianca's birthday. —To the furrier about Minna's coat. —Go and hear Fischer in the "Seraglio."—Two tickets for Berlioz. —Schedule free time for the portraitist. —Curriculum vitae for the Revue de Paris. —Supper with Liszt at Dumas's. —With the viola d'amore on the obligato.

The heavy agenda was a burden, but in a sense it was also a blessing because it shielded him from the awe of the ever-present need of confronting creativity, the need to make decisions, the need to gather energy to complete all these unfinished tasks.

He was the very model of insecurity and hesitation; every new idea gleaned from outside would drive him to change course. Every criticism uttered, from wherever it came, would spur him to reconsider everything. Friends would plead and foes would snicker, "Where is Meyerbeer's new masterpiece, the one we were promised years ago?"

Time and again he would violate agreements and be unable to meet deadlines. He paid a fine of thirty thousand francs to Véron, the director of the Opéra, for failing to complete *Les Huguenots* by the deadline specified in the contract. As it so happens, he was able to obtain a refund of the money from the infuriated Véron, who had been unable to break the solidarity of fellow composers who flatly refused to even consider a substitution.

Even his wife Minna—his first cousin, by the way—who had been watching his career with such a deep understanding and unmitigated love, would at times give up the hopeless task of coming to terms with the strange and adventurous way he managed his affairs. I wonder if this is why she so often fled from Paris to spend weeks at a time at health resorts all over Europe. I have in my possession one of the letters she sent from such a spa to her husband:

> I am very much aggrieved by the fact that you have decided to postpone, once again, starting rehearsals for Le Prophète. And according to the information reaching me both by word of mouth and through the press, L'Africaine, which we were justified in considering to be a completed opera, is far from being finished.
>
> How long must I plead with you not to act on momentary impulse to undertake obligations you cannot fulfill, or whose fulfillment would impede your other activities? You promised to stage in Paris a new work you have not yet composed. But at precisely the same time your presence will be needed in Berlin in connection with the reshuffling of the theater's management.
>
> But forget about that; when the king is behaving in such an irresponsible manner in all his decisions, he shouldn't expect responsible behavior from those people with whom he deals.
>
> But what's happening with Weber's unfinished opera Die drei Pintos? You promised his widow that you would complete the opera within a specific period of time. Did you really believe, even for a moment, that you would be able to do this? I don't hold cheap your noble motives, but this beautiful unselfishness and devotion is turned to derision and even to shame when it doesn't bind you to your promise.
>
> Your declaration that in the fall you will come out with a new opera (which means of course that you will start rehearsals in May or at the latest in June) was made to ease the pressure and buy you some additional time. But when the deadline nears, you will find yourself

empty-handed—the wrath and disappointment you will face will be trebled, not to mention the fine you will have to pay to Scribe and his collaborators.

My dear husband, if it were not for my unsteady health I would have chosen a bolder and more penetrating wording; but in the meantime I have given you enough to chew on, in hopes of helping you reach new decisions and give you the strength to stand by them.

Your faithful wife,

Minna Meyerbeer

But when the job was done, when the lights went out and the curtain rose, the audience was ecstatic, and so was I. So I'm not surprised at his mother's recollection of one of the most moving experiences of her life:

He didn't know that I was sitting amongst the audience in the Salle Le Peletier on this evening of November 21, 1831, as the curtain rose on Robert le Diable. I sat huddled in the corner, almost completely hidden, and tears poured from my eyes, tears of bliss and gratitude. The wonderful sounds, sounds that my firstborn son's imagination had created, together with the breathtaking sights, the colors, the lights, the movement and the dancing, all were mixed in one huge melting pot to form an allegory of the primeval battle of the sons of light against the sons of darkness, of the ancient struggle of good against evil.

When the curtain came down and the elated audience exploded in thunderous applause, I wrote, my hand trembling with emotion, a few verses on a sheet of paper, and sent this with one of the ushers to my son backstage:

May the Lord bless thee and keep thee,
May the Lord make His face shine upon thee and be gracious unto thee,
May the Lord lift up His countenance unto thee, and give thee peace.[6]

And I, what can I add to the blessing of a loving mother?

This is not the time to open a debate on whether the man who is now making his way by railroad to his final resting place, the man who wrote *Robert le Diable, Les Huguenots, Le Prophète,* and *L'Africaine* will be remembered amongst the great men of this era, or whether the saying about being "immortal during his lifetime"—a lifetime that has now come to its end—will prevail. I have my private opinion on this subject but I would rather not voice it now. But I think we should all be advised to ponder the saying a great musician, an avowed Wagnerite and Jew-hater who was never accused of showing undue love for our composer. Here is the wise advice given by the conductor Hans von Bülow:

> Those who wish to paint our good Giacomo as a composer who is outdated are making a big mistake. They would be better advised to listen to his music instead of making a sour face; they might learn something. Instead of holding their noses let them bury their noses in his scores.

There are those, like Meyerbeer, who have conquered immortality during their lifetimes but lost it when they died. And there are those who, like Bizet, fought all their lives in the futile hope of attaining a glimpse of recognition, and it wasn't until their deaths that they were granted immortality.

---

6   This is the traditional Jewish priestly blessing (*birkat kohanim*).

5

GRAND OPÉRA

The rehearsals for *Carmen*, which started at the Opéra-Comique three months ago, were interrupted yesterday for one full day. But even Bizet, with his usual witty sarcasm, did not utter a word of protest about this disturbance because yesterday, Tuesday, January 5, 1875, thirteen years after the cornerstone was laid, the Palais Garnier was inaugurated in a lavish ceremony. Many call it the eighth wonder of the world. It is, of course, the new opera house of Paris.

For week after week we have been fed with rumors about the marvels that the new "palace" harbors: a thousand marble stairs stretching from the entrance hall to the upper galleries; the statues and frescoes that had supplied tens of Prix de Rome laureates with work for years; the lounges, the ballrooms, the entrance foyer, all of which are decorated even more splendidly than the actual main hall; and above all, the sophisticated machinery behind the stage, a model of modern engineering with no equal in the whole world.

I am indebted to my dear sister Léonie for the privilege of having been present at the opening gala, amongst the two thousand handpicked guests. The artistic part of the program included two acts from Halévy's *La juive*—hence the complimentary tickets to which Léonie, Halévy's widow, was entitled. She chose me to accompany her that evening.

I probably would be hard put to name all the places that sheltered the Paris Opéra since its creation under Louis XIV. But the different names it has used since it was established are well-known to me. It was born as the Académie royale de musique. The Revolution brought a change of name and it became the Théâtre des Arts. Napoleon brought back the old glory with a tiny change: instead of "royale" the Académie would become "impériale." When the emperor went into exile, "royale" became fashionable again. Then came Napoléon le Petit, and reawakened the customs and the titles of the empire. Now we hope that with the advent of the Third Republic, the name Académie nationale de musique chosen by this venerable institution four years ago—while performances were still being held at the Salle Le Peletier, opposite the famous Trattoria of Paolo Borgi—will remain and bring with it fame and glory.

I do not ask why an institution like the Académie de musique should cling so desperately to bygone days, be they "royal" or "imperial." (It seems to me that a nation licking its wounds is justified in drawing some comfort from its glorious past. In my humble opinion, we are better off now that those days are behind us, but the memory of heroic times is still a treasure to be cherished.) But if I don't ask this question, there is another one that needs to be answered: Where are the contemporary operas that are expected to come before the public in this new temple of the arts? Or was it erected only to celebrate again and again the old, hackneyed favorites that have become loathsome?

Still, with all the pride we took at hearing *La Juive* on such a festive occasion, we couldn't avoid the obvious question: How is it that the Académie Nationale de musique didn't think it appropriate to commission a new work for the historic consecration of this palace?

If the program as advertised gives any indication as to the preferences of the management, the future of the youngest generation of French composers is in jeopardy. To witness, here is the program: the overture to Auber's *La Muette de Portici*; two acts from Halévy's *La Juive*; Rossini's *Guillaume Tell* overture; two acts from Thomas's *Hamlet*; a scene from *Faust* by Gounod; and, to close this grandiose event, *La source*, the successful ballet with music by Delibes.

Three of those composers are in various stages of decomposition by now. Two others are respected elderly figures, and another one is middle-aged. Perhaps it's not such a bad balance sheet after all— that is if the program had been performed as advertised. But the incompetence of the organizers was such that even this conventional and uncompromising program had to be abandoned. A dispute broke out between the management and Christina Nilsson, who had been brought from London to sing the roles of Ophelia and of Marguerite. Nilsson—who, by the way, created Ophelia in 1868—packed her suitcases and crossed the Channel back to England in the midst of the rehearsals. Instead of *Hamlet* and *Faust*, in a last-minute act of salvage, Meyerbeer's forty-year-old *Consecration of the Daggers* was staged. Gounod, accustomed as he is to mishaps, shrugged; Thomas cried sky-high vengeance. Delibes, that charming fellow whose *Coppélia* had taken Paris by storm, was the only living composer remaining to be represented at that historic gala evening.

I asked Bizet why in his opinion the management had seen fit to put together such a hackneyed program. His answer was a lesson to me, a lesson I will never forget. "I agree with you," he said. "In the same manner that they provided work for all those sculptors, they could have made at least one young composer happy. But remember, there is no such a thing as hackneyed music. *Every day dozens of new babies are born in France and they have never heard Mozart's* Jupiter Symphony."

When the lights dimmed and the orchestra strummed the first bars of the overture to *La Muette de Portici*, a strange silence fell upon the audience. It felt as if all the grumbling about the changes in the program suddenly gave way to a gigantic wave of nostalgia for those long-gone days, on the eve of the July Revolution, when those sounds were the heralds of hope—the hope for a new way of life, for a new world where all is for the best.

I was not yet sixteen on that historic evening of February 29, 1828, when we witnessed the birth of the Grand Opéra, the French romantic music drama, on the stage of the Salle Le Peletier.

For two years Rossini, who had been called from the neighboring Salle Ventadour, seat of the Italian Opera, to save the situation, had been toiling to improve the technique of the singers and to scout for new talent. Rossini considered the immediate and unmitigated success of *La muette de Portici* a personal victory, because all three major roles were performed by singers who had benefited from his guidance. Laure Cinti-Damoreau, who sang Elvire, was actually brought over from the Théâtre Italien. Adolphe Nourrit was Masaniello, and Henri-Bernard Labadie was Pietro.

It was also a birthday present for him. In spite of being thirty-six, it was only his ninth actual birthday. Having the rare misfortune of having been born on February 29, he could claim an actual birthday only once every four years.

Today, as I write these lines, the era of the Grand Opéra is over, mainly because those unique artists who united their genius to give it life have all left this world. But with the perspective of time I can say today, with no danger of erring, that the epoch of the Grand Opéra started on that historical date with the premiere of *La muette de Portici*.

It also reflected the atmosphere of political discontent that would ripen two years later and bring about the July Revolution of 1830. This opera was also the primer of the revolt started in Brussels on August 22, 1830, which resulted in the separation of the nine southern provinces from the Kingdom of Netherlands and the rebirth, after several centuries, of an independent Belgian state. It was the duet from act 2 between Masaniello and Pietro, "Mieux vaut mourir," with its heart-lifting refrain "*Amour sacré de la patrie*," which inflamed the public in the Théâtre de la Monnaie to such extent that they spontaneously began the revolution that brought Belgium its independence.

My brother-in-law Fromental Halévy wrote about the Paris premiere:

> What the public saw that night on the stage of the Salle Le Peletier was one of the seven wonders of the world: a small fisherman's village on the shores of the Mediterranean had been transported in its entirety, as if on a flying carpet, onto the stage. A Spanish prince so lavishly dressed that his attire seemed to have been copied from a Velasquez painting. An imposing royal palace built on the background of Mount Vesuvius. And to crown it all, we witness this same Vesuvius erupting at the end of the opéra in an orgy of fire and brimstone, which seemingly endangered the public itself with its flow of boiling lava. For weeks to come this spectacular pageant of the eruption was the talk of all the salons, and even silenced, for a while, discussions about the murky political situation.

Who was behind this wondrous phenomenon that, as if with a magic wand, brought the public back to the opera house? It was the achievement of an incredible team of four.

Let's take a closer look at these four unique talents. First there was Eugène Scribe, the son of a silk merchant, who had been spellbound by the theater since his early youth. He was born in 1791 and was educated as a lawyer, but never actually practiced law. I have good reason to suspect him of being of Jewish descent; his father changed his name from Sofer to Scribe when he settled in Paris. He started his literary career in the field of the vaudeville, those satirical sketches on topics of everyday issues, strewn with popular tunes to which words referencing current affairs were attached. In a very short time, he ruled the stages of the theaters on the boulevards, and from 1820 to 1861 some 120 of his plays were produced there. He conquered the Opéra-Comique when he wrote the libretto for the charming *La dame blanche,* which Boïeldieu set to music. When, in 1836, he was elected to the Académie française, everyone agreed that this was an honor that should have been bestowed on him many years earlier. In his acceptance speech he denied that the theater's purpose was to depict society. Still, the characters he staged were the very people who sat in the audience: shopkeepers, civil servants, doctors, lawyers, bankers, and stock market brokers.

But for his great romantic operas he chose to salvage from oblivion historic events or legendary figures and then implant them in the middle of intricate plots, the brainchild of his fertile imagination. In accord with the trend of public opinion, he was a staunch believer in the fundamental rights of man to achieve political and religious freedom. But he was ever cautious not to stretch the rope too far. This is why he always painted the passions of his heroes with a hue of pink to soften the operatic conventions.

He summarized his political, social, and artistic credo with the motto "The public is always right." His outer appearance was that of a perfectly average bourgeois, shunning any kind of extravagance in dress or behavior.

For the production of his plays and librettos he required the assistance of a host of helpers who followed his instructions to the letter. In choosing his plots and their development he had one single aim: effectiveness. In his operatic work he followed a very simple but effective discernment: "Always remember," he said, "that the French public will never be so blinded by the music as to forgive defects and shortcomings in the libretto."

The second member of quartet, Daniel François Esprit Auber, was for thirty years head of the Paris Conservatoire. He was the bright comet of the Opéra-Comique and produced one new opera every year for four decades. For his fellow countrymen he was the archetype of the French composer; his music was witty, light, elegant, funny, and tasty. Heine, the *enfant terrible* of the Parisian press, voices a slightly different opinion:

> The poet Scribe and the composer Auber make a perfect team because both are endowed with a generous amount of esprit. The only trouble is that Scribe is lacking poetry and Auber doesn't have any music in him!

> After his guest appearance at the Académie royale with his historic milestone La muette de Portici, Auber swiftly returned to the familiar and easygoing atmosphere of his permanent abode, the Opéra-Comique. He considers himself cursed by being condemned for life to compose music. He takes respite from his adventurous incursions in the land of the muses in the company of cheap ladies or riding one of the thoroughbred horses he raises in his private stables. He tries to hide his natural shyness behind a screen of affected authority. He never uttered a single word on the subject of his Jewish origins (if indeed he really is a Jew, as rumor has it).

> The shrewd humility with which he regards his highly vaunted talent deserves our full admiration and respect.

When he wrote this, Heine must have been aware of what Auber himself said concerning his own work: "If someday I am forced to witness even a single performance of an opera of my own, I will never again be able to write a note of music."

But this disaster never took place because while all Paris swarmed to the theater to enjoy his works, Auber indulged in pleasures of a completely different kind, which were to him much more rewarding.

Now let's look at the third member of this wonderful team: the director Armand Duponchel. He was an amateur archaeologist, an architecture student who had discontinued his studies and never completed them. His natural pallor and shrunken looks reminded one of an undertaker. But he had an infinite internal reservoir of energy and determination. His passion was creating sets for the theater that were unrivaled in their daring originality and sumptuousness. His imagination knew no bounds when it came to inventing new tricks and stunts. He has been called the Alexander the Great of the opera stage.

In his first report on being appointed manager of the Opéra he wrote,

> When I arrived at the Académie de musique, I found only a terrible neglect in all fields, but the physical condition of the stage was the worst. The sets are in appalling condition. There is no future for the Opéra without the stage settings undergoing complete renovation to match modern innovations on a technical level.

The fourth wheel of this sumptuous carriage was Pierre Ciceri. As a youth he studied singing at the Conservatoire and was well on his way to a promising career at the Opéra. An unfortunate accident that left him with a noticeable limp, and cut short all hopes of becoming a star, forced him to reach the stage through the back door. This he managed thanks to his hobby: landscape painting.

He started painting sets for the boulevard theaters. Those were still the days of the classic scenes with the rosy shepherdesses baked in sunlight on a background of flowers and green foliage. He soon shifted to the revolutionary style with a more realistic approach to his subjects. At the time he was appointed to the Académie royale as principal set designer, he was overflowing with new ideas; this made him the ideal partner to help Duponchel achieve the results he craved. He told his staff,

> Effective scenery is based on the ideal marriage between imagination and precision. Every new production has to start with fundamental research in terms of epoch and emplacement: the study of landscapes, buildings, accessories, dresses, local color, and customs. There is no better way to bring the public face-to-face with the historic truth.

After *La muette de Portici*, the Académie royale had to make enormous efforts to keep the level of its productions up to the standard to public expected from then on. This would be the task of the new management.

Since Auber, frightened by his own success, had chosen to rest on his laurels, and his partner Scribe had been sent on provisionary leave, another team had to be called in. Rossini was now drafted to serve the new god, the Grand Opéra. In order to write a great work in the wake and spirit of the new manner that was taking shape, the Italian maestro had to make some far-fetched adjustments and compromises. He had already dressed two of his former operas, *The Siege of Corinth* and *Moses*, in French attire and changed their soft, melodious Italian language, the language of nightingales and scented winds, into the totally different accents of French. He was now asked to renounce the very inner soul and essence of Italian opera, the solo aria, for the benefits of the big choral masses—street scenes, banquets, ceremonial processions, public meetings, revolt, and victory.

The translation into French of Schiller's *Wilhelm Tell* had just been published. It would supply all the ingredients needed: an exalting historical plot in the romantic frame of the Middle Ages, where an oppressed population, led by a fearless and pure-hearted hero, stood up to a ruthless foreign ruler in the manner of *La muette de Portici*; two lovers whose family ties made them irreconcilable enemies like in *Romeo and Juliet*; underground meetings of plotters like in *Hernani*; and the paroxysm of tension, the father, renowned marksman, forced to shoot an apple from his son's head, saving a spare arrow for the tyrant.

The libretto was the work of three, two of them amateurs: Jouy, Bis and Marrast. Victor Joseph Étienne de Jouy was born in 1764. At eighteen he received a commission in the royal army and served oversees, first in French Guyana in South America, and later in India in 1785. At the outbreak of the Revolution, he returned to France and fought for the Republic in the early campaigns, attaining the rank of adjutant general. He resigned his commission on the pretext of his numerous wounds and turned to literature at the age of forty. His greatest success came when he wrote the libretto for Spontini's opera *La vestale*. He has always been a fighter in the cause of freedom.

Hippolyte Bis was born in 1789, the year of the Revolution. He was a minor poet but he should be remembered for his arousing rhymes in *Guillaume Tell*.

Marie François Pascal Armand Marrast worked as principal editor of *La Tribune* and later of *Le National*. He participated in both revolutions, in 1830 and 1848. He became a member of the provisional government in 1848 and was appointed mayor of Paris. He wasn't an actual partner in the writing of the libretto but he made the final revisions to the text.

As for the set designers, they also had their moment of glory: the breathtaking views of the Alps in the shifting golden light of dawn and the brazen skies of sunset, the picturesque marketplace, the forest hideout, and the tempest breaking out and transforming the lake into a foaming, overflowing milk pot.

One critic wrote,

> French opera adjusts to the ideals of a public that is not a music-loving public. These days, who cares what the composer has to say, even if it's the famous Swan of Pesaro, even Rossini himself? Today's heroes are the stage designers, the set painters, the costume tailors, the jewelers, the embroiderers, and the upholsterers. Music and poetry have become a pretext for initiating a giant industry of illusion, an industry that swallows the greatest slice of the theater's budget and is the main attraction, both for the responsible authorities and for the general public.

> May I be allowed to remind all those concerned that an opera is, first and foremost, a musical work, and that the institution responsible for its care is supposed to concentrate its effort and means in forwarding and cultivating the progress of this art before anything else? Is it really necessary to insist before the manager of the Académie de musique and his helpers that all the illusions of the scenery and the lure of the sets are meant to serve the music and not to distract the audience's attention from it?

This review is only a sample from what filled the critics' columns in the Parisian press.

I am sure that the composer of *Guillaume Tell*, the Swan of Pesaro as he was called here, would gladly have signed his name to this protest himself. The fact that music had become the slave of the spectacle was unpalatable to the maestro. Those who try to explain his thundering silence for the forty remaining years of his life in terms of external circumstances like the July Revolution, the political upheavals, the new appointments to the managements of the Académie, the breach of contracts, the complaints, the litigations, and so many other iniquities that in no way make life easier or foster creativity, are talking nonsense. All these nuisances could not have brought an artist of Rossini's caliber to retire completely from the stage. It was his unshakable belief that this road deviated from his own, and after a brief incursion down it he categorically refused to persist in following it. The fact that a new star had appeared, who adopted this new road with all his might and with stunning success, did not bring Rossini back to the scene; on the contrary, it strengthened his resolution to turn his back on it. It is by *not* coming back to the arena, by *not* facing him in open confrontation, by scorn, contempt, mockery, or revulsion that Rossini settled his account with Meyerbeer.

I found something Heinrich Heine wrote in the *Augsburger Allgemeine Zeitung* that has bearing on this subject:

> Meyerbeer is the man of his time, and time, so eminently able to choose its messengers, proclaims his reign high and loud. When Rossini witnesses this victorious procession he turns around with an ironic smile on his thin Italian lips and complains of bellyaches.

Meyerbeer produced his grand opera *Robert le diable* shortly after the July Revolution. The inner struggles of his hero, unable to make up his mind about what path he should take, reflect the moral dilemmas of those tormented days, swinging like a pendulum between good and evil. There was this incident at the premiere when the repenting hero, enacted by Nourrit, suddenly fell into the very gaping hole that, seconds earlier, had swallowed Satan, the living image of sin and evil. We were afraid that the life of France's greatest singer had been snuffed out by one of those modern mechanical trapdoors of which Duponchel was so proud. But to everyone's relief Nourrit was back on stage soon enough, his voice as vibrant as ever, and not the slightest bruise to be seen on him. We could again be confident in our belief of light's victory over darkness.

I never liked *Robert le diable* because this entire opera is ambivalent, not only in its content but also in terms of its execution. Meyerbeer lacks belief in his own strength, and instead of imposing his will on the public, he slavishly serves his audience. It seems to me that he believes in the rule of the people, not only in politics but also in the field of music, and he seems willing to adapt the craft of composition to the public's taste. Fears haunt the poor man day and night. Some even say that he is relieved whenever one of his admirers departs our terrestrial world; the departed at least will never be able to change their minds about Meyerbeer's music.

On the days when his operas are performed, the gods of the elements automatically turn against him. If it rains he fears that Mlle Falcon, his star singer, might catch a cold; if, on the other hand, the evenings are getting warm and cozy, he is worried that the audience might prefer strolling in the neighboring parks and woods or on the boulevards, shunning the theater entirely.

Success brings with it a growing sense of confidence and *Les Huguenots* is a far cry from *Robert le diable*. Connoisseurs say that in the future every composer who aims at writing for the Opéra will have to study this score in order to assimilate the innovations in the orchestration, in the musical form, and in the use of the choral masses. Some people claim that the use of these gadgets aims to mask the paucity of inventiveness, but I am inclined to think this is an exaggeration. Meyerbeer is an educated man with a broad range of interests, and those qualities generally exclude straightforwardness in thought and feeling, traits associated with "natural talents."

Bianca, Meyerbeer's eight-year-old daughter, was right in saying, while sitting at the window and watching other children playing cheerfully, "What a pity that I have such enlightened parents; I am doomed to sit silently all the time or to memorize all those boring things, while all the other children run freely around and enjoy life."

After the July Revolution, a new manager was appointed to the Académie de musique. He was Louis Désiré Véron, who took this assignment as a purely private commercial business (with a generous governmental subsidy) on the basis of profit and loss. Véron is a very unusual man. After graduating from the Imperial Lyceum he started studying medicine in 1816 at the age of eighteen. Shortly after getting his medical degree, an acquaintance of his, an apothecary named Regnauld, died, leaving for sole inheritance to his wife and children a formula he had invented for a paste to make lozenges. Véron invested all he had in the production of his late friend's invention. Thanks to his excellent connections in the press, he was able to launch a publicity campaign in several newspapers praising the therapeutic qualities of the "*pâte* Regnauld." And in no time at all, he gathered a huge fortune for the Regnauld family and for himself. In 1828, he abandoned medicine and founded the *Revue de Paris*.

His private carriage is known to all Parisians. He is, like Auber, fond of horses. He cultivates his ties with the press by inviting the more influential of its members to lavish dinner parties. There have been innumerable speculations as to whether the large white scarves he invariably wears hide some mysterious deformation or a physical infirmity.

♪ ♪ ♪ ♪ ♪ ♪ ♪

On reading these notes that were written a few years ago, I can add a few relevant details today. After leaving the Opéra in 1836, Véron purchased *Le Constitutionnel* in 1838 and was its managing editor until

1852. This is when he published Eugène Sue's *Le juif errant*. I don't have to remind anyone that he is the author of *Mémoires d'un bourgeois de Paris*, which he published in six volumes.

I met him shortly after his appointment and these are his own words:

Before I accepted this assignment I thought to myself, the July Revolution is the triumph of the bourgeoisie. This middle class, after emerging victorious from the struggle, will be eager to rule and to seek entertainment. The Opéra will be the new Versailles, the new center of attraction, and the new ruling class will swarm toward it in droves to fill the empty places left by the *émigrés*, the nobility that went into exile. The scheme to make the Opéra both popular and sparkling seemed to me a sure recipe for success. I accepted the appointment.

To achieve his goal, Véron needed a team of collaborators pliable enough to adapt their artistic outlook to the conditions needed for success: a librettist who could write what the public wanted to see; a composer who could produce music the public wanted to hear; a choreographer capable of bewitching; and a set manager and stage director eager to enthrall and astonish the audience. This ideal team came under his command in the form of Scribe, Meyerbeer, Taglioni, and the joint efforts of Duponchel and Ciceri. Add to them the incomparable voices and acting talents of the great trio Falcon, Nourrit, and Levasseur; the star dancers Taglioni, Ellsler, and Grisi; the conductor Habeneck; and the choirmaster, my future brother-in-law Halévy, and you have all that was needed to transform the Académie de musique into a gold mine.

The first thing Véron did after his appointment was order the removal of the "do not enter" sign that hung over the entrance to the stage, thus opening this hitherto forbidden sanctuary to supporters, admirers, and lovers who wished to enter into the magic world of romantic dreams behind the scenes. Some say that this single act doubled the number of tickets sold.

Under his stewardship the Opéra balls became the foremost attraction in Paris and eliminated all apprehension of a possible deficit. Véron had the press in his pocket. The paid claque had, for some time already, been a well-oiled machine, with an iron discipline ensuring that even the worst play could be saved from failure. The famous Auguste, head of the claque, was a giant next to whom the tallest men in Paris looked like grasshoppers. He led his platoons in carefully planned campaigns, adjusting to circumstances at all times and in full cooperation with the director. His fee was never less than that of the prima donna or the prima ballerina.

Véron diligently checked every little detail and happening in his realm. Even the dates when the girls from the corps de ballet were taking their monthly "sick leave," the "dancer's head cold" as they called it, were meticulously recorded in his red notebook, to the great displeasure of the young ladies who felt cheated out of an easy way to get some extra free time.

Here are his own words concerning his creed about the operatic repertoire and the proper way it should be performed:

> In order to enthrall an audience for an entire evening, a five-act op-era must be built on the potent and everlasting passions harbored in man's heart, as they express themselves in dramatic events through-out human history. Those dramatic plots have to catch the eye no less than the ear. This is why the visual organization must be clocked like a masterfully choreographed ballet. Special emphasis should be placed on the performance of the choir, which has to be pictured as one of the main characters in the action. Every act must put forward clear and effective contrasts in term of sets, costumes, and dramatic situations. The public is entitled to expect great things from an enter-prise housed in a huge theater with countless facilities, claiming an

orchestra of more than eighty musicians, a chorus counting almost as many singers, eighty extras (not counting the children), and a team of sixty well-trained stagehands. If those expectations are not met we can say without hesitation that the Opéra has failed in its mission.

Over forty years have elapsed since Véron formulated his creed and I can say that it has remained a guiding beacon to this day, as the same principles have been applied by various managements that have headed the royal, imperial, national, or whatever Académie ever since.

The last sounds fade away in the new opera house, the eighth wonder of the world. Endless applause and bravos have died out. The audience streams out into the salons, the foyers, and the passages, and gathers in small groups to exchange views and impressions, to exhibit their newest dress, and to decide how and where to spend the rest of the night.

Léonie and I have had our share of entertainment and we are ready to retire to our respective homes. On our way out we stop at the corner where the bust of Halévy, sculpted by my sister, stands. His wise and generous features look back at us as if wondering about his own destiny, not knowing whether his life has been worthwhile or not.

Outside, the dark winter night is chilly and bleak. The gas streetlights look like giant fireflies in the fog, throwing greenish-blue circles of light on the pavement of the big square. I cast a last look around; maybe I will find Bizet and Geneviève in the crowd. No, I don't see them. They probably rushed backstage to congratulate Delibes on his success, and in my heart I say a silent prayer: may God grant you the success you deserve with the coming premiere of *Carmen*.

6

ITALIANS IN PARIS

An Italian composer, Giovanni Battista Lulli, who changed his name to Jean-Baptiste Lully, was the founder of French modern music. Come to think of it, there has been an unending flow of foreigners who have concurred in the shaping of our national musical heritage, a respected handful of geniuses who have adopted France as their home, and have been adopted by France as her very own children.

Italy gave us Lully, Piccini, Spontini, and Cherubini, who was the director of the Conservatoire when I studied there. From our northern neighbor, what since 1830 has been Belgium, we gratefully received Gossec, Grétry, and César Franck. Prussia gave us Meyerbeer, Offenbach, and Flotow, and Austria was generous in sending Ignaz Pleyel. Farther to the east there is Poland with Chopin and Hungary with Liszt (who was never really a Frenchman at heart, being so torn between his love for German profundity, Italian warmth, and French beauty). And there are still those who like to ride two horses simultaneously: Bellini, Donizetti, Verdi, and Paganini are essentially Italian musicians living and creating mainly in Paris.

At one of Paris's high society drawing room parties, the hostess proposed an interesting piece of entertainment. The guests of honor at the party were Rossini and Donizetti, so why not ask them to each compose a small piece of music and the guests present would decide which of the two compositions they preferred? The two composers shrugged, but willingly agreed to cooperate in this unusual game. They were given a text, the same text for both of them, and were asked to improvise an aria based on those words. They were asked to retire to two separate rooms and were given forty-five minutes to complete the task. Rossini came out from his secluded room after twenty-five minutes. Twenty minutes later, when Donizetti joined the party, both men handed over their contributions.

The hostess took the sheets of music and went to the piano, but when she put the compositions next to each other she was amazed to suddenly realize that although the handwriting was different, the two piece of music were absolutely identical.

Amidst the general stupefaction, the hostess asked the two eminent guests, "How can you explain such a strange coincidence?"

"It's really very simple," said the smiling Rossini, giving Donizetti's shoulder a friendly slap. "We both stole the melody from Bellini."

Shortly after the premiere of *Guillaume Tell* in August 1829, Rossini had to leave for Italy. When he came back to Paris in November the following year, the Revolution had changed many things. The new government had repudiated the signed agreements under which Rossini was to receive a substantial annual royalty, and the composer went from court to court until, after five years of bitter bickering and unending lawsuits, the case was decided in his favor.

During all those years he refused all commissions and stopped composing altogether. But in 1832 his friend Aguado promised the Spanish minister Valera that he would convince Rossini to compose a religious work for him. So at Aguado's insistent request, and under the condition that the manuscript would stay with Valera, Rossini reluctantly wrote six of the ten parts of the *Stabat Mater*. The four closing movements were written by Giovanni Tadolini.

In 1841 Rossini was infuriated to learn that Valera's heirs had sold the manuscript to a Parisian publisher for two thousand francs. He immediately instructed Troupenas, his publisher, to forbid all performances and to stop publication of the work. At the same time, in order to have sole ownership of the work, he composed the last four movements to replace those originally written by Tadolini. Troupenas bought the entire work for six thousand francs and almost immediately sold the rights to Escudiers for eight thousand. They in turn succeeded in reselling those rights to the manager of the Théâtre Italien for twenty thousand francs. All these transactions took place in the span of less than one year.

With all his common sense and shrewdness where money was concerned, Rossini never understood how in a few months the price of a work could climb from two thousand, to six thousand, to eight thousand, and finally to twenty thousand francs.

I had no trouble understanding this; it's how I made my fortune at the stock exchange.

Letter from Giuseppe Verdi to Clara Maffei

March 2, 1854

Cara Clarina,

You ask if I intend to take root here. Take root here? Impossible! Is there any reason I should? To what purpose? For glory? There is no such thing here. For money? I can probably earn more in Italy. Even if I had planned to stay here, it would have been impossible. I love my privacy and the Italian sky too much and I have no intention to take my hat off for all those barons, marquises, and other high-ranking nonentities whose whims dictate the law here in Paris. Furthermore, I am no millionaire and can't afford to spend the few thousand francs I earn on publicity, bribes, the claque, and other similar filthy things, without which there is no hope for success here.

Alexandre Dumas wrote in his paper the other day about Meyerbeer's new opera L'étoile du nord: "How sad it is that Rossini did not stage his operas here in 1854. But Rossini lacked the German foresight to build success slowly, putting down the foundation six months in advance through a masterly campaign in the newspapers and setting the stage for a curious public eager to acclaim the much-awaited work on opening night."

This is a very accurate summing up of the situation here. The rumor goes that Mme Meyerbeer herself, her pockets lined with banknotes, visited the editorial departments of the newspapers. And what was the result? The public was almost hysterical. I was at the premiere of L'étoile du nord, and could make sense of nothing, or almost nothing, of it. But the public is frantically cheering and finds everything wonderful, beautiful, and sublime. And this is the same public that after twenty-five or thirty years still can't swallow Guillaume Tell, and permits the mutilation of Rossini's masterpiece, miserably produced in a truncated version of three acts instead of the original five. And this on the stage of what is considered to be the premier theater in the world.

So how come I've come in Paris again and again, and prolong my stays here even when I'm not mixed up with a mishap like Les vêpres siciliennes? The answer is quite simple: here no one pokes his nose in my private business, and no one tells me how to manage my life or with whom to share it. And this is no small relief.

I meet Verdi quite often by chance, walking in the gardens, on the boulevards, or on the banks of the Seine. He is a stout man, with strong features and piercing blue eyes. His face is cut in two halves by an imposing moustache and all of it is surrounded by a short, graying beard. This is a man with whom your heart yearns to make closer acquaintance, but this is not easily achieved: Verdi lives in complete isolation with his companion Giuseppina Strepponi. In abstaining from marrying her, he has made it very hard for himself to live in his native Italy, a country so terribly strict in matters of tradition and morality that it comes close to bigotry. As far as I know he has not yet tried to form ties with even the most prominent of his French colleagues, such as Berlioz or Gounod.

As for *Les vêpres siciliennes*, it has been given free publicity following the mysterious disappearance of the prima donna Sophie Charlotte Cruvelli, who eloped with her lover, the Vicomte Le Vigier, in the midst of rehearsals. Some say that Verdi was not at all sorry about how things turned out, since he was not really happy with this opera. It was built along the lines of the typical Meyerbeer Grand Opéra, and he was angry with Scribe for not making some radical changes in the fifth act. Above all, deep in his heart, he was secretly unhappy at having written the music to a play where the Sicilians, in a way his Italian brethren, are portrayed as the villains.

Since rehearsals on the *Les vêpres siciliennes* were discontinued, the management of the Académie de musique tried to convince Verdi to write a new opera altogether. This Verdi did not even consider, especially since a tempting offer had come from Genoa; a new opera house was being built there and the municipality would have liked to name it after Verdi and inaugurate it with a new Verdi opera, preferably *King Lear*. He had indeed begun planning a libretto with Cammarano, and since the poet's death has broached the subject with Somma.

As a result of the Cruvelli scandal, Roqueplan, the director of the Opéra, was relieved of his duties in November 1854 and replaced by Louis Crosnier. So it is Crosnier who bore the responsibility of trying to accommodate Verdi after receiving the following letter:

Monsieur,

It is my duty to point out a few unacceptable facts concerning the production of Les vêpres sciliennes.

I feel deeply aggravated and humiliated by the fact that M. Scribe flatly refuses to make changes in the fifth act, which is, as anyone will tell you, absolutely boring. I know perfectly well that M. Scribe is a busy man who has to cope with a thousand other things that are perhaps more important to him than my opera. But had I been able to predict that he would show such scandalous indifference, I would have remained in my own country. There, to be quite frank, my business was never managed in such a wretched manner.

I had hoped that M. Scribe would find for the end of the drama one of those emotionally charged situations that brings tears to the eyes of the audience; what's more, the plot calls for it. This would have greatly improved the work, which, except for the romance in act 4, is completely devoid of a truly passionate passage. I had hoped that M. Scribe would have had the grace to make an appearance from time to time at rehearsals so as to give attention to unhappy turns of phrases or words that sound harsh, and on all those things that need to be changed. He might have become aware on such an occasion that acts 2, 3, and 4 are identical in their structure (aria, duet, finale), a thing that surely doesn't add diversity or interest to the work as a whole.

And finally, I had hoped that M. Scribe would stand by his promise to change in the libretto all things that my Italian compatriots find offensive. I find here a great danger: on the one hand, he slights the French, who are portrayed as cattle brought to slaughter; on the other hand, he hurts the Italians' feelings by portraying them as lowly conspirators and unscrupulous murderers. God in heaven! In the history of every people there are moments of light and moments of darkness, and we are not worse than any other people in this regard. Anyhow, I am an Italian before anything else, and will not accept, at any price, taking part in harming my country's reputation.

I must add a word about the rehearsals. Here and there I hear remarks that are if not outright insulting, at least inappropriate. I'm not used to these kinds of things and will not tolerate them under any condition. Some of the people involved in the production think that my music does not fit the Grand Opéra style. Others think their roles do not use the full measure of their talent. As for myself, I also have severe reservations as to the style of the singing and the level of acting. In short, I find that we are in total disagreement concerning this production, and I see only one way to avoid an impending catastrophe: to annul the contract. You certainly will point out that the

Opéra has already invested much time and resources in this venture, but this is nothing at all compared to the year I have wasted here, a year in which I could have earned at least a hundred thousand francs in Italy.

Please allow me to express the fullness of my gratitude.

Yours,

Giuseppe Verdi

P.S. Please bear with the paucity of my French; the main thing is that you understand what I mean.

But Cruvelli suddenly reappeared with a very unlikely pretext (she would actually later marry Le Vigier) and the rehearsals of *Les vêpres siciliennes* resumed. The *King Lear* project was shelved and the new opera house in Genoa would bear the name of Paganini, who was actually born in that city.

The first performance of *Les vêpres* was held on June 13, 1855. It was a stunning success.

1855

Rossini's return to Paris was greeted here with general satisfaction. There are two topics of conversation here: the Crimean War and Rossini. The press is full of speculation about his health and the reasons that drove him to come back here after so many years.

I think the reason is rather obvious: Rossini was suffering from a stone in one of his kidneys and was set on having it removed. And he has more faith in our French doctors here than in those of his homeland. True, he is a real Italian patriot, but even this has its limits.

I heard that he has not yet overcome the shock of the incident near his house in Bologna, during the 1848 riots, when a gang of hotheaded demonstrators shouted at him, "Filthy rich reactionary!" This kind of nightmarish incident does not strengthen one's patriotic feelings. By the way, his health seems to have improved since his arrival, as a courtesy visit to Auber, the director of the Conservatoire, has been reported. Eyewitnesses say that he looked relaxed and happy. If so, he was right in putting his health in the hands of French physicians.

1857

Today I had a most interesting conversation with a Belgian journalist named Edmond Michaud, a member of Rossini's inner circle of friends. I asked him the obvious question, the question to which all the musical world would like to know the answer: What brought about the maestro's decision to retire from creative work at the ripe old age of thirty-six? Could it be that in the course of their frequent chats a hint had been revealed that could shed some light on this enigma? Here is what Michaud said:

> I think this is a complicated and tangled matter. Too many different factors are involved. One thing is clear: Rossini finds it difficult to

adapt to modern times. Not only in music, mind you, but in all fields of life. He once said, "An era directed solely toward barricades and armed struggles, robbery, plunder, and violence is not an era fit for music." He is no admirer of technical innovations either: "In places where trains are rushing, art is standing still." He himself rode in a train only once in his life, from Antwerp to Brussels, and almost fainted from fright. It took him several days to get over the shock.

A few days ago the maestro showed me a libretto sent to him by a young French playwright in the innocent hope that it might whet his appetite. Rossini said, "This libretto is in full accord with the current spirit. The trouble is I loathe the current spirit."

I told Michaud that I had heard that one of Rossini's admirers had once asked when he would endow the world with a new opera. His answer: "When the Jews are through with their Sabbath," which was a direct allusion to Meyerbeer and Halévy, maybe even to Auber. Is it possible, I asked, that jealousy and bitterness could have driven him to silence his muse? Michaud vehemently denied that Rossini ever said that:

That is a calumnious defamation, and it has certainly emanated from someone whose sole aim is to blacken both Rossini's and his Jewish colleagues' reputations. One seems to forget that he brought Meyerbeer to Paris, and staged Il crociato when he was director of the Théâtre Italien. Rossini does not consider himself to be in direct opposition to any composer. Naturally, he certainly would have had no objection if earnings from his operas equaled those of his successful colleagues...I don't deny that he disapproves of Meyerbeer's latest works, because they represent in his eyes the defective ideals of our era, ideals that he condemns with irony and scorn on every occasion given to him. One could find a link between the public blindly following the Grand Opéra and Rossini's retiring from this field, where he has stopped feeling at home.

I further asked if Rossini's proverbial laziness might also have been a major factor in his deserting the battlefield. After having worked so hard during his adolescence to earn his living and help his parents, building at the same time a worldwide reputation, it may seem natural that he decided to rest on his laurels. He had earned all the money and all the glory he needed. Michaud replied:

> You may be surprised to hear that the source of the legend about Rossini's laziness is Rossini himself. In my entire life I never met a man so set on projecting a twisted picture of his inner personality by spreading cheap, calumnious lies about himself. But if you change "laziness" to "the drying up of inspirational forces," you might come quite close to the truth. Rossini was used to having ideas showered on him like avalanches. Things have changed and he is unwilling to go out chasing those ideas. There is no doubt that his physical degradation has played a major part in this drying-up process that has befallen him at such an early stage of his creative life.

And when I inquired as to what brought up this physical degradation, Michaud averted his gaze and under his breath whispered almost inaudibly, "*Les péchés de jeunesse*, my friend—sins of his youth." This was all he said and I asked no further questions.

Without going into the reasons of Rossini's stubborn silence, Heine wrote about the phenomenon itself:

> The average gifted man will always be driven by his ambition and will strive to scrape all the talent he can muster to the last crumb. But in the case of a genius, he will not allow himself to descend

from the summits he has reached. As William Shakespeare returning to Stratford-on-Avon to show his scorn for the world and its
petty pretentiousness, so a smiling Gioacchino Rossini will stroll
the length of the boulevard des Italiens, his sharp and witty tongue
ready for spirited rejoinders.

I fervently share this hope of my dear friend and poet that we shall
all see the boulevard stroller return to the highest summit of his art.

Last week I went for the first time to one of the parties held by
Rossini every Saturday night at his home at 2, rue de la Chaussée
d'Antin, at the corner of the boulevard des Italiens. The two guests
of honor were Giuseppe Verdi and Franz Liszt. The quartet from the
last act of *Rigoletto* was performed to honor Verdi; our host himself
accompanied at the piano. Then Liszt sat down at the piano and played
a very impressive piece of his own; it was a breathtaking performance
of a staggering work. He calls it a sonata, but I would say it is actually
an elaborate fantasia in one continuous movement. He told us that his
favorite pupil, Hans von Bülow, had given the first public performance
of this work just a few months ago in Berlin.

Young Bizet, who was about to compete for the second time for
the Prix de Rome, was also there. Rossini asked him what he thought
his chances were and about his plans for the future, and very warmly
encouraged him. His generosity toward the younger generation is
remarkable. Saint-Saëns told me that two years ago, at one of the first
such parties Rossini held after his return to Paris, the maestro performed
one of Saint-Saëns's works. All present assumed that their host was the
actual composer. Only after all the guests finished heaping their praises
on the composition did Rossini, with a cunning and satisfied smile,
reveal the true identity of the young composer.

The persistent rumor that Rossini has resumed composing has, at long last, been confirmed. Unfortunately, it is not a new opera he is working on. His resolution in this matter is unshakable; he will never again write for the stage. His output is now mainly short pieces, mostly for the piano, with funny titles like "My Hygienic Morning Prelude," "A Toast for New Year's Day," "Aborted Polka-Mazurka," "A Little Pleasure Trip on the Train" (if my memory does not betray me, he did not really enjoy his one and only trip on this horrible vehicle), "A Would-Be Dramatic Prelude," "Muster from the Ancien Régime," and "Chorus of the Democratic Hunters." He has written dozens of those humorous miniatures and is gathering them under the general title of *Sins of My Old Age*. Rossini wants everyone to believe that he produces those gems spontaneously, like a hen lays her eggs. But the painter Guglielmo de Sanctis (not to be confused with the famous literary critic Francesco) has caught him in the act of copying some of those pieces from heavily corrected drafts. This reminds me of Michaud's remark concerning the gap between the image Rossini wants to convey and his true nature.

Just for the record, Rossini stubbornly refuses to publish his *Péchés de ma vieillesse*. They are securely locked in a drawer, and the key to this drawer is in his wife Olympe's hands. She jealously guards this treasure like a ferocious Cerberus.

June 1859

My close acquaintance with Ignaz Moscheles, the Jewish piano virtuoso currently staying in Paris, won me the privilege of an invitation to supper at Rossini's new villa in Passy, the luxurious residential quarter on the outskirts of the Bois de Boulogne. Rossini says that he purchased the property because its shape reminded him of a grand piano. The whole place breathes music, and even the flower beds are designed in the shape of musical instruments. In the four corners of the drawing room's ceiling the portraits of four giants of music— Palestrina, Mozart, Haydn, and Cimarosa—have been painted. A quartet of lesser importance decorates the ceiling of the dining room: Beethoven is flanked by Grétry, Boïeldieu, and Padre Mattei. The entrance gate is adorned with a gilded lyre meant to proclaim loudly that the composer has moved for the summer from Paris to his new abode. In the autumn, when Rossini returns to the rue de la Chaussée d'Antin, the lyre will be removed to the basement until next summer.

We were granted the great honor of having a glimpse at his collection of wigs, which he keeps in his bedroom. Rossini changes wigs several times daily, according to his whim, mood, or circumstances. Even in the presence of his servants he is shy of being without a wig on his head. De Sanctis (who started painting a portrait of the maestro) is among the very few who has seen his head unadorned. He is completely bald but, according to the painter, he is endowed with a beautifully modeled cranium, reminding one of Cicero's or Scipio Africanus's head.

Apart from Moscheles and myself, there were only a handful of guests, among them Rossini's intimate friend, the composer Michele Carafa di Colobrano who since 1827 has made his home in Paris. He is a member of the Académie des beaux-arts and was appointed professor of composition at the Conservatoire in 1840. Three Belgians were also there: the cellist François Servais and his wife, and Edmond Michaud, armed with his eternal notebook in which he kept writing, maybe with the intent to use this as material for a future biography.

I was surprised at the frugality of the menu, which was in sheer contradiction to the maestro's reputation. This reputation, not in the least fostered by Rossini himself, was that of a gargantuan glutton. But the food, in all its simplicity, was exquisite and of the highest quality. And as much as the palate rejoiced, the stomach felt no strain, as everything was light and easily digestible.

The table talk was animated and touched on three topics: the decline in the art of singing, the pitiful condition of church music in Italy, and, befitting Moscheles's presence, the noisy way the new generation of piano virtuosos play nowadays. On this last subject Rossini expressed himself in unambiguous terms: "They play as if they were intent on shattering not only the piano but the piano stool as well."

Moscheles was anxious to learn about Rossini's preferences and asked him which of the composers of the past was his favorite. Rossini didn't even have to think to give his answer: "Beethoven I'm willing to have twice a week and Haydn twice as much. But Mozart! Give me Mozart every day!"

"Speaking of preferences, maestro," Moscheles insisted, "amongst your own work, which do you prefer: the high-spirited *Barber of Seville* or the dramatic *Guillaume Tell?*"

Rossini's reply was characteristic of the man: "I will have both the gaiety and the drama if you let me choose *Don Giovanni.*" And after everyone laughed at this witty reply, Rossini added, "The Germans were always the great experts in the field of harmony. We Italians were the great masters of melody. But when the north gave birth to Mozart we were irremediably beaten on our own soil. This genius surpasses both northern moods and southern nature and unites in his music the charm of Italian melody with that of German harmony."

A host of guests who had been invited for after supper had started gathering in the drawing room. In no time at all there was not a single free seat left and even the corridors were crowded with small groups, standing, sipping their drinks, and busy in animated conversation.

Rossini chose to stay in the dining room with Carafa. The door to the drawing room was wide open and the guests, every one of them in his best attire, came in turn to greet our host. It was a kind of ceremony with undertones of officialdom to it that has never taken my fancy. This is the reason I prefer the gay and informal evenings at Offenbach's home to this meeting of glittering society. But on the other hand, the musical program was of the highest quality, especially Moscheles's fiery playing. He played several interesting études and three *allegri di bravura*, which he himself had composed. After him, Rossini sat at the piano to accompany the formidable and massive Mlle Marie Saxe, who made a brilliant debut at the Théâtre Lyrique, and who is said to have already signed a contract to start next season at the Opéra.

But when asked to play some of his own *Sins of My Old Age*, he flatly refused. "You will be better off asking Moscheles to add a few encores," he said. And when Moscheles complimented him on his playing, our host said, "Everyone knows that I am a fourth-rate pianist. But I must admit that on *that* level no one can compete with me."

September 1860

I met young Bizet after he had just come back after three years in Rome. He told me a very amusing story. When he left for the Villa Medici, he secured letters of introduction from Rossini and from Rossini's dear friend Carafa. Rossini's recommendation was very helpful. But when it came to Carafa's letter, Bizet felt uneasy and decided to open the letter and check its contents. This is what he found: "The young man who bears this letter has had solid musical training and has earned the most coveted prizes at the Conservatoire. But in my opinion he will never amount to anything as an opera composer, as he is lacking even elementary...talent." (I added the ellipsis in place of a rude word that I cannot use here for fear that the paper will blush.)

A few days after his return to Paris Bizet met Carafa on the street and when asked if he had had any use for the recommendation letter, he replied, "Whoever is lucky enough to have a letter from an illustrious person like you, Monsieur Carafa, will never agree to part with it."

By the way, Carafa's nomination as a member of the teaching staff of the Conservatoire was due to Rossini's unceasing pressure. Auber, who was not enthusiastic about the nomination, is said to have warned him to learn the didactic material at least one lesson ahead of his pupils.

March 15, 1864

Yesterday, before an audience of handpicked guests, the first hearing of Rossini's *Petite messe solennelle* took place at the home of the banker Pillet-Will. Judging the work only according to the restricted number of participants needed for its performance—it is written for four solo singers, a small choir of eight singers, two pianos, and a harmonium— you could call it a chamber mass, I guess. But the emotional content of the work, and its unusual length (its performance takes close to two hours and it is longer than any mass I have ever heard) makes it, in my opinion, a major addition to the repertoire of sacred Christian music. After the performance I was able to take a closer look at the score, and I must say it is in full accordance with Rossini as I have learned to know him: a jester's cloak hiding a serious and sensitive personality.

The word *petite* in the title is a fierce and blatant mockery. On the front page Rossini wrote, "This composition is the last sin of my old age." On the last page I read this cryptic message:

> My dear God, at last this poor little mass has come to an end. What is it I have written? De la musique sacrée ou de la sacrée musique?[7] As Thou well knowest, I was born to the world of the opera buffa, which means a little knowledge and some heart. That is what I have. Blessed and sanctified be Thy name, and bring me to rest in Paradise.
>
> Gioacchino Rossini
> Passy, 1864

Those lines, though written tongue in cheek, truly reflect the composer's inner feelings. The work is a serious one, written with impeccable musicianship and deep feeling. It shows again that Rossini is unwilling to disclose the hidden earnest side of his personality, and he hides it behind a screen of humor. This is why he writes, "I was born to the world of the opera buffa." Even when he writes a festive mass he wants to show his true colors as a master of laughter.

Auber himself chose the eight singers for the chorus, and the solo parts were sung by four of the foremost singers at the Théâtre Italien. Rossini contented himself with turning the pages for one of the pianists and with hinting from time to time as to the right tempo. Giacomo Meyerbeer and Ambroise Thomas were among the guests of honor.

The enthusiasm that greeted the composer at the end of the performance was unbelievable. All present, the performers and the audience, clapped their hands and stamped their feet in a frenzy amidst spontaneous shouts of "Bravo! Bravissimo!" The last notes had hardly died away when Meyerbeer sprang to his feet and, with fire in his eyes and his brow flushed, embraced his old rival with such vigor that

---

7   "Sacred music or blasted music?"

Rossini had to remind him with a smile that they were both well past their prime and such physical violence might not be approved by their physicians. (It is true that Meyerbeer did not look well at all.)

I overheard him a few minutes later telling Auber,

> What are we compared to him? We just grope in the dark, hesitantly going our way, searching in vain for something that we are unable to find. If this man had resumed his work for the stage after *Guillaume Tell*, he would have been the uncontested ruler of the theater today! Look at what he did; in the short span of two months he created an entire cosmos. He is the Jupiter of our era, and holds all of us in the palm of his hand.

When I asked the maestro whether he had any plans for an orchestral version of this full-blooded work, he said that the piano version was preferable in every regard. But since he was sure that if *he* wouldn't orchestrate the work, someone else would do it quite soon, and maybe not at all to his taste, he considered it his duty to prevent this by doing the job himself. "They might even entrust my poor work to the hands of M. Adolphe Sax and his new saxophones," he added sarcastically.

April 21, 1865

I just came home from the Théâtre Lyrique, where they have staged the revised (French) version of Verdi's *Macbeth*. The public was bored and indifferent. The composer himself did not come from Italy for the renewed premiere. I suppose he guessed that this rough tragedy, gloomy and violent, was not at all what today's Parisians, intent on lighter entertainment, were looking for. During the intermission no one spoke of Verdi's *Macbeth*. The topic of conversation was the late Meyerbeer's *L'africaine*, which will open posthumously next week at the Opéra.

Verdi to Camille Du Locle, director of the Théâtre Lyrique:

Dear friend,

I have read some strange things in the press concerning Macbeth. I suppose that the people who wrote this know what they are talking about. But there is one thing I absolutely refused to accept: I may have failed in the writing of the music, but no one can claim that I don't know, don't understand, and don't feel Shakespeare's work. This is too much! He is one of my favorite poets; I have kept his works at hand since my early youth, and read and reread them all my life.

April 1867

To Camille Du Locle:

Dear friend,

I am deeply grateful that you asked me to contribute a new work for your theater in spite of the failure of Don Carlos, but I have made up my mind not to bend anymore under the yoke of the French stage. There are too many experts in your theaters; everyone wants to pass judgment according to his own wisdom and his own taste—with no regard at all for the personality and the intentions of the composer.

Everyone voices his opinion, everyone proffers his doubts, and the composer, exposed for a long time to this atmosphere, starts to have doubts about the legitimacy of his ideas. He ends up correcting his work, or to be more precise, he wrecks it. I'm searching in vain with your compatriots for the quality called enthusiasm. I believe in inspiration, you believe in construction. I believe in art, you believe in a system. I can succeed only when I compose according to my heart's command, with no outer influence and without reminding myself all along that I write for Paris and not for, say, some inhabitants of the moon. When I bring a new work to an opera house in Italy, no one will venture an opinion on it until he has studied the work most thoroughly, and everything is clear to him. No one will dare to have unwarranted demands; there is respect for the work and for the composer. As for the judgment, it is left the public.

But in France, after hearing the first four chords the whispering starts: "Ah, ce n'est pas bon—this is vulgar, not in keeping with good taste. This will not do for Paris." What is the meaning of words like vulgar, good taste, Paris, when we are concerned with a work of art that belongs to the whole world?

My conclusion is that I am not the composer you need for the Parisian spirit, and if I had been tempted to accept your commission for a new opera, there is no doubt that you would have been forced to take it off the stage after a dozen performances, exactly as happened with Don Carlos. To this I will not agree.

Warmest regards to your charming Marie and kiss little Claire for me.

Yours,

Giuseppe Verdi

1868

As we are in a leap year, Rossini enjoyed a fully official birthday. Due to being born on February 29, 1800, he is on a four-year cycle for his birthdays. Two weeks ago *Guillaume Tell* had its five-hundredth performance at the Opéra. To commemorate this event, most of the performers, soloists, choristers, and orchestra went to the rue de la Chaussée d'Antin and serenaded the maestro. Rossini, who is not feeling too well lately, sent his wife Olympe to convey his thanks to the musicians. He himself appeared very briefly at the window and was greeted with enthusiastic applause.

Rumor in town has it that he is about to undergo an operation to remove a tumor from his intestine. May God keep him under His holy protection.

Rossini died at Passy on November 13. The funeral service, which was a grandiose celebration, took place at the newly built Trinity Church. It was attended by a host of foreign delegations, representatives of the government and the Institut, and the top world-renowned artists, who sang excerpts from Pergolesi's *Stabat Mater,* and naturally Rossini's own *Stabat Mater* and the prayer from *Moïse* as well.

At the end of the ceremony (I almost said the concert), I spotted Berlioz in the crowd. He was one of the members of the delegation sent by the Institut. He looked almost like a ghost with his bandaged head and lifeless eyes—eyes that normally looked like burning coals—in a face that had thinned almost beyond recognition. I went to him and he clapped me gently on the shoulders.

He said,

Three months ago it was my friend Hubert Ferrand; last month I accompanied Léon Kreutzer on his last journey. And I know I'm next. I don't regret anything. I feel I am the last vestige of this generation. I hope my funeral will be half as brilliant as this one, but this is naturally a futile hope. The French have somehow come to respect me, but to find understanding and enthusiasm for my music I had to go to London, to Brussels, to Berlin, to Vienna, to Prague, and to Pest. I had to face the torture of a frozen trip to faraway Russia to get that. Maybe when I'm gone they will play some Berlioz here in Paris.

Verdi's initiative to have twelve Italian composers cooperate in writing a requiem mass to Rossini's memory was a complete failure. He was the only one to fulfill his part of the assignment, by composing the *Libera me*. Maybe in view of his fellow Italian composers' unwillingness to participate in the proposed scheme, Verdi will, when the time is ripe, see fit to complete the task all by himself. That would be something to enrich the musical world.

There is talk of exhuming Rossini's body and reburying him an in his native Pesaro. What a pity we can't ask for his opinion on the subject of where he would like to rest: at the side of Bellini, Cherubini, and Chopin in the Père Lachaise Cemetery in Paris, or with neighbors like Galileo and Michelangelo in the Santa Cruce Church in Florence. Whatever it will be, rest in peace, dear maestro. Amen.

7

THE FANTASTIC SYMPHONIST

I think it must have been in January or February of 1833 that I saw *Hamlet* at the Odéon Theater, with Henriette Smithson playing Ophelia. The audience was sympathetic and gave her a warm, though not enthusiastic, reception. My personal opinion was somewhat different as Mlle Smithson's acting left me rather cool and perplexed.

In all the years of my friendship with Berlioz, I never mentioned having seen her on stage.

My friendship with Berlioz began after the first performance, on December 6, 1846, at the Salle Favart, of *La damnation de Faust*. The theater was only half full and the audience gave the work a lukewarm reception. But I was stunned. Admittedly, the quality of the music was unequal throughout the work, and I even thought that some passages were quite tedious. But there were pages so beautiful, with sublime and heart-lifting music, that I at once decided that I must meet the composer, who, after all, was already a well-known personality. At the end of the concert I went behind the scenes to meet him and we got acquainted. When I told him that I would like to acquire a printed copy of the score he said it had not yet been printed, but that the second performance was scheduled for a fortnight later and that he would have complimentary tickets for me if I was interested. I was overjoyed!

But the audience gave the second concert an even cooler reception than the first one, while my personal assessment of the work grew twofold. When, at the end of the evening, I went backstage again I found the dejected Berlioz unable to hide his deep disappointment. I gathered that he must have lost quite a lot of money in this venture and I told him, without making any fuss about it, that I was able and willing to help. He looked at me, very perplexed, and said,

> I will not hide the fact that I'm completely broke and that I am left with a debt of almost ten thousand francs following this rout. But I really don't think…we hardly know each other. I met you only two weeks ago, though I admit I've heard about you and have since made inquiries about you. This is how I discovered that on top of being a very successful financial wizard, you have also had the privilege of being a pupil of my beloved teacher Lesueur. But I really would not dare to presume upon this new friendship of ours…

I replied, "Believe me, I will consider your acceptance of this loan an honor. For me it is like fulfilling a duty toward this noble art we both venerate: music."

Two months later Berlioz set out for his first trip to Russia. When he came back, his pockets lined with Russian gold, he reimbursed me to the last centime.

February 1854

I just read an article in the *Gazette musicale* written by a young German composer of the Lisztian school. His name is Peter Cornelius and he puts Berlioz on a pedestal. He has coined a new expression: "The three big 'B's.'" This is how he concludes his article:

> On the summits where Bach and Beethoven have been dwelling for some time already, there is a place reserved and waiting for the third big "B." Let me raise my voice in praise of the beloved Meister, my favorite among contemporary composers, on behalf of the proud and audacious hero, Hector, for the many-voiced composer and the versatile writer. Three cheers: Bach, Beethoven, Berlioz!

To be quite frank, the article has stirred up more sarcasm than agreement, and it seems that the old saying, "No prophet has honor in his own country," has made its mark again. Everyone seems to respect the talented writer. The witty critic is much feared in musical circles. And the humorist, as he has proved himself to be in his recently published "Evenings with the Orchestra," is enjoying tremendous popularity. But Berlioz the musician is, methinks, the least played of France's composers. The Opéra has closed its doors to him because of a rift between him and the chief conductor Girard. For similar reasons he is unable to have his works performed at the Conservatoire. The Société philharmonique, which he created in 1850 to promote masterpieces and open the field for bringing his own works before the public, has crumbled after less than two years of existence. If we can hear some of his music (a very rare occurrence), it is always a truncated version: two excerpts from *La damnation de Faust*, two movements from the Requiem, or an occasional excerpt from *L'enfance du Christ*. Whoever wants to listen to Berlioz's works in their entirety has to go to Weimar, Prague, Baden-Baden, Vienna, or Saint Petersburg. Not surprisingly, Berlioz is bitter about this and he feels like a stranger in his own country. And though he is only fifty-one, he talks like a man at the end of his career.

This is how he sums up the situation:

I may not be at the end of my career, but I am certainly going down a very steep slope that leads me faster and faster to the end. The flame has consumed me completely, but I am still burning, and here and there bursting with energy, a frightfully powerful energy.

I think I can safely say that I have mastered the French language; that I'm finally capable of writing a sheet of music, of poetry or of prose in a decent manner. I can conduct an orchestra and instill life into otherwise bored players. I admire art in all its forms. But I belong to a nation that has forsaken its interest in the higher expressions of the spirit and recognizes no other god than the golden calf. The Parisians have become a barbarian horde. Out of ten households of rich people you will be hard put to find one with a library. I don't mean, God forbid, a music library. People have stopped buying books. Cheap novels, available at public libraries for pennies, are enough to satisfy their needs for literature. In the same manner it is possible to subscribe for a few measly francs a month to a music publisher, and to choose the requested composition among the huge heap of garbage filling their stores.

In short, Paris is a city in which I am unable to do anything, a city in which I should consider myself lucky to act as a music critic—a role for which, according to many people, I have been predestined since birth.

One night, at a time when my wife's health still left us with some hope for her recovery, I dreamed that I was composing a new symphony. In my dream I heard the work very clearly. When I woke up in the middle of the night I still remembered the first movement almost in its entirety: it was an allegro in a minor key in common time. I decided to get up and commit it to paper. I was about to sit down at my desk to write it down when I suddenly realized the meaning of it all. I thought to myself, if I give in to the temptation and write this now, I will be bound to complete the work by adding the remaining movements. As my ideas have a tendency to develop on a larger scale lately, the symphony will thus reach huge proportions. The actual writing will take me some three or four months during which I will be unable to deal with any other work. My income will dwindle to nothing. When the symphony is completed I will be unable to resist my copier's entreaties and I will have him copy the parts. As a result, I will immediately contract a debt of 1,000 to 1,200 francs. When the parts will be at hand, I won't have my peace of mind until the work is performed, and I will organize a concert, the proceeds of which will, in the best of cases, cover half the costs. My debts will swell and I won't be able to take proper care of my poor invalid wife, to cater to my personal needs nor pay my son's allowance (he is soon due to board a ship as a sailor). I shuddered as all of this dawned upon me. I threw away the pen that was already poised over the paper and I thought, with God's help, the music will be forgotten by tomorrow. And sure enough, when I awoke the next morning this wonderful allegro was completely forgotten and lost to posterity for all time.

March 4, 1854

Today we brought poor Henriette, Berlioz's wife, to her final resting place in the small cemetery of Saint-Vincent. Twenty-five years ago, all of Paris was enthralled by her magnetic personality when she acquainted the French public with the stunning world of Shakespeare's plays. Today, only a handful of friends came to pay their last respects, and not out of recognition for the great actress she had been, but rather as a token of friendship for her husband. Berlioz himself did not come to the funeral and many an eyebrow was raised. It is true that he had separated from her years ago, but his bonds with his son's mother were nevertheless very deep, and he looked after all her needs, never abandoning her in her illness and suffering. Where was he hiding while we interred her?

A few months later, Berlioz himself showed me an entry in his private diary, and I think this is the proper place to reproduce it verbatim.

I could not bring myself to follow the hearse. I had suffered too much the previous day when I tried to find the Protestant clergyman in the suburbs at the outskirts of the city. Fate had it that the funeral procession passed near the Odéon, the very theater where I first saw her, twenty-seven years ago, when all the intellectual elite of Paris went down on bended knee before her. God! How much misery we brought to one another; we couldn't live together and we couldn't leave one another alone, and those last ten years we made life hell for each other.

Now I have come home after visiting her grave. She rests on the northern slope of the hill, facing England, where she never wanted to return. I have kept a lock of her hair. I write these words in the big drawing room, next to the empty bedroom where she died. In the garden outside, the trees are budding and spring is slowly setting in. Oh! To forget, to forget!

We were lucky to have our son Louis visit us last week, and she at least had the comfort of seeing him one last time. He is so tall and handsome, and in no way resembles the darling little child who used to run around in this garden. I somehow feel I have lost that child, and that the big youth I embraced six days ago is no consolation for the loss of the other one.

God be with you, my dear beloved sister. Thankfully time is moving on and crushes everything, kills everything, even the suffering and the pain…

Jules Janin, Berlioz's colleague at *Le Journal des Débats*, an intelligent, cultivated, and sensitive man who contributed the words for the cantata *Le chant des chemins de fer*, wrote in the same *Journal des Débats*:

How swiftly the godliness passes away from our ephemeral lives. How very delicate and frail they are, those brainchildren of Shakespeare and Corneille. Lo, it seems like only yesterday we saw her radiant in all her youth, a shining star on her balcony in the garden of the Capulet family. She was trembling like the leaves of those trees where the nightingale of the night and the morning's lark sang their heavenly serenade. All clad in white, her burning eyes turned to the immensity of the Verona sky. She was the focus of the world. Her deep and pure golden voice recited Shakespeare's lines in pure music. The universe was embodied in the magic of this young woman.

Mlle Smithson was not yet twenty when she captivated all of Paris with this new discovery. And so, unknowingly, she became the dream, the revelation, and the passion of the generation. She brought the new message to Dorval, Lemaître, Malibran, Victor Hugo, and

Berlioz. Her name was Juliet...Ophelia. She was the model for Eugène Delacroix when he painted Ophelia.

October 19, 1854

Last night I attended the premiere of my friend Gounod's opera *La nonne sanglante*. The plot was irritating, the spectacle pretentious, and the audience indifferent.

I don't remember that I ever went to an opera or to the theater with a fierce hope in my heart that the work would fail, but this is exactly what happened last night, and my wish was granted. All I can say is that it was poetic justice.

It all started with Scribe turning to Berlioz to ask him if he would consider writing the music to a five-act opera on a libretto he was working on, *La nonne sanglante* (The Bloody Nun). Berlioz gladly accepted and in no time a contract was signed between Léon Pillet (who was the director of the Opéra at the time), Scribe, and Berlioz. After completing the first act, Berlioz had to wait two years to get the text for the second act. In the meantime, Pillet had been compelled to give up the management of the Opéra. Nestor Roqueplan and Armand Duponchel were keen on getting the appointment as a partnership, but they knew that the minister of the interior was firmly against their candidacy. They also knew that Armand Bertin, the owner of *Le Journal des Débats* and Berlioz's friend, had the minister's ear and was able to bring him to change his mind on the matter. So they asked Berlioz to intercede in their favor. In return they promised that if they were nominated to the job, they would put the management of the musical side of the enterprise in Berlioz's hands, and also appoint him as conductor. When Berlioz pointed out that his friend Girard already held the post of conductor they suggested having two chief conductors with equal rights and told him they would take the matter up with Girard and convince him. Berlioz fulfilled his part of the bargain, and Bertin—quite unwillingly—managed to secure the directorship of the Opéra for Roqueplan and Duponchel.

A few days later, Roqueplan asked Berlioz to meet him. This was more or less the gist of the exchange between them:

Roqueplan said, "I understand that you have in your possession a libretto by M. Scribe that you are planning to compose. Surely you are aware that as a member of this institution you are barred from having a work of yours performed here."

Berlioz replied, "I gather you are referring to *La nonne sanglante*. I have already completed two of the planned five acts and I am still waiting for Scribe to forward the text for the remaining three acts. As for the ethical problem you hint at regarding the performance of works written by members of the staff, I wish to point out that Pierre Dietsch's *Le vaisseau fantôme* was staged when he was a conductor here. Halévy had two or three of his operas performed while he was choir master at the Opéra."

"Times have changed," said Roqueplan, "and this is not simply a matter of ethics; it is a rule of the house, and we do not want to infringe upon the rules. So I think you should reflect on the matter and perhaps hand over the libretto so as to enable us to entrust someone else with the task of composing the music."

"By the way," Roqueplan continued, "I have been talking with Girard and he is adamant in his stand not to share the conductorship with anyone. We thought of letting you conduct the choir, but as you don't play the piano this makes it difficult, to say the least."

As a result of all these ugly machinations, Berlioz was denied the position he coveted at the Opéra. He went to London where he conducted the Opera Orchestra at Drury Lane, and there waited for

Scribe to send him the three missing acts of *La nonne sanglante*. But what came was a letter that avoided the real issue and announced that the management of the Opéra was willing to stage the opera in a matter of weeks if it was ready for performance. Otherwise the whole scheme would have to be shelved, and Berlioz had better relinquish his rights and return the manuscript of the two acts he had in his possession—*which he did!*

Scribe turned to Delavigne for help in completing the text and then approached Verdi, Halévy, Meyerbeer, Grisar, David, and finally Clapisson to ask if they were interested in writing the music. But out of solidarity they all rejected the proposition; not one of them was willing to condone the slight suffered by Berlioz. As a last resort, they turned to Gounod who accepted the libretto. How right Bizet was when he wrote to his mother about Gounod, "This is once more proof that a great artist is not necessarily an honorable man."

At a certain stage, Gounod must have suddenly felt uneasy about the whole business because one week before the premier he wrote a letter to Berlioz. The exact content of this letter has not come to my knowledge, but from Berlioz's answer one can draw the conclusion that it must have contained some kind of apology. Berlioz's answer came to my attention in quite a devious way, at the hands of young Bizet. And how did Bizet get it? He says Gounod himself gave it to him as a token of friendship and as a bonus to his fees for arranging the voice and piano version of the opera. This is what Berlioz wrote to the man who behaved in such a shameful way toward him:

Paris, October 11, 1854

My dear Gounod,

I promise you, and you have to believe me, that I feel not an ounce of bitterness toward you in the matter of La nonne sanglante, and I wish you great success with all my heart.

Don't forget that I am indebted to you for the deep and inspiring experience you granted me when I heard your opera Sappho, and I am
happy to pay my debt. To hell with it all! We are artists, aren't we?

I am not sure I'll be free next Saturday evening, but if you would be
kind enough to send me tickets for the dress rehearsal and if you
can make sure that the seats next to mine will not be occupied by
unpleasant neighbors, I will do all that is in my power to come. This
in spite of my abhorrence for the stupid way in which, since time
immemorial, they hold this important event at the Opéra.

Adieu, be strong! And don't you worry yourself sick about Hector
Berlioz, who is devoted to you body and soul.

One additional result of this wretched affair was the falling out
between Girard and Berlioz that resulted in a permanent rift between
the two men. Roqueplan had given Girard a completely false and
distorted version of the facts, as if Berlioz had been seeking the post of
conductor for himself and plotted to oust him, while the truth is that
the idea of the sharing came from Roqueplan himself.

October 19, 1854

In the intimacy of a restricted circle of close friends, Berlioz married
the singer Marie Recio, with whom he had been living for the past
fourteen years. He told me in confidence that even though he was not
entering into this marriage with all the joy and bliss of a bridegroom,
he was morally bound to it by the ties he had woven in those long
years of living together. He said he could not cope with life without a
companion, and looking for a new female partner at this stage of his

life was out of the question. I do not wish to pass judgment on his decision.

On December 10 the whole of *L'enfance du Christ*[8] *was given in the Salle Herz. It was a stunning experience, an emotional pilgrimage. The composer had invited some of his oldest friends to this concert, some of them living in complete seclusion; amongst them were Heinrich Heine (whose physical condition seemed precarious to me), and Alfred de Vigny, the "invisible poet." Contrary to Berlioz's expectations, the concert proved a resounding success from the artistic point of view as well as the financial one. The concert was repeated several times in the next few days, particularly on Christmas Eve.* Even the *Gazette de la Cour*, the official organ of the court, which was never an admirer of Berlioz, remarked about the event that "Berlioz reaped in one day the fruit of many years of struggle and effort."

Cosima, Franz Liszt's daughter, brought him her father's blessing on the success of the oratorio. Heine, who had a few years earlier pronounced his doubts about Berlioz's ability in the field of melodious inventiveness, and thus deeply hurt the composer at the time, apologized in a friendly letter in which he admitted how mistaken he had been, and said he had found in the work "wondrous melodic flowers."

In spite of the natural satisfaction it brought, Berlioz was not overenthusiastic with his success. He was even tempted to find it a

---

8   In 1850, at one of the concerts of the late Société Philharmonique, we heard a work called "Farewell of the Shepherds to the Holy Family" by a seventeenth-century would-be composer named Pierre Ducré. The work, which was written in a pseudo-archaic style, was very warmly received by the Parisian public. Only a few weeks later was Paris made aware of the mystification: Pierre Ducré was a figment of Berlioz's imagination and had never existed; the "Farewell of the Shepherds to the Holy Family" had been composed by Berlioz, probably as a kind of hoax. Anyhow, this "Farewell of the Shepherds to the Holy Family" was not really a farewell at all, as it was to become the starting point of *L'enfance du Christ*!

trifle slighting. He wrote of it: "Well, well! It seems I have become a well-behaved boy: human, clear, and pleasant to the ear. I have finally come to write music like any normal composer."

He is angry because the public simply does not understand to what extent the chosen subject influences the style. According to him, had he come upon the idea of this subject twenty years ago, he would have written the oratorio then exactly as he wrote it now. He complained to me about the fickleness of the public: "One day they shower you with praises, the next you are abused in the most brutal manner."

"The problem in your relations with the public," I said, "is that they never know what to expect from you. Every new work of yours is a surprise and displays a different style. Does the *Symphonie fantastique* in any way herald the Requiem? What does the Requiem have in common with *La damnation de Faust*? The public is confused and embarrassed. And how do you get from *La damnation de Fa*ust to *L'enfance du Christ*?"

"That is their problem, not mine," said Berlioz. "I don't choose a style when I compose. The composition itself dictates the appropriate language that has to be used. In general terms, one could say that my style is daring, but it is not intended to destroy any of the basic foundations of music. It never occurred to me to write music 'without a melody,' as some French critics have called it. I am not in a position to judge the merits of my melodies, their scope, their originality, or their charm. But no one can deny their very existence—this would show either a complete lack of integrity or that one is being deliberately obtuse and offensive. What are they going to say when I produce my new opera? They will complain bitterly, 'Here he is again, returning to his old wretched self. What a pity.'"

The world has, all of a sudden, discovered Berlioz. He received so many tempting propositions that he doesn't know where to turn. He has been extended an invitation for a concert tour in the United States of America. He was promised $20,000 to conduct in New York, Boston, and Philadelphia. He has been asked to inaugurate a new concert hall in London. His presence is needed in Sweden for the impending festivities in connection with the king's marriage. But he is faithful to his true love and has decided to stay in Paris with his opera.

April 1855

Berlioz's *Te Deum* was performed in the church of St. Eustache, as a kind of solemn opening of the Great Exhibition. The sheer might of the work stunned the public—and even the critics. Amongst those who congratulated Berlioz after the outstanding performance was the journalist Nestor Roqueplan, the former director of the Opéra and Berlioz's erstwhile opponent. The composer winked an eye at me and whispered to my ear, "*C'est la fin du monde*—the end of the world is at hand!"

November 1855

Among the events marking the end of the Exhibition was the great concert organized by Berlioz at the Palace of Industry, in the presence of Napoleon III, Eugénie, Prince Jérôme, and the Duke of Cambridge. On the program there were works by Handel, Gluck, Beethoven, Meyerbeer, and Rossini, and, crowning the evening, Berlioz's grand cantata "L'impériale" (this is the new name he has given the cantata "The Tenth of December" that had first been performed in January). But to the composer's (and the public's) great consternation, the music was interrupted when the emperor decided he had heard enough and that it was time for him to give his closing speech.

The next day the concert was repeated—this time without the presence of the big brass and without interruption—in front of an audience of thousands. Berlioz had asked an engineer from Brussels to build an electric metronome for him, a machine with five branches, with which he could control five different musical groups in five different locations in the hall under five assistant conductors, by a simple movement of his finger, marking time and synchronizing all the musical bodies into one big entity. This electrical device was a tremendous success and has already been adopted by many other musical groups.

February 1856

On February 17 my friend Heinrich Heine at last found eternal rest. Or has he? For the last eight years he has been almost permanently confined to what he called his "mattress tomb," almost paralyzed by an unbearable backache. He had been living here in exile since 1831. His relations with the community of politically exiled Germans in

Paris was very strained, to put it mildly. But he was on the warmest, friendliest terms with a swarm of Parisian artists of all kinds: writers, poets, playwrights, sculptors, painters, engravers, and musicians. He was especially close to my cousin Olinde Rodrigues, as he was a staunch believer in Saint-Simon's doctrines and went out of his way to advocate them. In spite of his having been baptized in 1825—a thing he thought might make his acceptance into society easier and promote professional advancement if the need arose, which it didn't— he himself told me that in his heart of hearts he was, and always has been, Jewish. And when he was asked once why he hadn't returned to Judaism, he answered, "How can I return to something I never left?"

On his deathbed he said, "God will forgive me; after all, it is His profession."

He was buried in the small cemetery in Montmartre, not far from Henriette Smithson-Berlioz's grave. He asked to have this poem of his engraved on his tombstone:

Wo?
Wo wird einst des Wandermüden
Letzte Ruhestätte sein?
Unter Palmen in dem Süden?
Unter Linden an dem Rhein?

Werd ich wo in einer Wüste
Eingescharrt von fremder Hand?
Oder ruh ich an der Küste
Eines Meeres in dem Sand?

Immerhin! Mich wird umgeben
Gotteshimel, dort wie hier,
Und als Totenlampen shweben
Nachts die Sterne über mir.

Here is an approximate free translation:

Where?
Where will the weary wanderer's
Last resting place be someday?
Under palm trees in the south?
Under linden near the Rhine?

Will a stranger's hand hastily
Bury me in the desert?
Or will I rest in the sand
At the seaside?

For all that, I will be surrounded
By God's heaven, there as here
The stars at night in abeyance
Will shine over me.

It is a realistic mirror of his ambivalent feelings about the duality of his allegiances as a Christian Jew, as a German Frenchman. Has he really found the answer to those soul-searching questions that pursued him all his life? I wonder.

June 1856

Last month, on May 3, Adolphe Adam suddenly died after a very short illness. He was Berlioz's senior by only seven months, thus nine years older than I am. He was a very respected and honest, hardworking man who, like Berlioz, added journalistic activities to his work as a composer in order to round up his income. Most of his works were staged at the Opéra-Comique or at the Théâtre Lyrique. The last two are *Falstaff* (after Shakespeare) in January, and *Les pantins de Violette* as recently as last April at the Bouffes-Parisiens.

But I think future generations will remember him mainly as the composer of the inspired music for the ballet *Giselle*. He had been a member of the Institut de France since 1844.

A few days ago this august assembly held a meeting to commemorate the memory of their departed associate at the end of which they elected Berlioz to the vacant seat. The only thing I can say is that it's about time. In his three former attempts to get elected, lesser men were chosen. In 1851, Ambroise Thomas succeeded Spontini. Two years later, on Onslow's death in 1853, Reber was chosen to fill his place. And two years ago, in 1854, when my brother-in-law Fromental Halévy was elected to the office of secretary for life at the Académie des beaux-arts, they found it fit to have Clapisson sit in the vacant seat at the Institut.

The Institut. What an exalted institution. It was created in 1795 to unite under one roof the five great state academies: the Académie française created by Richelieu in 1635, the Académie des inscriptions et belles-lettres (1663), the Académie des sciences (1666), and the Académie des beaux-arts, this last one uniting three separate academies created in the seventeenth century: the Académie royale d'architecture, the Académie royale de peinture et de sculpture, and the Académie royale de musique. The Institut's official aim is to protect, propagate, and help develop all aspects of French culture. To that end, it subsidizes many cultural foundations, museums, etc., rewards some of the greater minds of the time by granting them recognition (and sometimes a state pension), and encourages young talent—for instance, by awarding the well-known Prix de Rome.

Within the Académie des beaux-arts, there are five separate branch-es: painting, sculpture, architecture, engraving, and musical composition. There is a sixth branch for unattached members. There are fifty seats called *fauteuils* (armchairs),[9] forty of which are for French artists and ten of which are reserved for foreigners. The members are elected by their peers, which means that the members of any specific academy elect the replacement for a fellow academician who has passed away. Every branch has its own seats; the music branch has six seats numbered from one to six.

On the day I'm writing this, *fauteuil* one is occupied by Clapisson, *fauteuil* two by Auber, *fauteuil* three by Thomas, Berlioz has just been elected to *fauteuil* four, Reber is in *fauteuil* five, and Carafa in *fauteuil* six.

Everyone was convinced that now, as a respected member of the Institut, as one on whom society has bestowed the highest honors, Berlioz would at last mellow and stop spitting flames and brimstone. But the Institut was to become just another battlefield for him, another arena to fight in for his uncompromising artistic beliefs.

His first battle was on behalf of young Bizet, and he succeeded, in the face of mighty opposition, in convincing a majority of colleagues to vote to grant him the much coveted Prix de Rome.

After this first victory, he went to battle again—this time for his new protégé, the painter Eugène Delacroix, a close friend of mine, who, like Berlioz, had always been spoken of with words like, "Yes, he is rather gifted, but..."

Delacroix had been rebuked seven times in his endeavor to get elected to the Institut. Berlioz, ennobled by the experience of his Bizet campaign, was once again able to mobilize the forces needed to achieve victory.

The next vacant *fauteuil* was for a foreign member, and Berlioz backed the candidacy of his old friend Franz Liszt. This time he was

---

9   This is why upon being elected Berlioz said," Until now I've sat on bayonets; from now on I will sit in an armchair!"

defeated. But this defeat was almost as sweet as a victory, as the newly elected member was Giuseppe Verdi.

Berlioz's assessment of Verdi was unequivocally positive; he said of him,

> This is a man to my liking, a proud, brave, and stubborn man. He is a far cry from Rossini's joviality, or from Meyerbeer's snakelike wriggling. He hates laziness, sloppiness, and indifference, and he makes this categorically clear in all contact he has with ministers and theater managers alike.

Paris has become an incredible center of musical activity. At eight different places, eight recitals are given at virtually the same time. And the public readily goes to listen to those would-be new virtuosos who are on the brinks of their musical careers.

A new craze has set in here: receiving messages from the beyond. Berlioz went to one of these séances out of curiosity and reports,

> Beethoven arrives and signals through the table legs, "Here I am." The medium then asks the composer to dictate a new sonata to him. The composer doesn't have to be asked twice: the table starts wobbling and knocking. The work is written down. Beethoven then goes home. The medium, followed by half a dozen shaken witnesses, rushes to the piano to play the sonata. Is it a game? Is it a vision? Not at all; this is the Paris of the Second Empire.

When asked which of his own compositions is his favorite, Berlioz answers,

> I think that in this matter there is no diversion of opinion between me, my fellow musician colleagues, and the general public. The best and most inspired music I have ever written is the adagio, the love scene from Romeo and Juliet. Many of the spontaneous praises I have received over the years were related to this composition. Once, at a concert in Hanover, the orchestra had just finished playing this movement; I felt something odd happening behind me. I turned around and looked: the orchestra members closest to me where kissing my coattails.

At a rehearsal at the court in Weimar, the conductor, Herr Seifrids, after having played the adagio without interruption, stood still for a second, then, with tears in his voice, he said aloud for everyone to hear: "There is nothing more beautiful in all the music literature I know!"

8

PARIS AGAINST WAGNER

November 1, 1859

Richard Wagner is back in Paris. He has been here only six weeks but he has already managed to be everywhere and to meet everyone who might be of any help to him in the future. "This man generates an atmosphere of excitement," young Saint-Saëns told me. "Suddenly things seem to be happening in this city, proving that besides the pursuit of easy profits and cheap pleasures, other aspirations still exist. Wagner's presence has changed Paris. This is a different city, a city with new expectations, with a new dimension. Do you understand the meaning of what I say?"

"I do indeed, my friend," I answered with a sly smile. "I understand perfectly. I can see that you are a new conquest of his."

"To be conquered by Wagner I do not need the man," was Saint-Saëns's reply. "It is enough for me to look at his scores."

In my own library I possess the scores of three of Wagner's operas, *The Flying Dutchman, Tannhäuser,* and *Lohengrin.* I am not immune to the special inebriating fragrance this music emanates. But I must say that I find much truth in what Liszt says about his music: "There are some moments of the most sublime elation, but so many tedious quarters of an hour." I'm much less enthusiastic about his essays on the creation of art in the future, parts of which have been published here and there in French periodicals. There is no doubt that the man is a visionary, but I refuse to concur with his opinion that all the accepted forms of music on which we have been reared and that have nurtured our spirits and souls, are pathetically outdated, that they have served their purpose and have no place in the future development of the art of music. His creed is that the future belongs to the "unified artistic creation" in which music, poetry, movement, and stage setting will join together in an effort to bring before the public the message of a new era.

I heard that Baudelaire and his circle are staunch supporters of those ideas. I must ask Baudelaire if he also agrees with the ideas proffered in Wagner's calumnious and nauseating essay "Judaism in Music." This is an essay full of venom that, since its publication nine years ago, has already brought harm and misery in many quarters. At first I chose to turn a deaf ear to the rumor saying that "Karl Freigedank," who signed it, was actually the same Richard Wagner whom I had known (and supported with handsome sums of money) twenty years ago, during his first stay in Paris. But soon enough the mystery ended and the veil was lifted, leaving no doubts as to the author's true identity. In the immediate future it means for me that I have no wish whatsoever to renew the acquaintance from days past. But I will not be surprised at all if one of these days this man will be sitting in my office, arrogantly asking for funding. The fact that a Jew is unfit for artistic creation does not bar him from advancing the arts by supporting his gentile brethren with generous offerings from his overflowing cashbox.

I vividly remember our first meeting in 1839, in Paolo Borgi's Italian restaurant on the rue Le Peletier, opposite the opera house. I had been asked to join the meeting by our mutual friend, the late Samuel Lehrs. Lehrs was a Jewish philologist from Königsberg who barely made a living by translating classical Greek literature for the Didot publishing firm. He had brought to Wagner's attention the figure of Heinrich Ofterdingen, who had participated in a song contest at the Wartburg, thus initiating the labors that would give birth to *Tannhäuser*. Meyerbeer, as usual full of conviviality and wisdom, as well as Heinrich Heine and his young wife Mathilde, were also present at this meeting. Heine's wife told us in the most charming manner about her struggle to master the secrets of reading and writing. Not so long ago, she had worked as an assistant in a small shoe shop on a little street near the law courts.

There was something eerie in this meeting: four Jews, two of them world-renowned artists, getting together to find ways of advancing the career of a young composer of uncertain extraction, whose main claim to fame was the plans he had for his own future. His artistic inventory at the time was rather meager: two operas, *Das Liebesverbot* and *Rienzi* (which Hans von Bülow so wittily dubbed "Meyerbeer's best opera").

When I left the meeting I was somewhat bewildered and stunned—stunned by two and a half hours of listening to an endless flow of arguments in heavy German-accented French, seasoned from time to time by the refreshing gush of Mme Heine's friendly prattle, and stunned most of all by the personality of Richard Wagner and his brilliant discourse about the state of music. He praised Auber's output before that composer fell into the pit of routine. He talked in the warmest of terms about my brother-in-law Fromental Halévy. But most of all I was bewildered by the overinflated self-esteem and unshakable self-confidence of this anonymous foreigner, who claimed that the very act of supporting him and his work was the holy duty of every art lover.

He almost succeeded in convincing us that in endeavoring to pave the way for him, we do ourselves a favor more than favoring him! I think that behind his deep belief in himself lies the explanation for the complete lack of gratitude and cynical arrogance that characterizes the man. This explains how, after having exploited Meyerbeer's goodwill to the hilt and needing his help no more, he threw him to the wolves like an empty wrapping, in his ill-reputed way. With Heine the task was much more difficult and the arguments needed to be more sophisticated and far-fetched, because, deep down, he really and honestly admired Wagner.

Wagner argued,

We have said that the Jews have not produced even one real poet. And truly in the days of Goethe and Schiller we never heard of a Jew who was a poet.

But when poetry became polluted and no true poet grew on our overexploited, scorched soil, a gifted Jew took it upon himself to un-veil this lie, this prosaic desiccation, in a sweeping mockery. He also tormented his famous brethren, Meyerbeer and Mendelssohn, with his whip slashes, on their masquerading as creators. But ultimately he stumbled too; after having scattered the illusions of the self-de-ceivers, he, too, was caught in the trap of self-deception and showed himself to us in the guise of a poet. And, sure enough, he succeeded in deceiving some of our best composers, who threw themselves on his work as if it were some hidden treasure, thus strengthening the deception instead of shattering it to pieces!

When Wagner left Paris after three years of unsuccessful struggles, disappointed and embittered, he said, "An impoverished artist, as exalted as his artistic goals may be, is doomed to failure in Paris!"

The Théâtre de la Renaissance, which had accepted his *Liebesverbot* on the strength of Meyerbeer's recommendation, went bankrupt before the work was even put on rehearsal. As for *Rienzi*, it was actually produced thanks to Meyerbeer's insistence, but not on the Parisian opera stage; it was performed at the Dresden Royal Opera.

If he came back to Paris in spite of all this, it is because of political reasons. His revolutionary articles and the active part he took in the uprising of '49 in Dresden have made him an exile. After fleeing to Weimar, where he benefited from Liszt's hospitality, he had to run again when a bounty was offered for his arrest in Germany. He found refuge in Switzerland where he lived on the hooks of a rich silk merchant of Zurich, Otto Wesendonk. There he got entangled in a love affair with his patron's wife, Mathilde Wesendonk. He tried his luck in Italy and in England but achieved nothing worthwhile there. What other haven could he turn to but our effervescent, corrupt, and murderous Paris?

Richard Wagner is back in Paris. Riper, more experienced, more settled in his ideals, but neither wiser nor more moderate. And sure enough, I agree with Saint-Saëns's verdict: "Paris, with Wagner within its walls, is not the same Paris, for better or for worse."

Upon his arrival he had to look for a place to live, in accordance with the needs of his work and keeping in mind his wish to be reunited with his wife Minna after a year of separation. He found an apartment on the rue de Newton, a quiet little street abutting the Champs-Élysées near the Barrière de l'Étoile. It is a nice and cozy little house but it was in miserable condition when Wagner arrived. He had to renovate it from top to bottom at his own expense, as the landlord refused to contribute financially. He sent for his furniture in Switzerland and hired a servant for himself and a lady's maid for Minna. He immediately got down to business; he contacted theater managers, stock exchange tycoons, and patrons of the arts.

His drive to make his music known and to bring the public to accept his musical idiom is a basic foundation for his social behavior and his actions in general. This drive brought him to arrange for a series of concerts to be given to remind the older generation of his name and make it known to the new one. To this end, he tried to enlist the aid of the emperor in order to have the Salle Ventadour and the Théâtre Italien put at his disposal. Getting no response from that quarter, he decided to rent the Salle Herz at four thousand francs an evening. For the delicate task of putting an orchestra and chorus together he turned to Berlioz. He was unaware that the days of his friendly relations with Berlioz were over, poisoned mainly by Berlioz's second wife, Marie Recio, who out of pusillanimity had set her husband against the German. So Wagner asked his good friend, pianist and conductor Hans von Bülow, to help him with the organization of the concerts that were so important to him. Bülow is married to Cosima, Liszt's daughter, and like his father-in-law is a staunch advocate of the "music of the future."

The programs were naturally pure Wagner: music from the operas *Tannhäuser*, *The Flying Dutchman*, *Lohengrin*, and *Tristan and Isolde*. The first concert was held on January 25, 1860.

Paul Bernard wrote in *Le Ménestrel*:

One thing we must admit: the "music of the future" has created quite an uproar—in the present. This is not the place to try and predict what the future has in store for this music, but it has achieved one thing: in this Paris of January 25, 1860, which in the morning hours was still wrapped in a sweet artistic slumber as usual, a violent storm suddenly broke out, the kind that awakens indifferent people, shakes placid onlookers, and drives the enthusiasts out of their minds. Whoever missed the Salle Herz that evening has never witnessed tumult in his life! Even before the first sound was heard, the audience was simmering, as if attending a sitting of the National Assembly or expecting the nomination of a new provisional government. When Wagner entered the hall the excitement grew to a thunderstorm; Germans and Frenchmen, classicists and romanticists, conservatives and those hoisting the banner of revolt, everyone was preparing and polishing their arguments—those who had made up their minds beforehand to formulate their support even without a hearing, and those who were set, in advance, on dispensing a guilty verdict.

All of artistic Paris was assembled here last night because no one was willing to miss meeting with this German, the Christopher Columbus of music. Even during the intermission, after listening to excerpts from Tannhäuser and The Flying Dutchman, the public rushed to the entrance hall to start loudly voicing their opinion.

"This is sublime, like Meyerbeer!" "This is a willful and outrageous corruption of Weber!"

"Heavenly sounds!" "Infernal screeches!" "A parody of music! Hurly-burly!" "A feast for the spirit, for the soul, for the senses!"

The commotion continued after the second part of the concert, which ended with the beautiful sounds of choral excerpts from Lohengrin. The noise increased and the heated discussions frightened a few shop owners in the Passage Choiseul who decided, as a safety precaution, to close their businesses.

They say that for M. Wagner's next concert, on February 1, they will double the security and circle the Théâtre Italien with a battalion of policeman. We seem to have returned to the good old days when the Gluckists and Piccinists turned our city into a battleground.

And Charles Baudelaire published an open letter to Richard Wagner:

Immediately with the first few bars I sank into those blessed depths of bliss that are known to men only in their sleep. I felt as though I was freed from the restraints of gravity and I floated, liberated, in other spheres. Only in my opiated visions have I experienced such fancies. No music ever instilled in me the deep desire to go back and drown in the nebulous, wide spaces, the shreds of a dream.

At the other end of the spectrum there is Berlioz's virulent attack against Wagner in *Le Journal des Débats*. This is, in my opinion, a direct result of his deep emotional distress at the activities undertaken by the German guest in our city. And not surprisingly, there are already talks that *Tannhäuser* will be staged at the Opéra, while *The Trojans* is being postponed indefinitely. How can one keep an objective and balanced outlook under such circumstances? But even more painful than the murky future of *Les Troyens* is what seems to be Berlioz's friend Liszt's betrayal; he feels Liszt has abandoned him in favor of Wagner, his new protégé. I tried to soothe his bitterness, but to no avail. Had he been willing to join the Wagnerian camp, his work would have benefited from the broad legitimizing and massive support of those growing circles of "representatives of progress." But his conscience will not allow him such a step. As a result, he finds himself completely isolated; the modernists have turned toward Wagner and the conservatives keep ostracizing him as a "dangerous revolutionary," as they have done in the past.

Berlioz told me,

This young man, Hans von Bülow, is one of the most enthusiastic representatives of the extravagant school that in Germany is called the "music of the future." I have been unceasingly pestered to put myself at the head of this movement here in France and to be its standard bearer. I have kept silent. Wise people will no doubt understand what direction the wind blows.

A few days later I found this letter on my desk:

Monsieur,

The three concerts I gave have amounted to a net loss of eleven thousand francs, money that I borrowed from different sources. My situation is too bad for words. Since I remembered your great generosity in the past, I turn to you to solicit your help in extricating me from these straits, into which I have been driven due to the distorted aspects of musical life in Paris.

With gratitude from old times,

Richard Wagner

This letter upset me more than I can say. I was well aware of the catastrophic state of Wagner's financial situation. I knew, for instance, that he had sold to the publisher Schott and Sons of Mainz the rights to *The Ring of the Nibelung*—an ambitious project he has been working on for a few years already, which still seems to be far from completion—despite the fact that the rights to *The Ring* had been promised to Otto Wesendonk since Wagner started working on it.

In some of the circles I move in, there is talk about the debts Wagner has contracted all over the place, not to mention the huge debts he left behind when he fled from Germany. But he didn't ask for a loan; he asked for a contribution. What should I do? A loan I surely would have refused with regard to Wagner's reputation with his creditors. But a gift was a different matter. I hesitated between several possible paths available to me: I could simply ignore the letter, or send it back with a fitting note to put the impudent Wagner in his place; I could also comply with his plea and send a check and mention the word "Jew" under my signature. In the end I took the most illogical path: I sent a very generous check without adding a single word to it. For days I ran around sullen and angry, wondering about the unfathomable motives that had driven me to act the way I did.

A week later an invitation was delivered to my office for a dinner party at Wagner's home at 15, rue de Newton. A short note had been included with the invitation, thanking me in rather official terms for my contribution. I angrily shoved the invitation aside—but on the evening of the party I found myself sitting in a carriage on my way to the rue de Newton. What did I want there? God knows.

It was a flamboyant party: the upper strata of the Parisian elite, an abundance of refined delicacies both for the palate and for the ear, and a choice of wise remarks thrown around by the leading French intellect. Mme Minna Wagner juggled in the most efficient way the ten words of French she had mastered, and ruled over the whole evening in the most regal fashion. I was rather surprised to meet a handful of my coreligionists there, among them an eighteen-year-old poet, Catulle Mendès, who arrived from his native Bordeaux only last year and has already rallied around him a circle of young writers calling themselves Parnassiens. Maybe he was there on the strength of his father—with whom I attended the synagogue school as a toddler to learn the rudiments of reading Hebrew, by the way—being a wealthy banker?[10]

Émile Erlanger, Wagner's honorary financial adviser, was also there; so was Stephen Heller, the composer and pianist from Hungary who would soon settle in Paris and become a close friend of mine.

Wagner's reputation as a womanizer has long since placed him in the center of spicy gossip in the corners of society's parlors. His latest affair seems to be, according to this gossip, with Blandine, Émile Olivier's wife. Olivier, a prominent socialist member of parliament and one of the republican minority known as the Five, is also a gifted

---

10   Six years ago, in 1886, Catulle Mendès wrote the libretto for Chabrier's opera *Gwendoline* and published an essay in defense of Wagner's cause (J.H.R.).

writer. His wife Blandine is the daughter of Franz Liszt and Marie d'Agoult.[11] Every word and look she exchanged with our host was subject to general scrutiny and would provide additional fuel to the envious, to the bigots, and to the anti-Wagnerian campaign.

Twenty years of creativity and struggle have added a look of distinction to Wagner's features. He was at his best on this evening. With much charm and geniality he apologized for the terracing work the municipality had undertaken on the street. For us, the guests, this construction had required acrobatic exercises to gain access to his house! It appears that they are planning to join the street to the new boulevards and have to lower its level to do so. There is even talk about tearing the whole house down within the framework of the new urban redesign, and this after Wagner has invested a small fortune in its renovation. It now transpires that the landlord was well aware of those facts at the time Wagner signed the lease, but chose to keep his peace so as not to jeopardize the chance of a cheap swindle.

The Opéra has agreed to stage *Tannhäuser* thanks to the active support of Princess Metternich,[12] who interceded with the emperor.

Wagner has described in a mixture of humor and bitterness the devious adventures of the French translation of the text.

---

11 Blandine Olivier died one year later, in 1862, at age twenty-seven (J.H.R.).

12 Pauline Metternich, Princess de Sandor, is the wife of the Austrian ambassador to Paris Richard Metternich (J.H.R.).

To start with, I took advice from some knowledgeable people, and they sent me to a courteous young man, M. de Challemel-Lacour. We met a few times and I explained to him extensively what my purpose is. But it soon turned out that this nice youngster was utterly incapable of producing verses adaptable to the music. At this point the whole project was postponed due to the fact that our man was not up to the task. He passed the job over to another acquaintance of his, who, naturally, also demanded full remuneration. I brought my plight before Hans von Bülow, who suddenly remembered a music-loving Parisian physician named Auguste de Gasparini he had become acquainted with in Baden-Baden. He might be able to help. Gasparini was out of town at the time, but I secured his address and wrote to him soliciting his advice. He answered immediately and recommended me to a good friend of his, a music teacher called Leroy. After a long hesitation, Leroy eventually proved shy to accept the task and sent me to Gustave Roger, the popular opera singer who has been obliged to temporarily leave the stage following an accident. Roger is living outside Paris, in a palace surrounded by a magnificent forest full of game, and is passing the time playing at dominos. He received me very cordially, listened patiently to my story, and pulled a few excellent rhymes from up his sleeve. He promised to take on the job and put his heart into it. Happy and content, I left him…and heard nothing from him again. It so happens that between his caring for his wound and the game of dominoes, he has neither time nor energy left for my business.

The next candidate was one Herr Lindau who proposed to get the translation done in collaboration with an acquaintance of his called Edmond Roche. As it so happens, I have met Roche before; he happens to be an employee at the customs office and had been very helpful when I had to go through all the paperwork and gruesome arrangements for having my furniture sent over from Switzerland. At that time he told me that my portrait was displayed in a place of honor on his piano, and that playing my operas is the only pleasure of his drab life. Gasparini vouched for the man's talent; the only trouble was that he didn't know a word of German. We surmounted this obstacle thanks to the aforesaid Herr Lindau, who was to prepare a word-for-word translation that Roche would then shape into a well-rhymed libretto. Lindau and Roche met daily at my house to put in a few hours' work. More than once I felt like grabbing Lindau by the neck and throwing him out; I kept my cool only out of respect for Roche, who worked assiduously and with much talent. This unbearable situation went on for several months. In the meantime I busied myself with putting together the team of solo singers. The rehearsals were about to start.

At this point, M. Royer, the director of the Opéra, told me that the translation put together by my pair of amateurs was inadequate, be it only for the fact that both of them are absolutely unknown. He proposed I trust one M. Charles Truinet with the job. Like Roche, Truinet didn't know German either. But his father, who had lived in Germany for a while, was willing to help in deciphering the text. I explained to M. Truinet that we didn't need his father's help; all we asked was to have him polish poor Roche's verses a little. I was sorry to find out that M. Truinet lacked elementary poetic fantasy; he is a lawyer by profession and works at the Opéra archive in an administrative capacity. But at this point, I was firmly resolved not to involve yet another translator, be he good or bad.

In the end, this Truinet, writing under the pen name of Nuitter, wrapped up the job and gave me a workable translation, even though it was completely devoid of luster.

But, as might be expected, the translation adventures are not the only trouble lurking around the preparations for bringing the opera to the stage. Pauline Viardot, who has completely and fervently passed over to the Wagnerian camp, told me about the talk she had with the composer. She says that she had tried to open his eyes to some of the facts of life, but was dismayed at his stubbornness, which was a clear indication of his unbelievable naivety and his total disregard for Parisian reality.

"I heard that you flatly refused to insert a ballet in the second act of *Tannhäuser,* as the custom is here," Viardot told me she said to Wagner. "Is this true?"

"Certainly," Wagner replied. "Where would I find a place for such a ballet in the second act? During the song tournament on the Wartburg? Or maybe during the procession of the pilgrims to Rome?"

"Willingness to adapt to the customs of a place is basic wisdom, my friend," Viardot countered. "This refusal may prove very costly to you."

"I have reshaped the Venusberg scene at the beginning of act 1," said Wagner. "I have woven into it a grandiose bacchanal: nymphs, naiads, mermaids, and satyrs break into an orgiastic dance. Is that not a sign of goodwill?"[13]

"There may be goodwill in it but no wisdom," Viardot explained. "The *petits rats* from the ballet school are little fit for this kind of production, and as you know you haven't been allocated the real corps de ballet. But this is not the main point. The important thing is that the members of the Jockey Club are having a late dinner and are used to arriving at the theater only at the end of act 1."

"What business do I have with the gentlemen of the Jockey Club?" Wagner asked.

"They are the ones who set the tone. If they have made up their minds to cause your failure, your opera has no chance at all. Their avowed aim in coming to the theater is to admire their lovely paramours from the ballet company. If they are deprived of this pleasure, they will make trouble."

---

13   Is it a coincidence that Berlioz had already used the very same ingredients at the beginning of act 4 in his *Les Troyens*, during "The Royal Hunt and Storm"? Or did Wagner knowingly adopt (steal?) Berlioz's idea?

"I will ask Princess Metternich to intercede in the matter with the emperor; he promised her that the theater would meet all my demands."

"The emperor will not act in any way against the members of the club," Viardot insisted. "Those young aristocrats are the main pillar of his regime. He needs them more than they need him. If they abandon him, he is lost."

Wager replied, "I don't believe they will abandon him for the ballet of an opera."

"In Paris, anything is possible."

"I also mean to demand that I be allowed to conduct my opera myself. Dietsch is a complete dummy, lacking intelligence, lacking memory, and lacking hearing. Never in my life have I met such an unmusical conductor. We have held over 150 rehearsals—not for the singers, but mainly to get Dietsch used to the right tempi. But it's a lost cause; even 300 rehearsals won't help."

Viardot begged, "Don't come out against the regular conductor of the Opéra; the entire team will rise up against you and all of Paris will follow."

"I act only according to the directives of my conscience."

"Does your conscience also order you to put a pack of hounds on stage? Those dogs have become the laughingstock of the salons," Viardot said.

"He who laughs last laughs longest," Wagner replied.

"Have you come to terms with the leaders of the claque?"

"There will be no claque at my opera. The audience should pass judgment, not a gang of paid applauders."

"You're giving the impression that you are set on digging a grave for *Tannhäuser* with your own hands."

"I will reveal something to you, dear Madame Viardot: I came to Paris in order to produce *Tristan* in German here. Instead, I end up producing *Tannhäuser* in French. I am cut off from this opera today;

I have come a long way since I composed it and I am immersed in a completely different world now. What's more, the production is far from meeting with my approval. If it fails, I can take it. It will not be my failure but the failure of the bureaucracy that rules over the arts in Paris. At least I will not have to carry the burden of having taken part in this conspiracy."

The first performance, on March 13, was interrupted by the members of the Jockey Club. For the second performance, five days later, the anti-Wagnerian faction had brought various unmusical instruments (whistles, toy trumpets, drums, and so on) to render the performance of the ballet inaudible. The third and last performance was a total imbroglio. The conductor was Pierre Dietsch; Venus was Fortunata Tedesca; the role of Tannhäuser was played by the German tenor Albert Niemann, and Signor Morelli was Wolfram. Elisabeth was sung by the young and gifted Marie Saxe. In spite of this mishap, Mlle Saxe went on to have a great career, but I want to point out a mistaken notion about her: Mlle Saxe is in no way related to that inventor and builder of musical instruments, Adolphe Sax. It is true that both came here from Belgium, but Adolphe Sax's family is from Dinant in the south and Marie Saxe (whose family name was originally Sasse) was born in Ghent in the north.

I would be oversimplifying if I stated that the commotion at the three performances of *Tannhäuser* was solely due to the missing corps de ballet, or the bad behavior of young dandies who would not swallow the story of true love's victory over the venal satisfactions of the flesh. I think it was mainly a political demonstration, and it was waged with no sentiment and no compromise—a battle to the bitter end. The general public had no say and no chance to express its protest; it was simply impossible to overcome the pandemonium created by a wild band making use of whistles, piercing little flutes, rattles, and toy trumpets. Even the ostensible applause at the emperor and the empress's entrance to their loge was drowned in the sea of imprecations, shrieks, and the imitation of animal cries of many kinds. The masters of the theater had voiced their verdict.

When asked during the intermission what such a virulent commotion was all about, some members of the Jockey Club explained that they had nothing to protest against personally, but the disturbances were ordered from "above." Still, when the curtain was raised again they apologized and said it was time "to get back to work." On the other hand, there were also cases where members of the audience reacted forcibly and there were cries of "Out! Out with the jockeys!" The painter Czermak physically assaulted some of the noisiest troublemakers. Princess Metternich thrashed about in a fashion that was very unsuited to her rank and position. But all this was like a drop of water in the ocean; the brutal hubbub prevailed. Prince de Sagan, one of the ringleaders of the gang, confessed after the last performance that he had no idea what all the commotion was about: "We were told to have an uproar—we created one."

After the third performance Wagner announced that the opera was being withdrawn. I think this was probably a mistake; the scandal around the first performances promised a full cashbox for the coming evenings, had he just let the first torrents of the storm abate.

As for the musical critics, one of them wrote: "The twelve hounds of the landgrave were beautiful animals. But what did we need them for? We'd have better use for twelve melodies in the score. But M. Wagner probably estimates that it is easier to find dogs than melodies."

But the one who really disappointed me was my good friend Berlioz. In his review in *Le Journal des Débats* he unveiled all his human weakness: "God in heaven! What a spectacle! My compliments to my fellow Parisians; they derided this defective style. They laughed at the tricks of a prankish orchestra and the pretentious innocence of the oboe. They fully understood that there is a thing called style in music."

Most of the other critics, even though many of them are Wagner's adversaries, denounced the disturbances as a scandal. It is possible that the challenge of men of Baudelaire's stature got them pondering and gave them second thoughts.

Baudelaire commented,

Gentlemen of the Jockey Club: Keep your seraglio, but don't deny us our theater, where some spectators, who do not think like you, may find pleasures more fitting to their taste. Free us from your presence and yourselves from ours. Everyone will be happier."

But let me tell you this, and not only you—if someone thinks he has gotten rid of Wagner, his joy is premature. One who believes this has no inkling whatsoever of the game of seesaw that occurs in the history of man, nor of the high and low tides of human feelings. Even today the reverse of this cycle has started. It was born at the very moment when malice, wickedness, stupidity, routine, and envy allied themselves to bury achievement.

I just read in the newspapers that Princess Louisa of Baden has secured a pardon for Wagner's unruly past and his misdemeanors. He is now allowed to go back to Germany. He is leaving in the next few days for Karlsruhe to help in the staging of *Tristan* at the local opera house. He is leaving but the storm has not abated. Baudelaire is right; the last word has not yet been uttered when it comes to Wagner—not in Paris, and nowhere else in the world either.

9

Trojans Seek Refuge

(or Paris, No Place for Trojans)

Around 1854, I don't remember exactly when or on what occasion, Berlioz told me,

These last three years I have been haunted by the idea of an opera on a gigantic scale, for which I would write both the text and the music, as I did in my religious trilogy *L'enfance du Christ*. The way it takes shape in my imagination, this work is imposing and most exciting, which is a sure indication that Parisians will find it shallow and dull.

March 1855

Berlioz had just come back from another concert tour in Germany where he conducted *L'enfance du Christ* in Hanover last month. On his way back he visited Liszt and Princess Sayn-Wittgenstein in Weimar. That is when he discussed with them his idea, an idea that has been haunting him for years, of writing a monumental opera based on his beloved Virgil's *Aeneid*. Liszt, and to a greater degree Princess Carolyne, were so enthusiastic about the scheme that Berlioz felt obliged upon his return home to start sketching the general lines of the work.

Virgil had been one of his father's favorite authors, and Berlioz had grown up venerating the Roman bard. But on starting his work, he became aware of the toll he would have to pay to bring the work to completion and decided to give up on the idea. He wrote the princess that he could not find the strength or the courage to live up to the task. She answered in no ambiguous terms:

My dear Berlioz,

If you shirk the upcoming difficulties, if you flinch before the effort, and if, in your weakness, you abstain from endangering everything for the sake of Dido and Cassandra, then don't come here again—I will refuse to see you again.

Berlioz's answer was short, swift, and businesslike: "Your threat was the decisive factor; *Les Troyens* will come to life."

I think his decision to tackle this grandiose project is a very courageous undertaking considering his health, which has deteriorated lately. He is fully aware of the obstacles he will have to overcome as well as the jealousy and opposition surrounding him, and in view of the slovenly ways and general indifference that rules here. But what can I say? He is so full of renewed energy and in such high spirits, so happy that he has made up his mind, that I think a physical improvement of his general condition is underway.

November 1857

Berlioz told me yesterday,

Within a couple of months I will have the composition of *Les Troyens* completed. But my ordeal with it will start only then. Where will I find the theater manager, the conductor, the singers needed to stage it? My new opera will be stranded like Robinson Crusoe's raft, until the sea sees fit to launch it on its way—if for works such as this a sea exists at all. Sometimes it seems to me that the sea is only an invention of ship builders.

Berlioz has finally completed his magnum opus. After struggling with it for years, the score for *Les Troyens* is in hand. But will we ever see it on stage? The chances seem rather slim. Anyhow, I want to copy here the letter Berlioz wrote to his sister upon putting down his pen.

March 11, 1858

My darling Adèle, my dear little sister,

At this very moment I've just written the final bar of Les Troyens. This is a great moment, an exalted moment, as this score holds within it all I have—or rather all I have left—after five years of slowly consuming me.

I may sound a trifle haughty with what I'm going to write now, yet I feel compelled to write it, as I am convinced that it is the truth. If the great Gluck could come back to our world and hear my work, he would say, "I recognize you as my son." This deep conviction that I have fills my heart with renewed strength, tremendous strength. And truly I need every ounce of this strength, now more than at any other time in the past, as I am about to launch the last battle of my life: the battle to have Les Troyens become a reality on the stage.

I feel scared at the thought of the struggle awaiting me—a struggle against indifference, against slovenliness, against envy, against malice. But I can't avoid the issue, because if I do, my life will be like an epos without the last chapter.

Be well, my little sister, and if you want to wish me well, wish only this: be strong, strong and mighty.

And another letter he wrote:

Paris, March 28, 1858

Sire,

I have just completed my new opera for which I have written both the text and the music. In the scenery and staging I have implemented several modern and daring gadgets, but nothing in it is beyond the capacity and resources of the Paris Opéra. I would be grateful, Sire, if you would permit me to read the libretto for you, and if indeed you feel it worthy and deserving, as I hope you will, I would freely ask your protection and patronage for it.

The Opéra is now managed by one of my old friends, who, in spite of his being a friend, does not appreciate my musical style. The two conductors in office there are my enemies. Sire, defend me from my friend. As for my enemies, as the old proverb says, I can defend myself from them.

If, after hearing the text of the libretto, Your Majesty thinks it unworthy, I will respectfully accept your decision and judgment. But I will not permit my work to be judged by people who are biased or driven by prejudice, and whose opinion is in my view worth nothing. Those amongst them who find fault with the text will denigrate the music without so much as listening to it. As for those whose lack of sympathy for my music has been a lifelong religion, their antipathy for the score will bring them to deny the value of the text without even giving it a glance.

I believe that under your patronage and with your help I will be able to conquer the Latium.

With the most profound respect and devotion, I am Your Majesty's humble and most obedient servant,

Hector Berlioz

Member of the Institut

Berlioz never conquered the Latium. Napoleon III never read this letter because Berlioz did not send it. The Duke of Morny convinced him not to as, in his opinion, it was absolutely unfitting. And it is clear that without the emperor's support the gang at the Opéra would make sure that any proposed plan would fail.

Louis Berlioz has returned from overseas. He is a captain in the Merchant Navy and is really a decent young man. For years he had been estranged from his father, because he strongly disapproved of Berlioz leaving the conjugal home to share his life with Marie Recio. But since poor Henriette Smithson's death, father-and-son relations have resumed and have grown slowly but steadily into mutual love. In order to be able to extend some financial help to his son, Berlioz has once again turned to his literary talents and has started publishing autobiographical reminiscences in *Le Journal des Débats*. The paper's circulation has risen sharply; Berlioz's music is under constant criticism, but his literary talent meets with general approval.

Léon Carvalho, the director of the Théâtre Lyrique, has asked Berlioz to stage Gluck's *Orphée et Eurydice* for him. He probably remembered the inspired way in which Berlioz had staged Weber's *Freischütz* in 1841 at the Opéra. Maybe he even knew that Gluck was Berlioz's favorite composer when he was a student. Back then Berlioz spent most of his free time at the Conservatoire's library copying Gluck's scores; this actually triggered his decision to stop studying medicine and devote his life to music. When his father, who was a physician himself, reproached him for his "ill-fated decision," young Hector Berlioz replied that he'd rather be a dead Gluck or Méhul than a featherbrained youth in full physical fitness.

As could be expected, Berlioz eagerly accepted Carvalho's invitation and went to work with quasi-religious fervor. He felt it was like paying a debt he owed to the composer who has had such a stupendous influence on the course of his life. With his usual meticulousness he checked the score and threw out all the additions that had not been made by the composer himself. Carvalho had planned to make use of the overture to *Iphigenia* and one of choruses from *Armide* in this production, but Berlioz was adamant that it would be all or nothing, and he had his way.

The role of Orpheus will be sung by that great artist, Berlioz's friend, Pauline Viardot. She invited Berlioz to her house in the country for a few days to properly study the part, as the style of singing he has in mind is totally different from the style in vogue today. She readily complied with his demands and worked hard to adapt to his straightforward and unembellished style, which is actually a declamation in music. Berlioz had to cut short this pastoral interlude as he suddenly fell ill with some sort of colitis. He made some excuses and returned to Paris. There, in bed, he continued working on the score.

Orpheus has been a resounding success. The public is ecstatic and connoisseurs are having a ball. I saw Jules Michelet beaming, Dickens shedding tears of happiness, and I heard Gustave Flaubert telling anyone willing to listen to him that he would go to the Théâtre Lyrique every evening until the last performance. Have people here really begun to realize what a real opera should be like? Everyone marvels at the new discovery: Berlioz, the super stage director who taught his team to sing, to dance, to act, and to dress properly. At his side at all times he had his young friend and admirer Camille Saint-Saëns who, thanks to his devotion and his extraordinary musical gifts, proved an invaluable help, mainly in training the singers.

At the Théâtre Italien they have revived *I Capuletti e i Montecchi*, Bellini's version of *Romeo and Juliet*. What most people, among them Berlioz, seem to be unaware of is that Felice Romani had based his libretto on the sixteenth-century *Giulietta e Romeo* by Bandello and the play of the same name published in 1818 by Sceola. So it really is not surprising that it differs from Shakespeare and that the secondary personae are totally different in both tragedies. Berlioz told me he had heard the opera at the Teatro della Pergola in Florence, and he was very much distressed that the role of Romeo was written for a woman. He has the most ardent yearning to treat the subject as an opera, notwithstanding his *Dramatic Symphony* of ten years ago. In the meantime he has published an extensive article on the subject in *Le Journal des Débats* (without, however, mentioning his own work even once).

January 1860

Berlioz's second wife, Marie Recio, has, because of her stupidity and her misplaced jealousy, brought about a rift between Berlioz and Wagner. These two geniuses, who were on such friendly terms in the past, are now exchanging harsh words in the pages of *Le Journal des Débats*. It started a few years ago when Berlioz and Marie visited Liszt and Princess Sayn-Wittgenstein in Weimar. Marie made some uncalled-for remarks about Wagner's personality and his music. Berlioz blushed but chose not to rebuke his wife in front of their hosts.

March 1860

Berlioz has of late suffered a few painful setbacks. He had applied for three different conductorship tenures. The post of conductor at the Opéra was given to Dietsch. Tielemann was chosen as conductor for the orchestra of the Conservatoire. And a protégé of Auber, whose name I don't even remember, was elected to conduct the Imperial Capella.

An additional blow came when he got news that his beloved sister Adèle, ten years his junior, had died. Of her he used to say, "She is the only person in the world who could really thoroughly understand me."

March 7, 1862

Last week the Opéra opened the season with Gounod's new work *The Queen of Sheba*. It was a disaster.

The Opéra had closed its doors to Gounod since the failure of his two previous productions on its stage: *Sapho* in 1851 and *La nonne sanglante* in 1854. But the tremendous success of *Faust* at the Théâtre Lyrique three years ago had given a new luster to his name and the Opéra gladly accepted the score of *La reine de Saba*, only to regret it bitterly on the morning of March 1, when they were forced to shelve the work after only a single performance.

Berlioz was at a loss to find the right words to soothe Gounod's grief. Writing in *Le Journal des Débats* he did his best, reminding readers of Gounod's natural melodic gift and his supreme confidence in the treatment of lyrical moments in *Faust*. He also wrote, "No composer can write a dozen operas worthy of that name. Paisiello wrote 170 of them, but what is their value? Where are they today?"

Berlioz was well aware that the failure of *La reine de Saba* would negatively impact the chances of him being able to have *Les Troyens* staged. The management of the Opéra would be much more cautious, as its financial reserves would be depleted by another failure.

There is only one opera drawing the public today: Offenbach's parody *Orpheus in the Underworld*. Strangely enough, Berlioz, with his revival of Gluck's *Orphée,* has unwittingly contributed to the success of this farce. The real trouble with it is that Offenbach has put antiquity as a whole to derision and made it impossible to consider staging another play with a theme of antiquity on the serious stage for a long time. This has naturally had a direct impact on *Les Troyens*.

But in the meantime Berlioz has started work on another opera, which is in absolute contrast to *Les Troyens*: short and compact, sparkling and entertaining, in chamber music guise. He has once again written the libretto himself Shakespeare's comedy *Much Ado about Nothing* as the framework. The opera was commissioned by the Baden-Baden Summer Festival and will be called *Béatrice et Bénédict,* and Berlioz has summed it up with one sentence: "A capriccio written with the point of a needle."

Berlioz convinced me to go to Baden-Baden and attend the premiere of *Béatrice et Bénédict*. I had a very good time there. I like the place, with its gardens, the shaded alleys, the forest, and the old castle on the mountaintop. I readily admit it: I enjoyed this combination of luxury, lightheartedness, and making the most of the pleasures of life, things that characterize both the place and its guests. The town has really earned its nickname of Little Paris. There were so many beautiful women around! Sticking to my principles, I avoided the casino; the time I saved was well spent walking through the woods. I'm quite confident that this was a net gain. As for the opera, I will share with you Berlioz's own impression:

August 19, 1862

Last night, Béatrice et Bénédict was a stunning success. The troublemakers and the provocateurs where left behind in Paris. In their place came writers, artists, and real music lovers. It was a magnificent production. Mme Charton-Demeur outdid herself both in her singing and in her acting in the role of Béatrice. Bénazet, who does all things in a big way, spent huge sums on the dresses, the scenery, the soloists, and the choir. He was intent on inaugurating the Neues Theater in the most splendid way. The press is full of praises—the critics suddenly discovered that I am endowed with melodic inventiveness and, lo, even with a sense of humor. The same story again as with L'enfance du Christ.

Berlioz really felt welcome in Baden-Baden. For the past few years Bénazet had put together an orchestra especially for him, the core of which was formed by some of the best instrumentalists in Europe. And Berlioz conducted a number of concerts in the luxurious atmosphere of the small town for the benefit of a congenial and cultivated audience every summer.

Charles Gounod was also amongst the many musicians who came to Baden-Baden for the occasion. He fled Paris after the failure of *La reine de Saba*. Jouvin, Berlioz's colleague at *Le Journal des Débats*, was surprised to see him, as the rumor in Paris was that he had cut himself off completely (at least for a time) from music and all musical activities.

"What are you doing here?" asked the journalist Jouvin.

"I am making a pilgrimage to commemorate a death in the family," answered Gounod.

"Did you lose a next of kin, a dear one?" asked Jouvin.

"Yes," answered Gounod. "A lady I loved dearly: the queen of Sheba!"

"My dear Gounod," he said, "I hope you understand that there is nothing personal in what I wrote about your opera. It is a matter of professional ethics and, as you know, a critic has to put aside personal feelings and considerations and give as unbiased a judgment as his training permits, even if posterity will occasionally pronounce him grossly mistaken."

Bizet was very annoyed by the fact that he had to miss the premiere of *Béatrice et Bénédict*. He was stuck in Paris where he was busy with the preparations for *Érostate*, the two-act opera by his friend Ernest Reyer. *Érostate* was also scheduled for Baden-Baden alongside *Béatrice et Bénédict*. The Baden-Baden Theater, with its lavish and sumptuous productions, was putting up genuine concurrence to the Paris stages. It certainly surpassed Paris in its audacity and staunch support for everything new, daring, and deviating from the usual routine.

Reyer promised Bizet that as a reward for his relentless efforts with *Érostate*, he would intercede in his favor with Édouard Bénazet, the all-powerful theater director, and try to have him order an opera from him for the next season. Reyer himself was already in Baden-Baden with his librettist Paccini,[14] and worked feverishly on completing his opera. Every additional excerpt he finished he immediately sent to Paris to his diligent assistant.

The account Reyer gave to Bizet on that premiere is worth citing:

> The success of *Béatrice et Bénédict* was rather mild. A *succès d'estime*. In my opinion Berlioz's opera is a wonder of art and crafts-manship. This in spite of the fact that "Papa Haydn," who is the subject of so much jesting in this opera, played quite a trick on Berlioz by whispering in this ear the most wonderful phrases from *The Creation*, while he composed the duet. But what of it? Never has a sweeter, purer, and more wondrous thing been written than this duet.

And from personal experience—as I myself was also present at the premiere—I gladly agree both with Reyer's description and with his judgment.

In the end Bizet also arrived in Baden-Baden, laden down with the score and the parts for *Érostate*. He had supervised the copying of the parts himself and had painstakingly done the endless proofreading in place of his friend.

I don't remember ever seeing him so nervous and on edge as during that summer. I vividly remember a terrible altercation he had with Paccini. During one of the heated discussions held in the French-speaking group assembled there, Paccini inadvertently emitted an

---

14   Émilien Paccini has translated the libretto of *Der Freischütz* into French for the1843 production staged at the Opéra by Berlioz.

unhappy and ill-judged remark, saying that the failure of *The Queen of Sheba* was entirely deserved. I am not even sure Paccini seriously meant what he said, but Bizet at once sprang to his feet, flushed with anger, and showered him with abuse and even threats. All of us who were present were stunned, and before we could react to calm him down and stop him from doing anything rash, he challenged Paccini to a duel.

It took Gounod quite an effort to convince him to drop the matter, arguing, quite logically, that if someone had the right to feel slighted it was Gounod himself.

Only many years later would I come upon the reason for Bizet's strange behavior that summer: a dark cloud had estranged him from his father Armand. Marie Reiter, the young maidservant in Bizet's parental home, had just given birth to a healthy young baby, Jean. Since Aimée Bizet's death Reiter had become Armand's mistress, so everyone took it for granted that Jean was Bizet's half-brother. Only Reiter and the two men knew for a fact that Bizet, and not Armand, was the father of the newborn.

I can't disclose under what circumstances this secret came to be known to me, and I wouldn't be surprised if Jean himself finds out about his real parentage through this unwarranted indiscretion of mine. In any event, the atmosphere in the Bizet household was heavily charged and felt just like before the outbreak of a menacing thunderstorm. Adding to the burden of all the work he had to do for others and his feeling that he was treading water and making no progress whatsoever toward fulfilling his own artistic ambitions, this situation frayed Bizet's nerves and brought him to the verge of losing his usual self-control.

On June 13, the second Mme Berlioz died suddenly from heart failure. She was forty-eight. Her mother, who has been living with the couple since their marriage, will from now on be alone in looking after the composer's personal comfort. He has always been at a loss as far as keeping a household is concerned. Louis, Berlioz's son, has arrived from overseas to be with his father for a while to ease his loneliness.

Berlioz has an ardent desire to see *Les Troyens* on stage, so he can sum up the achievements of his artistic life. But he has given up all hope of having this work produced at the Opéra. So he had to seek salvation elsewhere. After the triumph of his staging of Gluck's *Orphée* at the Théâtre Lyrique, Carvalho, the director, feels he owes a debt to Berlioz. This is how the idea of producing a truncated version of *Les Troyens* was born.

Conscious of the fact that the Théâtre Lyrique does not have the technical means to put on the first two acts, Berlioz has agreed to stage the three closing acts as part two under the name of *The Trojans in Carthage*. (He's now calling part one *The Fall of Troy*.)

Even so, part two will have to undergo changes and amputation, but the important thing from Berlioz's point of view is to breathe life into the yellowing pages of the score. Flaubert, the author of *Salammbô*, has been retained as an adviser on local get-up. But this is a useless appointment, as the budget for costumes is inadequate and can't cope with the original instructions and compromise will also affect the production.

Berlioz is furious but doesn't have the courage to withdraw the score. "Better a mutilated performance than no performance at all," he says. What a change from the intransigent director who put on *Freischütz* and *Orphée et Eurydice*.

September 20, 1863

Today I attended the funeral of the great poet Alfred de Vigny. He died three days ago from cancer of the stomach. This is becoming quite depressing: all these giants disappearing, and no real replacements in sight. This is the third great artist whose hearse I have followed since the beginning of the year.

The year started with the death, on January 17, of my good old friend Horace Vernet, who had been the third generation in his family of gifted painters, and since 1829 he had also been the director of the academy at the Villa Medici in Rome. And last month, on August 13, a personal and dear friend of mine, Eugène Delacroix, died after having at long last received official recognition for his unique talent.

September 30, 1863

Bizet's *Les pêcheurs de perles* has failed to win public recognition at the Théâtre Lyrique. Berlioz has written a laudatory article in *Le Journal des Débats*, praising the work as being "full of beautiful, expressive pieces filled with fire and rich coloring" and declaring the composer to be "a genuine genius." But Carvalho is furious and the till is empty. The real loser is Berlioz's opera. The premiere has been moved up a month in the hope that this will replenish the theater's depleted cash.

This means that *Les Troyens à Carthage* will be even less rehearsed than planned. The only thing left is to pray and hope for the best.

I was very curious to see and hear the work even before the first night, so I arranged to be admitted to one of the dress rehearsals. On that morning they had worked only on the second act (act 4 in the original *Les Troyens*).

It begins with an impressive symphonic tableau. The action takes place in a forest near Carthage; naiads bathe in a stream and satyrs are running around.

The sound of hunting horns is heard from a distance, getting nearer and nearer, until the queen's entourage enters the clearing. A storm forces the hunters to seek shelter. Dido and Aeneas have left their escort behind and taken refuge in a nearby cave, where they reveal their mutual love and fall into each other's arms.

At the end of the rehearsal I went to the conductor's podium and had a good look at the impressive manuscript. This interlude is called "The Royal Hunt and Storm," and under the title I found this remark, probably meant to appear in the printed version of the score as well:

> If the theater is not big enough to allow for the performance of this grand, brilliant interlude; and if it is impossible to find female choristers capable of roaming the stage wildly with disheveled hair, and male choristers able to dress as satyrs and fauns, performing stage rite….if the fire brigade is scared by flames and the floor assistants are afraid of water; and if the director is afraid of everything—then it is better to forget about the interlude altogether and dismiss it.

On November 4, 1863, *Les Troyens à Carthage* was born on the stage of the Théâtre Lyrique. The public was deeply moved; there were tears and sighs, applause and "Bravos!" It is true that at the end, when the composer was called to take his bow, there was one harsh whistle, but it was nothing and lost in the sea of general approval.

The septet and the love duets were especially appreciated and the audience responded with a spontaneous and unanimous burst of applause. Mme Charton was sumptuous—a real queen! It really was a tremendous success. But all the compromises Berlioz had to make in order to bring about the performance were a heavy price to pay. The opera was taken off the bill after twenty-two performances, and I doubt very much if it will be seen again during Berlioz's lifetime. As for part one, *The Fall of Troy*, it is already clear that he will never live to see it; his beloved Cassandra will be left to come alive only in his imagination. There is one consolation: *Les Troyens à Carthage* has earned fifty thousand francs for its composer, thus freeing him once and for all from the slavery of writing for the press. His last article was the laudatory report on Bizet's *Les pêcheurs de perles*.

I am proud to point out that Meyerbeer went to the Théâtre Lyrique every single night to hear *Les Troyens*. He said he went there both to enjoy the show and to learn. Now there is humility for you!

May 1864

Meyerbeer is dead. A princely funeral ending in a slow procession through France brought him to his native town of Berlin. The general feeling is that the musical world has lost its ruler.

Berlioz has started of late to hold readings of Shakespeare's plays in a restricted circle of close friends. I was present at a long evening when *Othello* was read: it was a breathtaking experience. I will make every endeavor to hear his *Hamlet* in a few days. The emotional impact is almost comparable to a full-scale presentation at the theater.

June 1867

A terrible thing has happened. We had arranged, a few friends and I, to have a reception in honor of Berlioz at the Marquise de Visconti's private hotel. Some of the best musicians who happened to be in Paris during this time were present and had promised to contribute to the evening's program. The reception was due to start at six o'clock. By 6:30 Berlioz had not yet shown up—very uncharacteristic for such a meticulously punctual man. Embarrassment slowly gave way to worry. What could hold him back? We sent Theodore Ritter, a young pianist and composer , to look for him, but he failed to come back. Worry turned to anxiety and I set out for Berlioz's home. On the stairs I crossed paths with his mother-in-law; she was crying her heart out. She told me between sobs that Berlioz had just left the house on his way to the reception, when a neighbor stopped him to express his condolences on the death of his son. The unfortunate news had been published this very morning in the press, and not one of us, including the poor father, had seen it. Louis had died of yellow fever on June 5, in Havana. He was thirty-three.

When I entered Berlioz's room, I found him lying on the sofa, his head turned toward the wall. He was muttering, "It was my turn to die, it was my turn."

Why is fate so cruel? It knows perfectly well, as everyone does, that Berlioz's days are numbered. Was it really necessary to deal him such a merciless blow in the twilight of his life?

I have been told that one week after Louis's death Berlioz went to the Conservatoire and gathered from the drawers all the odds and ends that he had accumulated over the years—letters, posters, diplomas, decorations, batons, and all kinds of souvenirs—and threw them all into the fire.

When I went to visit him a few days later he told me,

My creative life has come to an end. I will write no more music, nor will I conduct concerts anymore. I will write no more verse or prose. I have resigned my position as a critic. All the musical enterprises I have undertaken have come to an end. I don't feel the urge to do anything anymore, and, sure enough, I do nothing. I just vegetate, reading, pondering, and fighting a deathly weariness of the soul. I am afflicted with an incurable neuralgia that causes me to suffer day and night.

March 11, 1869

Berlioz passed away three days ago, on March 8, at 12:30 a.m. He went to sleep peacefully and never woke. Two faithful women were at his bedside during his last hours: Mme Recio, his late wife's mother, and Paolina Charton-Demeur, the singer who had devoted her talent to creating the heroines of Berlioz's two last operas, Béatrice and Dido.

The funeral was held today. According to the custom for members of the Institut, a squadron of the National Guard on horseback was posted near the house on the rue de Calais. Bugles were sounded when the coffin was carried out. The pallbearers were Gounod, Reyer, Thomas, and Count Taylor. At the service held at the Trinity Church, the Pasdeloup chorus and orchestra played music by Gluck, Beethoven, Mozart, and Cherubini. And Berlioz's music as well, of course: the "Hostias" from the Requiem, the septet from *Les Troyens*, and the "Pilgrims' March" from *Harold in Italy*. Four months ago in this same church, after the funeral service for Rossini, Berlioz told me he would be the next to go.

From the church, the procession made its way to the cemetery in Montmartre where Berlioz's two wives are buried.[15] The orchestra marched in front of the hearse, playing excerpts from the *Symphonie funèbre et triomphale*.

A typical Berliozian incident took place when the two well-groomed black horses harnessed to the funeral cart panicked. They took the bit between their teeth and galloped on their own toward the gates of the cemetery, sowing havoc in the ranks of the orchestra, whose players scattered in all directions. Even to his last resting place, Berlioz, true to his principles, arrived alone.

---

15 Henriette Smithson had been buried in the cemetery of Saint-Vincent, but when the concession for the plot expired in 1864, Berlioz had her exhumed and reburied next to his second wife Marie Recio in Montmartre.

10

DAVID RIZZIO

July 1829

Next month I will be seventeen!

Two years ago my mother decided to change my piano teacher. I started playing at the age of five when we still lived in Bordeaux. When we came to Paris my father asked the cantor of our synagogue if he knew a reliable piano teacher in the Jewish community. Charles Gimenez recommended M. Joseph Wolf, a recent newcomer from Alsace. M. Wolf became my piano teacher until we moved to the rue de Montholon in 1826. As it was too far for me to walk from our new home to M. Wolf's house, my mother started looking for a teacher living closer to our place. She turned again to M. Gimenez and this time he came up with the perfect solution: in our congregation there was a young widow who was a certified piano teacher and eagerly looking for pupils in order to balance her precarious financial situation. Her late husband, David Ancona, who had been the synagogue's treasurer, had died of consumption three years earlier. She lived on the rue de Chantilly, just a five-minute walk from the rue de Montholon.

Mme Veuve Ancona had been married for five years and was twenty-four when her husband died. My mother knew her casually from the women's section (*ezrath nashim*) of the synagogue. She was a timid-looking brunette, her face always lit with a convivial smile. But when it came to the piano, she was merciless; the slightest deviation or slurring was sanctioned with a peremptory, "Again, please; bar thirty-five."

In the two years since she has become my teacher I have worked on Clementi's *Gradus ad Parnassum*, on two Mozart sonatas, and on a beautiful sonata by Beethoven. As my mother wished to be generous toward Mme Ancona without seeming to extend charity, I had two lessons a week instead of the weekly lesson I had had with M. Wolf.

I had just started working on the magical adagio from Mozart's Sonata in F Major; we had finished working on the first movement, the allegro, the previous week. What a magnificent composition this is, with its changing rhythms, countless surprising modulations, and a completely independent left hand.

On that Thursday I strolled leisurely, my satchel in hand, down the rue Pierre Sénard and crossed the rue de Bellefond at the corner of the rue de Chantilly. When I got to Mme Ancona's house, I climbed the stairs two at a time and rang the bell at her door. As she opened it, I greeted her as usual, "Bonjour, Madame Ancona," and got the usual answer, "Bonjour, Hippolyte." I went straight to the piano and opened the Mozart sonata to the page of the adagio, but she stopped me and said that she wanted me to play the whole sonata from start to finish. I was somewhat taken aback since we had not yet worked on the third movement, but I felt that I was up to the task, so I didn't say a word.

She came to sit next to me as she always did and I started playing. At the end of the allegro she got up without a word and stood behind my stool. I felt the warmth of her body on my back and I had a feeling that the pounding of my heart could be heard in the apartment next door. Ten bars through the adagio she suddenly leaned over my right shoulder, her right breast touching my ear, and put her hands on the keyboard, saying softly, "This is how I want you to play it."

Yes, we became lovers. She stopped being Mme Ancona and became Stella, my very dear, unforgettable Stella. For all practical purposes this was the end of the piano lessons. Stella and I went on meeting twice a week for two years. Then one day she told me that we had to stop seeing each other, as she had met someone and planned on getting married again. I don't think anyone ever knew about this affair; anyhow, this is the first time I've disclosed it.

March 1836

We are back in Paris, my wife and I, after a three-month honeymoon in Italy.

For generations it has been a tradition in my family—like in most Jewish households—that the parents decide whom and when their children marry, and this decision is normally taken at a very early stage of their children's lives (this is how both my grandmother and my mother got married at the age of sixteen). Thus it was that shortly after Benjamin and Flora Salome were blessed with the birth of their daughter Mathilde in 1817, they began looking for a match for her.

They agreed with my parents that, with the good Lord's will, Mathilde would marry me shortly after her eighteenth birthday. This is how young Mlle Mathilde Salome became Mme Hippolyte Rodrigues on January 7, 1836. I was already a promising young financier with a law degree to boot, and had, for almost two years, been head of our family bank, Les fils d'A. Rodrigues.

The marriage was celebrated in the Sephardic synagogue on the rue Causserouge in Bordeaux, the same synagogue where my late father had been a leading member and where I had learned to decipher the Hebrew alphabet and rudiments of our ancient language as a child, long before I started visiting the elementary school in which I began to acquire my normal education.

All of Mathilde's family was present: her parents, her four sisters, and a host of cousins. Naturally my mother was also there, as well as four of my sisters: Elisa Esther (she was forty and had married William Busnach in 1829); Laura, who was thirty-three at that time and had married Benjamin Gradis, a remote cousin of my mother's, in 1822; Nancy, thirty, who had married Henri Vieyra-Molina in 1825; and Léonie, the youngest, who was sixteen years old and would in due time marry my composition teacher, Fromental Halévy, in 1842. Practically the entire Jewish Portuguese community of Bordeaux came to pay their respects to my mother and congratulate the newlyweds.

Mathilde was a shy, well-mannered, and soft-spoken young lady. She was 163 centimeters in height to my 170. Her smooth skin had a natural tan and her head bent slightly forward most of the time. Her long eyelashes hid dark, almond-shaped eyes and an inquisitive, sharp glare that was a blatant denial of her timid bearing.

Love was no part of the bargain. Like our parents and our ancestors before them, we would certainly grow to love each as the years passed. Nonetheless, my unshakeable decision was that my own children would be free to choose for themselves when it came to matters of matrimony.

The Jewish community in Bordeaux was generally prosperous. Very few families needed pecuniary assistance from the community's welfare funds. The Salome family was an average middle-class family and Mathilde's upbringing had been in accordance with their social standing. Apart from her general education, she had learned a smattering of cooking and sewing, and had been given piano lessons as an additional bonus, as seemed fitting for a young girl destined almost from the cradle marry the son of one of the leading families of the congregation.

The day after the ceremony, we boarded the carriage that brought us to Nice, on our way to our Italian honeymoon. For Mathilde this was the first time she had ever left her native Bordeaux. She would have to get used to quite a new style of life, since after Italy we would go straight to Paris, to the spacious apartment I had purchased on the rue de la Victoire.

Our son Edgar was born in Paris on March 22, 1837. Our neighbor, Fromental Halévy, composed for the occasion music to Psalm 115. "The Lord hath been mindful of us: He will bless us; He will bless the house of Israel; He will bless the house of Aaron."

When we returned from our honeymoon, I immediately applied and was accepted to the class of musical theory at the Conservatoire. I had an interview with the director, the famous composer Luigi Cherubini, who sent me to be tested for piano playing by Marmontel; my solfeggio examinations were held by Victor Dourlen, whose harmony class I would join a few days later, after I officially became a registered student.

Jean François Lesueur was my first composition teacher. Unfortunately, he died in October, a few months after I was admitted to the Conservatoire. This is when I joined the class of my former neighbor, Fromental Halévy. Among my classmates were four students who would become Prix de Rome laureates. Louis Désiré Besozzi was the last of a long line of professional Italian musicians who were already active as early as the seventeenth century. His father, Henry, had for many years been the leading flautist at the Opéra-Comique. Louis was awarded the Prix de Rome at the end of my first year at this institution with his cantata "Marie Stuart et Rizzio." This was the first time I ever heard the name David Rizzio, the man who was to become the central figure of the opera I would write some thirty-five years later.

Charles Gounod, who was nineteen at the time and had become a friend of mine within the first days I joined the class, also competed and was awarded the second prize for his work (on the identical text, according to the regulations of the Prix de Rome). I think it worth mentioning that Gounod's father had also—years ago, naturally—won second prize in the same competition, but in the field of painting.

Georges Bousquet, who won the 1838 Prix de Rome with *La vendetta* was also in our class. And Charles Gounod was the next winner with his dramatic scene *Fernand*. I was so happy when Gounod was awarded the coveted prize that when our second son Georges was born that same year, I chose Fernand for his middle name. Gounod really was worthy of the prize as he stood head and shoulders above the rest of our class.

There also was Emmanuel Bazin, of course. He won the Prix de Rome in 1840 with his *Loyre de Montfort*. But I always knew that he was a very shallow person who did not harbor any real originality. So I'm not really surprised that all he achieved in the end was to become a third-rate teacher.

Early in 1863 I showed Berlioz some of the piano pieces I had composed and he exclaimed, "Hippolyte, you should try your hand at work on a larger scale, a ballet or maybe even an opera!" But then he suddenly recoiled and said,

> After due reflection, and from bitter personal experience, I retract what I just said. You can play these piano fantasies at home, for yourself and your entourage, and enjoy them to their full value. As for those two choral pieces you showed me, you could have them performed at your synagogue, I guess. But an opera? God forbid! You'll work on it for a year or two and then you will identify with it to such an extent that you will find no rest until you see it on stage. This means getting involved with so many unpleasant people that even you, in spite of your friendly nature and your powerful relations, will become nauseated. You will find it a Sisyphean task leading nowhere.

But the seed had been planted, and the idea of composing an opera never stopped gnawing at the back of my mind.

A few months later, I received with my morning mail an official invitation from the Institut to the award ceremony of the Prix de Rome. On the verso of the Bristol board there were two lines in Berlioz's neat handwriting:

> Come and join me. I'm sure you'll be interested.
>
> Your friend, Hector Berlioz

When I entered the big hall, half an hour before the ceremony was due to start, Berlioz met me and shook my hand. He said,

> His name is Jules Massenet, he is twenty-one, and there is something about him that I feel amounts to a very promising future. He has already caught my attention several times on his frequent visits

to the library at the Conservatoire. His questions are always to the point and the scores he studies are often of works off the beaten track. Truth be told, there is an obsequious side to his personality, a kind of sleekness, which prevents me from seeking a more personal interaction with him. But I'm sure you'll like the directness of his musical style and his daring, though always logical, harmonic progressions. It is a pity that his cantata will be performed only with piano accompaniment, because the score that he submitted to the committee is orchestrated in a lush, rich, and masterful manner.

The cantata was "David Rizzio." Again that same David Rizzio that I remembered from the Prix de Rome in 1837. This story of a professional musician who is murdered because he dared to become the lover of a lady of exalted rank, filled with political intrigues and religious unrest, haunted me. It was somehow associated in my mind with the story of Alessandro Stradella. In the forties, my good friend Friedrich von Flotow had written an opera on that subject and the public gave it a rather warm reception. But somehow it was washed away in the big wave of the fashionable Grand Opéra craze. Flotow has recently returned to Paris after an eight-year sojourn in his native Germany. I'm sure I'll seek his advice regarding my plans about composing an opera dealing with the murder of David Rizzio.

♪ ♪ ♪ ♪ ♪ ♪ ♪

My closest friends, Charles Valentin Alkan and Stephen Heller, never seriously considered writing anything but music for the keyboard instruments. At most they might try their hand at some chamber combinations but beyond that it was terra incognita for them. Heller once told me that he knew the piano intimately, and that the best way he had to express himself was through the language of the piano. He liked to say that even words were a clumsy means of expression for him. "I'm not a verbal person," he would say. "I can only express my real thoughts and feelings in the magical world of sounds, and for me that world is confined to the piano."

Alkan held the same opinion. He told me,

> You know—perhaps better than anyone else since we shared the same elementary education as boys—that from the start I was determined to be a musician. In the last few years I have given my full attention to the *pédalier*. I am, in my opinion and in that of many music lovers I know, the best performer of it in town. Because the literature for this instrument is so scarce I endeavored to enlarge its repertoire. I have played the *pédalier* since it was introduced to me; I teach *pédalier* playing, and lately the majority of my compositions are written for this instrument. I even composed a symphony for it and if you ask, "Whoever heard of a symphony for a solo instrument?" I will answer, "Go to Sainte-Clotilde and listen to César Franck play the organ." There you have another mighty symphony for one instrument.

I have raised the question of composing an opera with both Alkan and Heller; both had the same reaction: they shrugged and voiced their opinion that someone like me, who hasn't even competed for the Prix de Rome, could never have an opera staged in France. Nevertheless, my mind was already made up. The idea of writing this opera had haunted me for years. Now the gestation was nearing its term and there was no escape for me; some overpowering force drove me and I had to compose it.

For years I have been convinced that the librettists are the curse of opera composers. Assuming that their literary aptitudes are on a decent level, you will always have to fight your way through a maze of nonsensical actions or wrongly timed dramatic situations. That is, unless you have a Ranieri da Calzabigi or a Lorenzo da Ponte to do the task. So I decided that if I'm doomed to have a bad libretto, I'd rather write it myself.

I set out for Scotland on February 15, 1866. All my friends warned me about the discomfort I should expect both with the traveling conditions and with the accommodation available at this time of the year. But I had a precise goal in mind: I intended to visit Holyrood Palace on March 9. David Rizzio had been murdered there on March 9, 1566, exactly three hundred years ago.

The crossing of the Channel from Calais to Dover was a nightmare in spite of the modern paddle steamer; I would rather forget than describe it. In spite of the big leaps we have made in France, both in the expansion of the railway network and in the comfort of the train cars, the British are still very much ahead of us in this field. The railway connection between Dover and London has existed for over twenty years and I must admit I rather enjoyed the ride. This was my first visit to Great Britain and I intended to make good use of it. The weather in London was what you would expect it to be: cold, rainy, and foggy most of the time. Nevertheless, I was able to do quite a lot of sightseeing in the five days I spent there.

The highlight was my visit to the Tower of London. Having only a superficial knowledge of the history of the United Kingdom I learned a lot during those days. I also visited the theater where I saw Shakespeare's *King Lear*. At Her Majesty's Theater, Haymarket, I saw a very good staging of Verdi's *La traviata,* and I had the good fortune to be able to purchase tickets for Meyerbeer's *L'africaine,* a sold-out Covent Garden production.

The trip from London to Edinburgh with the Caledonian Railway took almost ten hours. When I walked out of the Princes Street station in the early hours of the morning the temperature was minus fourteen degrees Celsius. The streets, white with a thick carpet of snow, were deserted except for the few other people who had arrived on the same train I had taken. I was shivering despite the heavy cocoon of the best English wool that enrobed my entire body. I was lucky to catch one of the very few horse-drawn carriages parked across the street, which took me to the hotel where I had made a reservation.

On March 9, I rose early and left the hotel before daybreak. The surrounding trees sent their naked branches like so many arms in supplication, upward, toward the low ceiling of menacing gray clouds. The whole landscape was painted in many shades of black and gray on an immaculate background of white. As I walked slowly down the Royal Mile with Edinburgh Castle behind me, I was awed by the complete silence. Perhaps I should say the sound of silence, because the combination of the heavy carpet of snow and the low skies covered with bluish-gray clouds was, in a certain way, absorbing every sound in the environment before it could even materialize. It was like walking in a big cotton ball. I wasn't cold anymore. Maybe this was on account of the excitement burning inside me—the excitement of getting to the spot where this horrendous crime had been committed three hundred years ago.

At the far end of the road, the imposing complex of the Palace of Holyrood rose majestically out of the morning fog, with its foreboding background of high, snow-covered, rocky, and barren hills. The palace was not yet open to the public to visit at this early hour, so I strolled in the park, toward the chapel.

When I entered the palace courtyard, called the quadrangle, I was the only visitor on that bleak morning. I planned my tour of the palace so that it would end at the northwest tower, where the rooms occupied by Mary Queen of Scots were situated. The queen's suite of rooms was very well kept, especially the magnificent wooden ceilings. The initials MR (Maria Regina) and "IR" (Jacobus Rex, her son James VI) were strewn all over the place. The highlight of my tour was to be the north turret room, the very place where David Rizzio had been stabbed fifty-six times in front of his helpless, beloved Mary Stuart. She was pregnant with the baby that would in due time become James VI.

When I arrived at this room shortly before noon, I was surprised to see that there was some kind of religious service going on, under the supervision of several high-ranking members of the Scottish Catholic clergy. After the ceremony, I talked with some of the people there, including the French consul in Edinburgh. After all, Mary had also been queen of France, albeit for a very short time.

♪ ♪ ♪ ♪ ♪ ♪ ♪

Back in Paris, I immediately started work and planned the setup for my opera. It was already clear to me that I would have to concentrate on the last days of David Rizzio's life. So I had to leave out all the things I had discovered, after arduous research, about his youth in Italy, and the way he arrived in Scotland in 1564 as a member of Count Moretto's staff. As the queen was very musical (she could play several instruments) it took her no time to discover that this newcomer, with his solid, basic training and natural aptitudes, was a perfect candidate to lead the small court orchestra. It was just a matter of weeks before Rizzio was promoted to the queen's personal secretary; and soon enough he also became her lover.

I located the first scene in Holyrood Park, near the chapel. The queen and her ladies-in-waiting are kneeling and praying. Kennedy, one of her most trusted officers, comes to warn her that her husband has found out about her plan to meet Rizzio at this place, and that he's on his way with a party of his followers to catch them red-handed and kill them both. Without panicking even for a second, Mary asks her maid Nelly to take her place at the rendezvous and act as if she were Rizzio's lover.

While I was writing the text, the music came to me by itself, naturally, without any kind of cognitive effort; it was as if the versified sentences enrobed themselves with magical melodies. I curbed the feverish urge I had to gallop forward, and adopted a steady, moderate rhythm, a pace I was used to in all my endeavors and which fit my personality so well.

Early in 1868 I had to interrupt work on the opera because my editor, Michel Levy, reminded me that on publishing *Les trois filles de la Bible* in 1865 I had undertaken to supply him with a second manuscript about Christ's Sermon on the Mount. In the wake of that book came *Le roi des juifs*, in which I brought forward irrefutable arguments proving that Jesus had been condemned and executed not by Jews for religious reasons, but by the Romans on political grounds.

In May 1858, my son Edgar had married Louise Meyer. She came from a well-known and influential family in Alsace. Her great-aunt, Julie Meyer, was the wife of Élie Halfon Halévy, and the mother of Fromental and Léon. After the signing of the Treaty of Frankfurt in May 1871, Alsace-Lorraine was annexed by the German Empire. As a result, many Jewish families chose to leave those provinces and rebuild their future in France. Most of my daughter-in-law's family was among them. They settled in the northern city of Lille, near the Belgian frontier. The newly appointed spiritual leader of the community,

Rabbi Benjamin Lippman, was my personal guest when he came to Paris to consult with the Consistoire concerning the organization of the community under his guidance.

In May 1873, the Jewish community of Lille sent me an invitation to spend four days in their town in order to give a lecture on a topic that was dear to my heart: the early days of Christianity. I had just finished the orchestration of *David Rizzio* and felt I was entitled to a vacation, so I eagerly accepted.

Since I very much cherish my privacy, I declined Rabbi Lippman's generous invitation to host me during my stay. I preferred the accommodations of the hotel. But I was very happy to accept his invitation to share the Friday evening meal with his family.

They did not yet have a synagogue in Lille, and the congregation met for the Shabbat service in the restaurant that one of the Meyer brothers had opened two years earlier. The cantor had a beautiful and high, clear tenor voice. When I inquired about him, Émile Meyer told me that this young man was a soldier from the garrison that the German army held in Lille according to the stipulations of the Treaty of Frankfurt. The terms of this treaty stipulated that France would pay Germany an indemnity of five billion francs, and until that sum was fully paid, the Germans would keep an occupation force in the northern part of France. The costs of this occupation force would naturally be paid by the French people. Two other soldiers from infantry regiment number 130 stationed in Lille were Jewish, and all three had received permission to perform the traditional rituals imposed by their religion, and to keep Shabbat as a day of rest insofar as this practice did not clash with their usual military duties. (I don't know if this was the result of a general directive issued by the German general staff, or whether it was an initiative taken by a local officer with an open-minded and liberal outlook.)

On our way from the improvised synagogue to Rabbi Lippman's home where supper was waiting for us, Meyer explained to me the dilemma the community had been faced with when three young soldiers from the occupying enemy forces sought out the leaders of the congregation and asked for permission to join the sacred services. The congregation consisted of an overwhelming majority of people who had left their original homes in Alsace and Lorraine because they were genuine French patriots and refused to live in territories annexed by the hated enemy; they abhorred the mere sight of a German uniform. But on the other hand, they were all Jews and shared a common creed. Hospitality was an ancestral inherited duty, and a Jewish home, anywhere in the world, was always open to any Jewish traveler in need of shelter on his way from one place to another. This double allegiance has always been a troubling issue with the Jewish people wherever Jews were treated properly in their host countries. So the leaders of the community adopted a very reasonable decision: the young German Jewish soldiers were welcome to join on festive days and on Shabbat provided they wore civilian clothing and on the condition that the language spoken with their French brethren would be French, Hebrew, or Yiddish (despite the fact that everyone in the congregation was fluent in German).

Meyer explained:

To give you a more realistic picture of the situation here, I will tell you about two rather nasty incidents that occurred in the last few months. One day, two young German soldiers entered Mme Marx's grocery store intending to buy some kosher sausage. Mme Marx is a widow in our congregation, and one of her sons was killed on the battlefield at Sedan. At first she was sure that those Germans had come to tease her and to humiliate her. She flatly refused to even talk with them. But when they insisted and tried to convince her that they too were Jewish and that they wouldn't eat the meat served at their canteen, she flew into a rage, seized a heavy iron bar she kept there for protection, and drove them out forcibly, slightly wounding both of them.

The two soldiers refused to press charges or to complain to their superiors in the army. But they went to the rabbi, trying to explain their situation and by the same token asked to be permitted to attend Friday evening and Saturday morning prayers.

The second incident has caused quite a stir in our community. One of the three young Jewish soldiers of the garrison has fallen in love with Monique Lippman, the rabbi's youngest daughter, and she reciprocated his feelings. They had been seeing each other secretly for a few months already and two weeks ago the youngster went to see Mlle Lippman's father to get his consent to marry her. You can imagine the scandal this raised when it became public knowledge in our streets. Rabbi Benjamin Lippman refused to consult with the elders of the congregation; when they tried to broach the subject with him, he firmly told them that this was his personal problem and that he intended to find his way out of this mess with God's guidance. I personally know that he had three long confrontations with Monique after which he called both youngsters to his study for a long meeting. You know the end of the story: he will announce the formal betrothal tonight after the blessings, just before supper.

All three young German soldiers were also guests at the Lippman's Friday evening supper. Manfred Samuel Loewe from Mainz was the eldest of them. He was the youngster who had the good fortune to win the beautiful Monique Lippman's heart. He was twenty-four and had just finished law school when he was drafted. Most of his friends called him Dr. Loewe, which was actually the right thing to do, as a lawyer in Germany is automatically called doctor, just as here in France a lawyer is called *maître*. Loewe's French was fair, but he talked with a heavy Teutonic accent.

The young cantor's name was Felix Menahem Bernhardt and he came from Frankfurt-an-der-Oder. He only knew a very few words of French but his Yiddish was adequate.

Wilhelm Aaron Heidt had been born and reared in Cologne and his French was very close to perfect. He had spoken French as a second language since childhood because his mother was born in Metz. To my Parisian ears he had a very, very slight accent, but so did most members of the Jewish community of Lille. He acted as the spokesman for the three of them.

After the meal, I had a lengthy conversation with Felix Bernhardt. We talked mainly about music and he told me that his sole ambition was to become cantor at the synagogue in his hometown. I told him I had just finished composing a three-act opera and I was considering having some kind of concert performance at my summer residence in Saint-Gratien, a picturesque little town some fifteen kilometers north of Paris in the Val-d'Oise. I also told him that I liked his voice very much and appreciated his singing during the religious service. I asked him whether he would consider singing the title role in my opera. He was taken aback but readily agreed. He then told me about his sister Karolina, who had, in his opinion, a very nice mezzo-soprano voice. She was only nineteen but was intent on becoming an opera singer; he had made vain efforts to convince his parents to let her study music in Leipzig or in Berlin. We agreed on the spot that I would intercede with his parents; I would go to Frankfurt to listen to his sister's voice and try to convince her parents to let her come to France for the occasion, whatever the role I would find adequate for her to sing.

I was very much surprised at my sudden outburst of cooperation with this young German. Even before the war I had an instinctive dislike for almost everything originating from east of the Rhine (with the exception of German music and German literature, which I admired because of their depth, which was at the opposite end of the spectrum and so different from most of the shallow and superficial stuff our modern French writers and composers have been producing lately). Even in my professional life, before my retirement in 1855, I had always restricted my contact with German banking establishments to the absolute minimum. I suppose it was the general atmosphere around the table and the first-class Alsatian Riesling that made me forget and forego all my prejudices and my principles.

When I came back from Frankfurt, Mlle Lina Bernhardt sat next to me on the train. She was on her way to Paris and about to become a pupil in Pauline Viardot's class at the Conservatoire.

Marguerite Romain was born in 1836 in the Belgian town of Mons. At the age of sixteen, she became a pupil of the Conservatoire Royal in Brussels and soon became one of the most promising students in the opera class thanks to her brilliant soprano voice and the seriousness of her approach to her studies. Three years later she married Auguste Masson, a big landowner who was also the proprietor of a small sugar refining factory. He insisted that his wife relinquish all thought of an artistic career and fulfill her duties as a housewife and hostess in the framework of the upper bourgeois social circle in which they moved. Masson was forty-three when they married. He died four years later in an accident during a hunting expedition in the forest. Marguerite reverted to her maiden name after a suitable period of mourning.

I met Marguerite Romain in 1867 at a performance of Thomas's *Mignon* at the Opéra-Comique; Marie-Célestine Galli-Marié sang the title role. We started seeing each other rather often, thanks to our mutual fields of interest. I had been separated from my wife and living alone (except for my faithful servant Jeannette) for over four years. One day in 1871 I offered to introduce Mlle Romain to Pauline Viardot, who had just come back to live at her villa in Bougival. As you can imagine, Marguerite was overjoyed. Viardot agreed to take her on as a private pupil. We left Viardot's home together and Marguerite came home with me. We have been living together ever since.

On Tuesday, August 19, 1873, two weeks after my sixty-first birthday, a small crowd of friends and relatives was gathered in the big hall of my mansion in Saint-Gratien. The occasion was the reading of my opera *David Rizzio*. In the front row, next to Pauline Viardot and her husband Louis who had just turned seventy-three, sat my uncle, seventy-seven-year-old Edouard Rodrigues. Edouard was a true music lover and philanthropist. He had been a close friend of Meyerbeer. My wife Mathilde was there also. Since we had separated more than ten years earlier, I very seldom saw her now.

My two sons were there as well: Edgar with his wife Louise and their daughter Fernande; and Georges, who is a painter. So were my sister Léonie with her daughter Geneviève and her son-in-law Georges Bizet. That is it as far as the family is concerned. Except for my publisher Michel Levy and Catulle Mendès, all the other friends I had invited belonged to the musical world: Charles Gounod, Camille Saint-Saëns, Stephen Heller, Charles Valentin Alkan, Albert Cahen, Augusta Holmès, and Emmanuel Chabrier. Two of Pauline Viardot's pupils were to sing the main female roles: Marguerite Romain was to sing the role of Mary Stuart and my young protégée Karolina Bernhardt was to be her faithful lady-in-waiting and confidante, Nelly. Karolina Bernhardt's brother, Felix, was to play David Rizzio. Hector Salomon, the thirty-five-year-old conductor of the Opéra choir in Paris, had managed to gather a little improvised chorus and they had no difficulty in learning their parts, since all of them were professionals. The piano reduction of the orchestra was played by my very good friend Stephen Heller, who had read the score from the beginning to the end at first sight when I first showed him the work. I acted as a very unprofessional "conductor," whose role was actually to give the cues for entries, to keep the right tempo, and to coordinate this little troupe in its endeavor to make the performance worthwhile.

My opera ends when Queen Mary, from the depth of her despair and her ardent wish to avenge Rizzio's death, becomes the prey of the arch-villain Botwell, who succeeds in extracting from the helpless queen a promise that she will marry him if he murders the king in his sleep. As he strikes, three bars of empty E-flat in the lowest register bring the tragedy to its conclusion.

11

THE GIRLS OF THREE CITIES:

PERTH, ARLES, SEVILLA

August 1863

"Had we been able to gauge the true capacity of his talents, we never would have thrown this 'white elephant' in his lap."

This is how, in a mixture of embarrassment and admiration, Michel Carré apologized at the dress rehearsal of *Les pêcheurs de perles*. This was the first meeting of Cormon and Carré, the librettists of *The Pearl Fishers*, with the music written by this youngster whom they regarded as a greenhorn. In my opinion this description of the "white elephant" was paying an undeserved compliment to this commonplace imitation of Bellini's *Norma* and Spontini's *La vestale*. It used the same recipe of a sacred priestess invalidating her vows of chastity for the sake of love.

The action was originally set in Mexico, but during the course of rehearsal, for no apparent reason Carvalho, the director of the Théâtre Lyrique, decided to change the setting and transported it to Ceylon. Up to the last moment Cormon and Carré had no idea in which direction they should lead the outcome of the plot. They pestered Carvalho time and again asking him, "How do we finish this mess?" and "What shall we have for an ending?"

In the end, Carvalho, exasperated, called to them, "Throw them in the fire!" This came as a revelation, and that is indeed what they did. The opera ends in an apotheosis of flame; the whole village of fishermen is ablaze and in the general confusion that ensues the condemned lovers are able to make their escape.

The premiere had been scheduled for September 15, but Léontine de Maësen, who sang the main female part, was taken ill and the opening was postponed to September 30. I guess she had not fully recovered by then for her Leila was well below average for one of her performances.

Bizet heeded the opinion of one critic only, that of Hector Berlioz. As it happened, this was to be Berlioz's last contribution as the musical reporter for *Le Journal des Débats*. The tone of his criticism was rather encouraging. After a serious analysis of some of the opera's highlights he concluded:

> This work contains quite a considerable number of pieces that are full of beauty and expression, endowed of rich and blazing colors. M. Bizet, prize winner of the Institut de France, went to Rome, and came back from there without forgetting the essential qualities of music. His work *Les pêcheurs de perles* crowns him with an aura of glory. It seems we have to recognize him as a composer, in spite of his being such a superb pianist.

Les pêcheurs de perles was performed eighteen more times in the same autumn of 1863. I have not seen it since.

Barely five weeks later, on November 4, Bizet was sitting in the same Théâtre Lyrique, applauding loudly and calling, "Bravo!" at yet another premiere. This was the truncated version of Berlioz's *Les Troyens*. After five years of frustrated waiting, Berlioz managed to have acts three, four, and five of the opera performed under the title of *Les Troyens à Carthage*.

I was only eighteen in 1830 when the battle for *Hernani* was waged, but I vividly remember the riotous atmosphere of those days. The battle for *Les Troyens* was in the same vein, albeit on a smaller scale.

Bizet and the handful of friends who stood in defense of Berlioz's music were hard put to overcome the wave of whistling, meowing, and shouting of all sorts that greeted this noble work which, in my opinion, contains so many moments of sublime beauty. And, as in the case of *La reine de Saba*, Bizet's stubborn stand once again almost entangled him in a duel.

The direct cause was an abusive letter sent by Victor Chéri, orchestra director of Les Variétés, who had written the music to a song that was all the rage in Paris lately. In this letter, he stated that if "Monsieur Georges Biset [*sic*]" should be so bold and go to the next performance of *Les Troyens* and be rash enough to voice his approval in the scandalous and ridiculous way he did in the past, he, Victor Chéri, would regard it as a personal insult and would have no option but to kick his behind.

Bizet responded, "I sent two seconds to Chéri, Naftali Mayrargues and Ernest Guiraud. The poor thing started to shake all over and swore that he was not the author of the unfortunate letter and that he knew nothing whatsoever of the whole business."

When this story reached the gossip newspapers, they no longer portrayed Bizet as a young and unknown Prix de Rome laureate as they had in the past, but as the well-known composer of *Les pêcheurs de perles*.

Even the great Auber, the director of the Conservatoire, who was busy staging his own works, thought it appropriate to stop when crossing Bizet by chance on the street and say to him in a condescending tone, "My young friend, I have heard your work. It's very good."

Bizet's reply was rather unexpected. "I accept your praise," he said, "but I do not to reciprocate it." Then, as Auber made a face, Bizet grasped that he had been a little bit too blunt and quickly added, "A soldier of private rank may receive the praises of a *maréchal de France*, but it would be presumptuous and highly improper to return them." With a sour smile on his face Auber went on his way.

I broach this much criticized part in Bizet's life very reluctantly: his involvement with La Mogador. Still, I feel it is my duty as a serious, honest, and objective biographer to write about this phase of his life. I could have easily left it out, turned a blind eye to the facts, make believe that I had forgotten this sequence of events and act as if it had never happened...but forgetting or seeming to forget has never been my way of life.

I am aware that among the obstacles to Bizet's marriage to my niece Geneviève one of the highest hurdles was this black stain on his past. And as a fervent advocate of this marriage, this part of Bizet's life has brought me some very unhappy moments. His lighthearted behavior caused me much gnashing of teeth and dissatisfaction. On the other hand—and with some amount of hindsight—I must admit that without La Mogador Bizet would never have reached the depth of insight needed to create *Carmen*. The fires of passion that this woman kindled in this irresponsible youngster for the first time in his life brought about a transformation that years of experience and observation never could have achieved.

Her name was Elizabeth Vénard and she was known as Céleste. Her mother was a prostitute and she herself was almost raped when she was thirteen by one of her mother's clients. Sadly, she was unable to avoid following in her mother's footsteps and she also became a prostitute. Since she was a highly intelligent girl she quickly realized that in her profession there were castes as in every other organized society. On the lowest level roamed the common prostitutes—the streetwalkers—while the higher spheres of this "sisterhood" were inhabited by a very limited number of courtesans. To evolve from even that level and reach the status of mistress to a respectable member of society was the rarest of achievements.

Céleste's intelligence, tenacity, and wit made it possible for her to climb to the rank of courtesan in a very short time. She was one of the first to introduce the polka dance to the Parisian cabarets, and she became the most brilliant of its performers. She earned her nickname La Mogador when one of her admirers stated that it was easier to defend Mogador (a Moroccan town that had been under siege by French colonial forces) than to free Céleste from the grip of men dancing the polka in her arms. She also shone at the hippodrome in the acrobatic riding of the horse-drawn chariot she had received from a love-stricken duke.

With characteristic willpower and tenacity she had taught herself reading and writing, though she never managed to master proper spelling. Two of her prominent lovers—Alexandre Dumas the father, and Alexandre Dumas the son—helped her write novels and plays and bring them to performance in the theater. This gave her a foothold in the snobbier Parisian social circles. In the last stages of his general decline, the poet Alfred de Musset, after his relationship with Georges Sand broke down, was among her lovers. Some even called her "a poor man's Georges Sand."

And then she managed to accomplish the miracle: La Mogador, a former prostitute and courtesan, married, after a tumultuous and romantic love affair, the handsome and penniless Comte de Chabrillan.

To escape their creditors, the young couple fled to Australia. After her husband's sudden death in 1858, the countess returned to Paris with two little dogs and a parrot. With the help of her many friends in literary circles, she published her memoirs and with the royalties she earned she was able to repay almost all of her late husband's debts. She took over the management of the Bouffes-Parisiens when Offenbach sold his rights to her. There she ran a series of successful operettas, some of them to her own librettos.

In 1865, Georges Bizet was traveling on a train bound from Paris for the village of Le Vésinet. His father had bought some land there and built two small cabins that would become a kind of summer resort for them. On the train he met the famous La Mogador (actually Mme la Comtesse de Chabrillan), who, as it happens, had also built a summer home in Le Vésinet. Before the trip was over the two new neighbors were friends, and quite soon much more than that. She was forty-one; Bizet was twenty-seven.

That is also the time Bizet met a young man fresh from the province, who, together with Ernest Guiraud, was to become his closest friend until the end of his life. This was Edmond Galabert, the son of a winegrower in the south, who spent a few months in Paris every year in order to deepen his knowledge of music, and to quench his thirst for culture and art. He turned to Bizet to take lessons in musical composition. Galabert used to pay his fees with the lavish delivery of crates of first-class wine from the paternal cellars. He was a serious and diligent pupil, though unfortunately utterly devoid of creative inspiration. Nevertheless Bizet undertook his musical education with the utmost seriousness. I think Bizet was very much relieved when

Galabert decided that there were enough mediocre composers around and that he would make a much better winegrower than musician. The friendship between the two youngsters deepened when the teacher-pupil bond between them was removed. In the continuous correspondence that they exchanged, Bizet voiced his opinion on a wide range of topics and on his general outlook on worldly affairs of a social and political nature. He also stated his virulent opposition to the saber-rattling of Napoleon III.

In June 1866 Bizet left his lair in Le Vésinet and set out for Paris in order to meet Carvalho, the manager of the Théâtre Lyrique. The subject of this meeting was the commission of a new opera *La jolie fille de Perth*, based very loosely on one of the Waverley novels by Walter Scott. Those stories had proved their merit in operas like Boïeldieu's *La dame blanche* and Donizetti's *Lucia di Lammermoor*. The libretto was written by Bizet's friend Jules Adenis (an old warhorse in this field) in collaboration with Jules Henri Vernoy de Saint-Georges, second as a librettist in today's France only to the great Eugène Scribe. Amongst his works we find the ballet *Giselle*, which he wrote in cooperation with Théophile Gautier; two of Fromental Halévy's operas, *L'éclair* and *La reine de Chypre*; and the libretto to Donizetti's *La fille du régiment*. Still, this is the man who I can say gave Bizet the worst libretto he had ever seen in his life. Vernoy de Saint-Georges was sixty-seven at the time. Bizet, in the most irreverent way, described him thus:

> He is always the perfect gentleman, tall and slender, with an impressive face, his hair meticulously dyed, dressed with taste and perfumed like a marquis of the Ancien Régime. I spent days and nights

with his libretto—really a dog's life. Any resemblance to Walter Scott's novel is purely coincidental. Only the names of the characters are faithfully kept unchanged. But those characters are devoid of any kind of life and the dialogues...God help me, I'd rather not talk about it. To put those rhymes to music I have to start with forgetting the words.

This explains the many places in the opera where the emphasis of the musical phrase is in complete disagreement with the verse. With the perspective of time I can say today that in spite of the wretched libretto we can find much beauty and even a shred of dramatic power in Bizet's music. Still, I confess that when I compare it to *The Pearl Fishers* I can find no great progress. Many have blamed the work for its lack of local Scottish color, which would have given the action more semblance of unity and, perhaps, added some credibility to it. But it is not the composer who is to be blamed for this; it is the libretto that is so lacking backbone that poor Bizet could find no framework to adorn with his melodies. I think that his charming melodic inventiveness can compensate for many drawbacks, though I must admit that to some extent his musical language is colored by the blessed influence of his older friend Gounod.

The year 1867 brought the World Exhibition to Paris. Like all of his fellow Parisians, Bizet wanders through a jungle of Japanese temples, Swiss chalets, Balinese huts, Norwegian fishermen's cabins, Muslim mosques, and Mongolian tents. But his spirits are very low; all theaters and opera houses have gone out of business. Verdi's *Don Carlos,* for instance, was withdrawn after only fifteen performances at a disastrous financial loss. If Bizet had nurtured some hope for his *Fair Maiden of Perth*, all went down the drain.

The year 1867 is coming to an end—almost. December 26. At long last, the curtain rises at the Théâtre Lyrique on *La jolie fille de Perth*, conducted by Adolphe Deloffre. According to Bizet,

> I never have been so happy! My work met with a real success. I never dreamed of such an enthusiastic reception. I'm proud to say that I have met with approval from all sides. Suddenly I was greeted with respect. The audience, which in the beginning was not on my side, was completely conquered and followed me without reserve. I gave instructions to the leader of the claque not to start the applause; there was no need for it. The critics were unanimous in their approval...and now, will this be accompanied by some financial reward?

I'm sorry to say that the answer to this question was no. The success was real, but still, the public of the boulevards was not in the habit of going to the trouble of coming to the Place du Châtelet for the dubious pleasure of hearing a new work by a little-known, young composer. This brought about Carvalho's decision to stage, between presentations of Bizet's work, Clapisson's *La fanchonette*, a proven success. After eighteen performances, *The Fair Maiden of Perth* disappeared completely.

Bizet had not nurtured dreams of a big victory or of treasures coming his way. But this one time he was sure that the success was real and he had good reason to believe so. He was too proud to complain about his disappointment, even to his closest friends. Even so, he was so well aware of his true value that it was impossible for him not to feel a wave of bitterness at being denied the laurels to which he was so sure he was entitled. He made a tremendous effort to fight the gnawing pain that had taken hold of him and he threw himself headlong into work, strengthened by the conviction that in the end he would come out victorious in this struggle. But the blooming of his youthful energy was lost. The beautiful assurance of his early years was gone.

On October 3, 1867, in a letter to Galabert, Bizet exulted having met a girl worthy of his love, a girl with whom he wished to spend the rest of his life and would marry within two years. This girl was his teacher's daughter, my niece Geneviève Halévy.

A fortnight later, in a new letter overflowing with despair and bitterness he writes to his friend that the girl's family had had second thoughts and had withdrawn its approval of the betrothal. To me it was a shock, but also a tremendous challenge; this young man, whom I have admired since my friend Charles Morhange pointed him out to me in his early teens, and was on the brink of becoming a close relative, now needed my help and friendship to fight for his happiness.

I set out on this stubborn struggle, which lasted for almost twenty months, when I stood alone against the adamant wall of the united family. My foremost opponent in this confrontation was Émile Pereire, the family's financial adviser, and the one who had initiated me into the craft of becoming a banking wizard. At the outset, in view of my religious convictions, I was not wholeheartedly in favor of the union of my Jewish niece to this scion of an outspoken Catholic family. But when I found out that Bizet's mother's family had initiated a campaign against this marriage, ironically bringing forth religious reasons, and when I became aware of Bizet's firm stand, like a mighty oak in a furious tempest, against all the bigotry and attacks of the Delsarte clan, I resolutely shelved my prejudices and unconditionally put all my might behind the young couple in this epic battle of wills. It is this battle, during which we stood side by side, that has promoted my loose acquaintance with the young man I have admired for years into a true and solid friendship.

Perhaps I should have warned Bizet of the precarious condition of my niece's mental equilibrium. But the happiness of those two young people so very much captivated my heart that I really thought it would be a kind of betrayal to bring up the subject at such a critical time.

I really don't know anything about how the human brain works, about mental deviations or about how the soul reacts in situations of crisis. I sometime suspect that all those doctors who claim they can help patients with mental or nervous problems are actually groping in the dark. But I can point at some facts that have, in my opinion, played a major role in undermining my niece Geneviève's poise, which was so steady when she was a child.

She grew up in a household where her father was too busy with his professional occupations to take an active part in her actual upbringing. And with her mother disappearing from time to time for more or less lengthy periods, when she fled to Dr. Blanche's clinic in Passy to tend to her mental equilibrium, Geneviève must have felt totally abandoned and lost in this big world. And then there was the terrible spring of 1862. On March 17, Fromental Halévy died. He was not yet sixty-three.

Geneviève was a very sensitive thirteen-year-old child, and my sister, though endowed with a very acute maternal instinct, was too panicked to give her the protection she needed during those critical hours. The burden fell on her nineteen-year-old sister Esther, who immediately, as if it was the most natural thing to do, took the reins and became her little sister's protector. And then the second blow fell on this ill-fated family: two years had not elapsed since Halévy 's death when this beautiful angel, Esther, died after a three-day illness, the true nature of which the doctors had not been able to diagnose.

Esther and her cousin Ludovic, Léon Halévy's son, had been in love since they were teenagers, and were determined to marry in spite of all the difficulties facing them as first cousins. The family had accepted that, but, alas, fate decided otherwise. This union would never be realized.

For several days and nights Ludovic, lost in the immensity of his sorrow, did nothing but write furiously in his diary. No one ever knew what he wrote. After a while he came out of his trance and tore out all the pages, then he wrote a single sentence in his diary:

April 19, 1864

After three days' illness, Esther died.

In her grief, Léonie completely lost her self-control. It was impossible to get near her without her hurling incoherent accusations. Fifteen-year-old Geneviève, feeling completely abandoned and helpless, turned to the only person she thought could still become an anchor for her sinking ship: her mother. But in a moment of distress my sister uttered a few unpardonable sentences, accusing Geneviève of being somehow responsible for her sister's death. Geneviève, wounded to the core of her child's soul, ran away from home and came to me to look for a safe haven. Since then and until her marriage, she lived with me and my family most of the time.

Bizet and Geneviève had a modest civil marriage ceremony at one of the arrondissement town halls in Paris amid a restricted circle of family and a fistful of close friends. The bride's mother, my sister Léonie, and all of Bizet's mother's family were conspicuously absent.

The young couple spent their honeymoon at the small property I own in Saint-Gratien, a little picturesque town some fifteen kilometers north of Paris, in the Val-d'Oise. Their matrimonial bliss seems to have completely erased all bitterness concerning the daily problems they had faced those last years: the indifference of the public, critics, and theater managers, as well as the painful family mourning and estrangements.

They settled in Montmartre in an apartment at 22, rue de Douai, ten houses away from Pauline Viardot. Their apartment was one floor above Ludovic Halévy's and near friends like Guiraud and Gounod.

Then the storm that changed the world of every Frenchman and landed us in a new reality broke out. On July 19, war with Prussia was declared; on September 2, with the capitulation of McMahon's army in Sedan and Napoleon III taken captive, the carefree life of the Second Empire crumbled to emptiness. Then we had the Siege of Paris, the occupation, the Third Republic, and the Paris Commune. It is so painful to recall those terrible days that my hand is shaking as I write these words.

Bizet, like all his friends, had joined the National Guard. Geneviève, in spite of his exhortations, had refused to leave Paris. (This was to be expected if we remember the deep-rooted convictions she formulated on this topic in the letter she sent to me from Nice when she was only thirteen years old.) I myself, having no such qualms, found a relatively quiet haven in my house in Bordeaux.

Naturally, all these happenings were faithfully mirrored in our daily approach to life and the abysmal feeling of being unable to cope with the situation. It was a kind of spiritual suffocation. That is why so many people had tried to isolate themselves from the surrounding catastrophe by retiring to the relative protection of inner family circles and the warmth radiated by those we love.

I think that somewhere in the depths of his heart, Bizet always reached out for the motherly love he had lost when he returned from those formative years in Rome. That is probably why he tried to bring about reconciliation between his wife and her mother, a move that proved to be a calamity. When I left Paris at the start of the rout, I brought my sister Léonie with my entire household to the old family home in Bordeaux. Bizet had started a continuous correspondence with his mother-in-law, and they both thought it a bright idea for the young couple to join us all in the south. It turned out to be a disaster. The meeting between Geneviève and her mother turned into a nightmare for Geneviève and she completely broke down, to the point that Bizet feared for her sanity. The day after their arrival in Bordeaux he had to take her back to Le Vésinet.

Bizet himself went on maintaining warm and friendly relations with my sister through the steady stream of letters they exchanged. Only after Bizet's death did Geneviève confide in me that this correspondence between her husband and her mother, which built a bridge of understanding between the two that grew firmer with every letter, undermined her personal tranquility and made her feel like an outsider.

On July 10, 1872, Geneviève gave birth to a son, Jacques. Bizet was busy giving birth to his *L'Arlésienne*. I feel almost entitled to say *our L'Arlésienne* since Bizet chose to express a tangible token of friendship by dedicating this work to me.

Alphonse Daudet was born in Nîmes in 1840. After a short but disastrous career as a teacher, he came to Paris to join his brother Ernest, who was a journalist here. This is when he published his first set of poems, *Les amoureuses*, which was favorably received. As an immediate consequence Villemessant, the charismatic editor of *Le Figaro*, invited him to join the staff of his newspaper. Daudet was an out-and-out anti-republican, actually a monarchist. He also made no secret of his anti-Jewish feelings. Still, when his three-act play *L'Arlésienne* (based on one of the tales of his 1869 compilation *Lettres de mon moulin*) was published early in 1872, Bizet contacted him and they agreed that the play would be accompanied by incidental music that Bizet would supply. This common venture developed into a lasting friendship.

What is it that brought together those two youngsters with such diametrically opposed outlooks? The answer lies in one word: music. Daudet was a keen music lover, a real aficionado. He loved any kind of music and was bewitched by the mysterious hold music had on his very soul. This was all that was needed for Bizet's conquest.

I think there is one additional factor that has not been emphasized enough: just as Gounod's collaboration with Mistral was to produce *Mireille*, Bizet, perhaps without even being conscious of it, wanted *his own* Provençal heroine, and Daudet was heaven-sent to bring it to him.

The curtain went up on *L'Arlésienne* on October 1 and the audience's indifference drove Bizet to lose his Olympian poise. He immediately set out to draw an orchestral suite in four movements from the beautiful work and Pasdeloup played it at his concerts in November.[16]

As *Mireille* is, in my opinion, Gounod's second-best opera, so *L'Arlésienne* remains for me Bizet's greatest achievement after *Carmen*. But I must admit it: I am biased.

Sometime after *L'Arlésienne* Daudet again turned to Bizet, telling him he was working on a three-act play that could perhaps be turned into an opera. But by then Bizet was already wholly immersed in *Carmen*.

Carmen. Some people say that Don José killed Carmen and *Carmen* in turn killed Bizet. Well, in a way there is some truth to that. He put all of his soul into that masterpiece. He told me that this opera was not, as some people undoubtedly will think, the result of his having completely mastered his craft; his craft was *part* of him now and it was a tool at the service of his inspiration—and *Carmen* was entirely the brainchild of that inspiration.

---

16 After Bizet's death, Guiraud concocted a second suite based on music from *L'Arlésienne* that had not been used in what is today known as Suite no.1.

At the time they staged the ill-fated *Djamileh* at the Opéra-Comique, the managers of the theater, de Leuven and du Locle, had commissioned a three-act opera from Bizet and proposed Meilhac and Halévy as librettists. This pair had written a long string of successful librettos, many of them for Offenbach, including *Orphée aux enfers, La belle Hélène, La vie parisienne, La Périchole,* and *La Grande-Duchesse de Gerolstein.* Feeling they had sufficiently contributed in that field they decided to try their hand at the more serious side of the theater and produced *Frou-Frou.* Then came the war and the rout, and after that our entire world had changed.

Ludovic, Geneviève's cousin, came up with the idea that *Carmen,* Prosper Mérimée's short novel, would be a suitable story to wield a libretto for the new commission.

Prosper Mérimée! What a fascinating personality. Most people ostensibly avoided him; some even described him as a monster because he was so outspoken, cynical, and egotistical. But he always behaved in the most affable, pleasant, and courteous manner toward me.

Somehow he has always reminded me of young Saint-Saëns, especially in respect to the breadth of his interests. He was a lawyer by training, getting his degree at the age of twenty from the Sorbonne. But he was also an accomplished archaeologist, a full-fledged historian, and a polyglot with a fascination for comparative linguistics, having studied Greek, Spanish, English, and Russian. I think that in this field his main interest lay in Russian and other Slavic dialects. Among his early literary works we find a compilation of popular ballads from the Balkans, which he had translated from the Illyrian under the assumed name of Hyacinte Magdanovic. This collection (published under the title *La Guzla : ou Choix de poésies illyriques recueillies dans la Dalmatie, la Bosnie, la Croatie et l'Herzégowine*) has been translated into Russian by no less than the poets Alexander Pushkin and Mikhail Lermontov! In return he has made what seem to be masterful translations of four

Pushkin plays (including *La dame de pique*), Gogol's *The Inspector General*, and Ivan Turgenev's *Apparitions*.

He has written tales of horror and some of his stories are weird and fantastic, but his style has always been refined and crisp. His frequent travels took him to Spain, Greece, Turkey, and the Balkans. During his 1830 visit to Spain he befriended the Countess of Montijo. I think she was the person who drew his attention to an item of news in the daily press that was to be the kernel of his novella *Carmen*. She also asked him to act as a coach to her daughter Eugénie during her period of courtship with Napoleon III. And, indeed, when Eugénie became empress she showed her gratitude for services rendered by naming Mérimée a senator. One other little-known fact (as far as I am aware) is Mérimée's invaluable contribution to our rich French cultural heritage by discovering the series of tapestries known as *La dame à la licorne* (The Lady and the Unicorn), in 1841 at the Château de Boussac. This propitious discovery came just in time to save that treasure and halt the deterioration that time and improper care had wrecked upon the tapestries. Georges Sand, who was with him at the time, gave a written account of this stupendous discovery and thus brought it to the knowledge of the general public.

Prosper Mérimée died in September 1870—exactly three weeks after the Sedan surrender.

From the outset the librettists had a hard time convincing du Locle and de Leuven of the soundness of the idea of turning *Carmen* into an opera. They argued that they were at their best when painting a drama in brilliant colors against the background of a foreign and exotic landscape. Du Locle liked the idea but de Leuven was stubbornly opposed to it. He maintained that the Opéra-Comique was a family theater that should never antagonize its public by putting a bunch of smugglers, thieves, gypsies, and cigarette girls on the stage in a play where a whore is murdered by her lover, himself a deserter. The boxes of this theater were renowned grounds for matchmaking and there was no point in driving away their faithful public with a story of licentious behavior and murder.

But Ludovic coaxed him into reluctant acceptance by promising that they would soften the crude action by rounding out the sharp edges and by introducing Micaëla, a character who could not fail to move the public into feeling full sympathy toward her. As for the murder, it would be drowned in the bright coloring of the popular fiesta in the last act. "Just don't let her die," de Leuven asked the Meilhac-Halévy duo. On reading the finished version of the final scene, and unable to annul the contract for the commissioned opera, de Leuven resigned as codirector of the Opéra-Comique. I think du Locle had anticipated this and was exulting. Now that he was left as the sole manager in charge, he turned around and started a campaign against the work that his own theater was about to stage. It was impossible for him to recall the commission, but he missed no occasion to slander *Carmen*.

But for the Bizet household *Carmen* was also a great misfortune, as it brought about a rift between Bizet and Geneviève. After the birth of little Jacques, Geneviève had started leaning heavily on Bizet and had become more demanding on his time and attention. Bizet felt that this seriously slowed down his work on *Carmen*. He was torn between his genuine need for Geneviève's love and his new entanglement in the grips of the bewitching *Carmen*. Yes, she had cast a spell on him, just as she had cast a spell on Don José. There was also the matter of Geneviève's seemingly flirtatious behavior. Many men were attracted by her magnetic personality, her beauty, and her intelligence, and they were more or less openly courting her. She felt flattered by their attentions and the fact that she was not resolutely putting a stop to their advances hurt Bizet's pride and inflamed a helpless jealousy. By common consent the couple separated for a few weeks; Bizet stayed with their son in Montmartre and Ludovic put his summer home in Saint-Germain at Geneviève's disposal.

It was not an easy task for the librettists to transform Mérimée's tale into a viable opera libretto. Only the outstanding talent of the duo of Meilhac and Halévy, their long years of experience and of working as a team, could have produced a libretto of this high quality, a libretto that, in my opinion, sits atop the highest shelf of opera literature. Bizet would not be content to blindly follow everything he was fed. He contributed some pertinent changes—for instance, in the wording of the habanera and the seguidilla. But his influence on the libretto was decisive from the start when it came to shaping the image of Carmen. Mérimée's Carmen was a conscienceless thief, a whore, a cruel and pitiless instigator of murder. Bizet insisted on changing her into a real, attractive heroine, a woman with solid principles (though not principles anchored in the conventional moral code), a woman fighting and willing to die for her right to freedom—the same right Bizet also claimed for himself.

♪ ♪ ♪ ♪ ♪ ♪ ♪

Marie-Célestine Laurence Marié de l'Isle was born in 1840. Her father, who came from an impoverished aristocratic family, boasted a successful career as an opera singer. In 1855 she married an obscure sculptor named Galli. Her husband died in 1861. She started her professional career in Strasbourg in 1859 and appeared on the stages of various opera houses. During his short second tenure as director of the Opéra-Comique in 1862, Émile Perrin (du Locle's father-in-law) heard her in Rouen and enrolled her to join the staff of his theater. She distinguished herself especially in the role of Mignon in Thomas's opera.

When du Locle offered her the title role in Bizet's new opera, Galli-Marié immediately contacted the composer to get an idea of what was in store and get a first glimpse at the character she was about to play. When Bizet ran through the score with her, he knew at once that she was the Carmen he had been dreaming about. And she felt as if it had been written for her; she actually became Carmen. She rapidly became his friend and confidante. She also turned into a staunch supporter of his art, and has remained even today a courageous fighter in the struggle to bring his music in the best possible conditions before the public.

Galli-Marié also made her personal contribution to the final version of the opera. She was unhappy with the aria written for her first appearance on the stage, and she asked Bizet to change it; he rewrote it thirteen times, and she still was not satisfied. He then remembered a song La Mogador had liked to sing almost ten years earlier, a song he thought was a Spanish folk song. He reworked it and proposed it to Galli-Marié; she enthusiastically approved and thus the wonderful habanera of *Carmen* was born. In the Choudens edition of the piano score, which is in my library, a footnote says, "In imitation of a Spanish song, property of the Editors of the Ménestrel." It has since been revealed that this "folk song" was composed by Sebastián Yradier, a Spanish composer who died in 1865.

Escamillo also thought that his entrance lacked some luster. Bizet added the refrain, "*Toréador, en garde!*" to the toreador's aria, saying, "They want trash? I'll give them trash!" I always wondered what Bizet meant by this cryptic remark. I think this refrain, though quite catchy and popular, is still great music. I intended to ask him about it, but, unfortunately…

Bizet and Geneviève spent the summer of 1874 in Bougival. One of their neighbors there was Élie-Miriam Delaborde, a painter (he was a close friend of Claude Monet and exhibits his paintings under the name of Miriam) and pianist (he has quite recently been nominated as a professor at the Conservatoire). It was more or less public knowledge that Delaborde was my friend Alkan's illegitimate son. Bizet liked his company as he was a brilliant rhetorician, but also because, like Bizet, he enjoyed swimming in the cold waters of the Seine that flowed through the village. Like most men, Delaborde was also attracted by Geneviève's intriguing personality and they spent a lot of time in each other's company. Bizet not only accepted this, but seems to have encouraged this emerging closeness between them, as this freed him from the need to cater to her incessant demand for attention, and allowed him to concentrate on the task at hand: the orchestration of *Carmen*. And indeed, within two months he managed to write down all 1,200 pages of the complete score.

Rehearsals started on September 1. By mid-November they were being held daily. Some musicians in the orchestra complained that the parts were unplayable, but the main source of trouble was the choir. The choir singers were used to standing in a group and singing their parts like in any other opera. But here they were expected to move—actually, in some way, to act—and to disperse on the stage, as in the cigarette girls' chorus in act 1, Escamillo's entrance in act 2, and the fiesta scene at the beginning of act 4. They strongly resented this additional burden and threatened to go on strike. Du Locle's hostile attitude made things even harder to put up with. When Bizet came home at night he was a bundle of nerves.

The constant criticism thrown at them about the vulgarity and crudity of their opera had a negative effect even on Halévy and Meilhac. They asked Escamillo not to pinch the cheeks of some chorus girls when he entered Lila Pastia's inn, and then they begged Carmen and Don José to play down their realistic acting. They both flatly refused.

And when du Locle asked for the end of the opera to be changed, both Galli-Marié and Lhérie (who sang the part of Don José) offered their immediate resignations.

On the morning of March 3, 1875, the day of *Carmen*'s premiere, the Académie announced that Bizet had been awarded the Légion d'honneur. During the evening performance, one of the spectators said loudly, "They made haste to give the decoration in the morning. They knew that after tonight's performance it would be too late and impossible to grant it."

Two days before that, Bizet had sent me an urgent note stating that Geneviève had been afflicted with a sty, and could I help by spending a few hours with her? So it was that on the night of the premiere of *Carmen*, the composer's wife was confined at home, applying compresses to her sore eye. I was with her on that evening, and that is why I missed the premiere.

The next morning I visited Pauline Viardot in her spacious house in Bougival and she gave me a detailed account of what had occurred. I shall only summarize the important things she told me. Act 1 went quite well, taking into account the poisonous atmosphere with which du Locle so strived to infuse the work. The habanera and the duet between Don José and Micaëla were loudly applauded. The entr'acte between act 1 and act 2 was encored and the toreador's song was, as expected, a great success. But from here onward the atmosphere degraded frightfully: Don José's "La fleur que tu m'avais jetée" baffled the audience and the fact that there was no ballet in act 2, as tradition dictates, was very much resented. The scenery in act 3 was almost identical to that of Offenbach's *Les brigands* of '69 (whose librettists were, by the way, also Meilhac and Halévy) and this enraged many a spectator. And the last act, as du Locle had hoped, was greeted with an icy reception.

The press was almost unanimous in tearing the work to pieces.

I went to the second performance, two days later, with a predisposed conciliatory and forgiving attitude. To my great surprise, from the very first notes of the introduction I was transported into a magical world where the excitement that the music instilled in me was rapturous, while my pulse accelerated as the action progressed. The remarks I couldn't help overhearing in the foyer during the intermissions went, without exception, from the positively appreciative to the unreservedly laudatory. There was not even one wrong note in this chorus of positive approval. Is it really possible that the negative campaign initiated by du Locle and the prejudiced press could have been so influential that the public became blind and deaf to the beauty of this new work that first night?

I met Bizet a few days later and related my personal and enthusiastic opinion and gave a truthful description of the public's reaction on the second evening. He did not interrupt me even once. He looked at me without smiling, his face frozen in deep gloom. When I finished talking, he only asked in a whisper, "And the press?"

A few days later I visited my sister Léonie at Dr. Blanche's sanatorium in Passy. As I was about to leave, Dr. Blanche's son, fourteen-year-old Jacques-Émile, somewhat timidly approached me and asked why I had not attended the premiere of *Carmen*.

"Ah, and you were there?" I asked.

"Yes, Gounod took me with him," he replied. "He has taken to me, and whenever he is here, we spend many hours together. I'm sure you know that he is one of my father's regular guests here."

"I know," I said. "I think he needs a place to isolate himself from the outer world and to renew his strength. As for myself, I went to see *Carmen* on the second night. It was a perfect success. But Mme Viardot told me that on the first evening it was…well…not so successful. I'm eager to hear a second opinion, especially from such a bright young man like you."

"I liked it very much, but I must confess that I am rather partial to modern music and prefer it to the moth-eaten Méhul and Boïeldieu they feed us so much of. I was much taken by those Spanish rhythms and the general pace of the music. As for the action, it was unbelievably realistic. I mean, very realistic compared to what I am used to seeing at the Opéra. Anyhow, to be quite honest and in spite of what I hear, it was much to my taste."

"Something in your tone of voice betrays some kind of reservation. You can be truthful with me. Something bothered you—what was it?" I asked.

"It really has nothing to do with my opinion of *Carmen*. It is Gounod's reaction to it that baffles me. But I'm not sure it is fitting for me to talk about that."

"If it is a matter of conscience, I leave it to you. I won't insist, though I'm extremely curious to know what Gounod thought about it. Considering his friendship with Bizet, I thought that he would estimate the work at its true value and be proud and happy."

"That is what bothers me. You see, during the first and second intermissions we went backstage to compliment the composer and Gounod hugged him warmly. At the beginning of the third act, after Micaëla's aria in the mountainous gorge, Gounod leaned out of our box and applauded loudly, as if needing to express unequivocal support. Then he returned to his seat next to me and muttered, 'That aria is mine. It is written entirely in my style; Bizet has robbed me.

If you take out my music and the Andalusian tunes from this opera, you are left with a little bit of Mérimée and a lot of platitudes.' I was stunned, as you can imagine. So what was all this show during the intermission and the overenthusiastic applause? I'm still trying to get over the shock."

"Well," I said, "you have learned something. There are some men who are able to create great works of art while they themselves are just ordinary people, sometimes even pusillanimous people. They just happen to be the instruments of Providence who are able to translate the inspiration of the muses into an intelligible work of art. Gounod is a great composer, one of the greatest of our generation. He can also be a faithful and supportive friend. But he is a small person, sometimes even a coward. Still, in spite of this character flaw, I love the man no less than the composer; maybe because he's so much in need of love, and certainly because of his convivial behavior. But if you take Wagner, for instance, there is a man who earns no respect from me as a human being, though I admire much of his work. As great as his music is, his character is so base and his conduct so reprehensible. But don't quote me."

And now I must add a last few lines to end this chapter, this chapter so close to my heart, the chapter about Georges Bizet.

What was it that drove him to take the crazy plunge into the icy waters of the Seine, fully aware that his chronic throat ache might not be able to cope with it? Was it a defiant gesture telling fate, "Here I am! If you want me, come and take me!"? Was it an act of despair in view of the disintegration of his conjugal life? Was it some kind of final acceptance of what he thought was his total rejection by the public as a creative artist, the complete destruction of his beautiful serenity, and the loss of self-assurance concerning his talent? Or maybe it was nothing but a passing moment of madness. I can give no answer to that riddle.

On the morning of June 3, I received a telegram from Ludovic: "The most horrible disaster. Bizet died last night."

12

THE KING OF SHEBA

October 1884

I was strolling slowly on the Pont des Arts, enjoying the soft autumnal afternoon, when I saw Gounod walking briskly toward me. He said,

Hippolyte, how happy I am to see you! Just a few minutes ago, we concluded the meeting at the Institut whose purpose was to choose the Prix de Rome laureate for this year in the field of music. The vote was unanimous, without even the slightest hesitation or discussion. The cantata submitted by young Debussy, a pupil in Guiraud's composition class, is the winner this year. I would like you to meet him. He is a very interesting chap—maybe a little bit obstinate and unruly, but very talented, overflowing with wisdom and endowed with a razor-sharp mind. I'm sure he's going to go very far. And on top of all that, what a good-looking lad. Ah! There he is on the bridge, leaning over the parapet and watching the boats sail up and down the Seine. I must go and talk to him—I don't think he yet knows that he has won the prize.

But suddenly Gounod froze in his tracks, and it was as if some cloud suddenly hovered over his head and his eyes filled with some dark gloom. Without knowing what the reason was for the sudden sadness that had fallen upon him, I felt a surge of warmth and sympathy, and a need to comfort my old friend.

He felt the need to explain. "I suddenly feel very queer," he said, "as if I had traveled back in time. I put my hand on young Bizet's shoulder and he stared at me with his steady, frank look and said, 'I hope I'll love Rome as you do. If I write to you, will you answer me?'"

And I thought to myself that this old man now regretted that there was no way to undo the past, to erase some things that are best left forgotten. I gave him a light hug, turned around, and carried on with my afternoon stroll, wishing for him to have a good and peaceful old age.

Throwing a quick glance behind me, I saw him walking toward the youngster on the bridge.

July 1888

The fact that Charles Gounod was awarded the title of *grand officier de la Légion d'honneur* was prominently advertised in the Parisian press. It is true that this honorific title is, by tradition, almost exclusively reserved for the highest ranking military and political officials. Still, the fuss was somewhat exaggerated. Moreover, when most of the newspapers reported that Gounod was the first musician to enjoy this exalted honor, they made a gross mistake: Have they all forgotten that a few months ago, in March, to be exact, Giuseppe Verdi was also made a *grand officier*? And I think I remember that someone once told me that during the Hundred Days, Napoleon bestowed upon Cherubini this same distinction.

Gounod, who turned seventy last month, is considered to be the very incarnation of French music. When will Berlioz, who has been dead for almost twenty years now, be granted similar recognition? Or for that matter the composers of the Société nationale de musique—Franck, Lalo, Saint-Saëns, and Chabrier—most of them in their fifties and still struggling to get some kind of recognition in the second or third rank?

How strange it is that this unusual high honor has been bestowed on a composer who for the last twenty years, since his 1864 opera *Roméo et Juliette* to be more specific, has not produced one single work worth mentioning. The religious works in which he has been engrossed for so many years are remarkable for their exalted intentions and their nonexistent inventiveness. They appear to be a vain effort to recapture some of the inspiration that has eluded the composer for so long. Remembering his wonderful mass composed in the fifties, the requiem from 1842, and the *Messe solennelle à Sainte-Cécile*, you can't help wondering if it is the same hand that wrote down those notes. Whatever comes from his desk today can without hesitation be named after the Shakespearean comedy *Much Ado About Nothing*.

I must confess that in spite of all his drawbacks, I have kept friendly relations with Gounod all these years; after all, we were classmates at the Conservatoire, and this goes back over half a century. But still, it is my private opinion that much of the glory and fame Gounod is enjoying is due to his manners and outer appearance: his white beard framing even features in a sober face and the black gown, like a priest's cassock, that he invariably wears. With his angelic physiognomy he bears a striking resemblance to some of the apostles as they are represented in Rubens's or Titian's paintings. Who is not awed when he walks slowly toward the piano, like the high priest marching to the altar, sounds three times in a row the note D, and asks his followers watching with mouths agape, "Do you grasp, my dear friends, that those three notes are the symbol of eternity?"

It took me some time to wake up to reality and ask myself what all this was about.

One could surmise that this aping of holiness is unfit for a man throwing lecherous looks at any pretty girl on the street. For someone who deserted his home and country for years amidst a scandal of adultery, which, notwithstanding its histrionic and ridiculous aspects, is still a most serious matter. But such is the fame of the man and so great is his fascination that all is forgiven and forgotten. And not a week passes without one of his witticisms, those epitomes of wisdom, perspicacity, and eloquence, being made public by those who attend the salons or by being quoted in the newspaper. Just to get acquainted with them, here are a few such "pearls":

Bach and Beethoven are the marble columns of the temple of music—and Mozart is the high priest.

Children are the roses in the garden of life.

Melody is the soul of music; music without melody is a contradiction.

Parody is what witticisms contribute to success.

As far as we are concerned, the musicians Palestrina and Bach are the fathers of the church.

I like to compose in C major, because this is God's favorite key.

He told me once in confidence that he had abandoned his dream of becoming a priest because he didn't have the moral strength to hear a woman's confession without conceiving sinful thoughts. This small detail draws the full picture of the man. The truth of the matter is that the earthly sides of the man's character and his craving for worldly pleasures have made his longing for spiritual elevation and purity an ephemeral dream.

Listening carefully to his music, you will find in it the same contradictions that characterize his personality: sensitivity opposing introversion, depth versus outward sweetness, true emotion side by side with hypocrisy, and refined taste neighboring pitiful exhibitionism. This is the man Gounod—a saint deviating from the righteous path, an intellectual whose main interest is his material success, a true friend who proves to be a hollow cane; a protector, guide, and supporter who gives in to pusillanimous jealousy. His charm and authority, peerless amongst French musicians, made it possible for him to surround himself again and again with faithful followers who had in the past turned their backs on him in anger and disappointment. My dear Bizet was first and foremost amongst them.

And all that in spite of all the changing moods that so characterized Gounod. I remember a scabrous incident when Gounod, because of his strained relations with his publisher Choudens, asked Bizet to act as a go-between in some negotiations concerning the royalties for *Faust*. When the negotiations did not come to a favorable conclusion from Gounod's point of view, he started accusing Bizet of plotting with the publisher to divert dividends due to the composer.

How very touching it is to see the younger artist, forgetting all grievances and bitterness, turning again and enthusiastically toward his senior, recognizing in him the leader of his generation. And this happened at a time when Bizet's musical faculties were ascending to their zenith, the time when *Carmen* was taking shape. In a very moving letter, Bizet acknowledges his debt and voices his gratitude for the decisive influence Gounod had on his artistic development. And let's not forget that Gounod really loved Bizet. Notwithstanding their minor stumblings, the older man has always been a friend who gave support and encouragement when the younger man so desperately needed it.

Some time ago, I came across the booklet in which Gounod wrote his reminiscences. I read it through in a single evening. There is nothing in it that I didn't already know, but it's nicely narrated. It somehow leaves the reader in a pleasant mood, and sometimes even brings him to the verge of elation. Some of the stories relate to the composer's childhood, and their touching candor mirrors some of Gounod's better traits.

I'll copy here some passages I liked most.

Music I started drinking at my mother's bosom. She used to sing while she was breast-feeding me. I can say without blushing that my first lessons in my art I got effortlessly and without being conscious of it, as if from nature itself. At a very tender age, I learned to discern the intervals, and I developed a keen ability to differentiate between melodies in major or minor modes. I was told that one day, on hearing a street singer's sentimental song, I asked my mother, "Why does this man's music weep?"

From his father, the painter who died when Gounod was still a youth, he inherited most of his talents. He was hard put to decide whether to follow in his father's footsteps or to side with his mother, who was wholly and solely immersed in music.

The book relates in very lively pictures the years the young Prix de Rome laureate spent in Italy and in Germany, his encounter with the two Mendelssohn youngsters, Fanny and Felix, and the lasting friendship that grew between them.

The city of Rome was to be a second home for him, as it was for young Bizet years later.

In his hour of need he returned to Rome several times, looking for shelter, consolation, and support. In the book he paints, with an exquisite pen, the portrait of his beloved mother. After her husband's death, she was left impecunious and struggled with great courage to face the task of managing the household and supervising the education of her children.

Gounod also states in the same book:

I was never jealous of any man, except for that great artist Franz Liszt. And it is not his immense talent that I envy, nor his art, nor his overwhelming success. All those are blessings that are rightfully his. What I'm jealous of is the fact that he has been ordained a priest, which is something I have aspired to all my life.

Not so long ago we met in Rome and had a lively discussion about Thomas Aquinas and Ernest Renan's book Vie de Jésus. Then we sat down and played to each other excerpts from our own religious works. I played from Rédemption and from Mors et Vita and he played from Christus and from The Legend of Saint Elizabeth. Suddenly, a spell of mischief over which he seemed to have no control made him plunge into his Fantasia on the Waltz from Faust. What masterful piano playing it was! I sat dumbfounded...how good it was to be reminded that with all our repentance for the sins we committed in our youth, we also have some achievements to be proud of from those very days.

The famous waltz reminds me of an interesting remark Gounod made. After the festive three-hundredth performance of *Faust* I asked him whether he considers this opera, so popular and beloved, to be his best work. He looked at me, and with a boisterous wink he answered, "I view success as a chain of happy events that turned out well, and not as a means of measuring quality. Does this answer your question?"

This made me wonder again about the many facets of this man and the depth of insight he so often instinctively showed.

All his life Gounod needed a strong woman behind him. After he left his mother's tutorship he chose Pauline Viardot as a protector. She lent her voice and her unique personality to his very first opera, *Sappho*. But things turned sour when Mme Zimmerman, the wife of his adored piano teacher at the Conservatoire, decided that he was the right husband for her elder daughter. Without batting an eye, Gounod sacrificed his former friend and benefactress to contract a loveless marriage.

Anna Zimmermann was a plain woman, but a wife with an iron grip. She bore him two children, his daughter Jeanne and his son Jean. After her father's death, Anna inherited the summer house in Saint-Cloud, a place where Gounod often took refuge from the stress of everyday life, and from the disturbance of editors, singers, music critics, and theater directors. By the way, this house was spared destruction during the Franco-Prussian War as the result of a personal letter written by Gounod to the Prussian crown prince, in which the composer stressed his affinity for German music. It goes without saying that this letter caused turmoil at the time, but like all other mischief committed by the great man, it was soon forgotten.

During those troubled days of war, the siege, and the short-lived but bloody days of the Paris Commune, Gounod and his family took shelter in London, while his colleagues and friends found themselves bearing arms in defense of the fatherland.

Gounod remained in London from 1870 to 1874. He avoids talking about those years. Whenever I try to broach the subject, he adroitly diverts the conversation to a different subject. So I have no firsthand information about this matter and what I know is only hearsay; nevertheless, here it is.

When the new Royal Albert Hall was opened in '71, it was inaugurated by a choral concert sung by a choir called the Royal Albert Hall Choral Society. Gounod had been asked to be the musical director and conductor of this choir and he must have done a first-class job judging from the reputation this choir enjoys to this day. One of the soprano singers in this choir was a semi-professional singer named Georgina Weldon, whose marriage had recently broken down. Gounod took Weldon to Paris to sing the solo in the performance of his new cantata "Gallia." When he returned to London, he chose to leave his family in Paris and went to live at Weldon's place—it is there that he composed his opera *Polyeucte*, the Corneille tragedy dealing with an Armenian Christian martyr. The role of Pauline, Polyeucte's wife, was to be sung by Weldon. But at some point their relationship deteriorated and Gounod returned to the bosom of his family.

After the contrite composer's return to the nest, his wife tightened household discipline even more to punish him for his misdeeds and to prevent the recurrence of such behavior in the future. I have been told that the family's budget is entirely in Anna's hands and that she has sole control of the purse strings. Some even say that poor Gounod receives a weekly allowance for pocket money, like his children were allotted in their youth. As for her prowess as a public-relations wizard in forwarding her husband's interests, I was able to judge for myself as an eyewitness to a recent incident.

I was a guest at a reception held in honor of the English musician Charles Hallé. Gounod, full of verve, poured a handful of compliments on Hallé's performance at the recital he had given the previous night: "The phrasing of that wonderful passage in the Beethoven sonata—only you are capable of playing it that way. Even with eyes closed I would have recognized Charles Hallé's style from the very first notes."

At that very moment Mme Gounod landed among us with a glass of wine in her hand and took control of the situation. "My dear Monsieur Hallé, my husband is so sorry we had to miss your recital yesterday evening, as we had a previous engagement that we were unable to cancel."

I like Gounod's *Faust*. I think it is a beautiful work, enjoyable and very effective in the opera house. I especially fancy the first meeting between Faust and Marguerite, the song "Il était un roi de Thulé," Mephisto's "Le veau d'or," and the finale of the second act, where the singing is interwoven in the most masterful manner against the background of that wonderful waltz. There is no doubt in my mind that these are some of the most beautiful pieces ever written in the entire repertoire of opera music. But the work as a whole is, to my taste, lacking homogeneity. Then again, is it really reasonable to expect homogeneity in a work coming from a man whose character is so full of contrast and contradiction like Gounod's? It is always hard to maintain a purity of style and at the same time satisfy the public's taste, or to express a sincere feeling without being dragged into cheap sentimentality.

Some epicures see *Faust* as a grotesque falsifying of Goethe's masterpiece. Wagner puts it this way: "Two students from the Latin Quarter chasing after a skirt. Gounod is a very gifted composer, but he should be choosier in picking his librettos."

Notwithstanding my admiration for Goethe, I refuse to adhere to this view. The reason is quite simple: the link between Gounod's opera and the philosophical play by the great German poet is fortuitous at best. The libretto by Jules Barbier and Michel Carré is based mainly on Carré's play *Faust et Marguerite* from 1850. This was loosely based on Gérard de Nerval's classical translation of part one of Goethe's *Faust*.

In Germany some creative and practical thinking found a quick remedy to the problem that seems to have bothered Wagner and many other German intellectuals and admirers of Goethe. They rebaptized the opera and stage it there under the name *Margarete*. In this guise they can enjoy Gounod's music and the Barbier-Carré libretto with a clear conscience. They just watch a routine love affair, followed by betrayal and abandonment, which gets entangled in a foul struggle between heaven and hell.

Carvalho, the newly appointed director of the Théâtre Lyrique, was very much incidental in many of the changes Gounod made to the opera before it even went to rehearsal, during the time of composition. This was mainly due to the fact that his wife Marie Miolan-Carvalho was to sing the role of Marguerite. For instance, the mad scene that Gounod intended for Marguerite in the last act was omitted, because it did not fit Mme Carvalho's voice, style, and inclinations. And the famous "Soldiers' Chorus" was added as an afterthought. It was written originally for the Paris Orphéon Choir, to which Gounod had been appointed director in 1852, and was inserted in *Ivan le terrible*, an opera Gounod left unfinished. One evening, as Gounod was playing excerpts from this discarded opera for a restricted circle of friends,

Carvalho sprang to his feet and demanded vehemently that this chorus be incorporated into *Faust*.

Gounod protested, saying that there were no soldiers in the opera, but Carvalho was adamant, and when Ingres, his old friend from his Villa Medici days in Rome—who, in addition to being a first-rate painter, is also a fine musician—supported the director's point of view, Gounod gave in.

It seems worthwhile to mention here this curious coincidence: in his 1846 *La damnation de Faust* Berlioz did exactly the same thing. He decided to insert his Hungarian March that he had orchestrated for his Budapest visit, met there with such remarkable success, into one of his more substantial works. This seemed to be the surest way to ensure that this small gem would not sink into oblivion. So exactly like Gounod did thirteen years later, and in complete disregard of credibility or common sense, he introduced into *La damnation de Faust* a group of soldiers on the banks of the Danube. Those soldiers played no role in the action; their sole function was to justify including The Hungarian March.

When *Faust* was staged in London in 1863 at Her Majesty's Theater, the great British baritone Charles Santley demanded that Gounod insert an aria for him, and suggested a solemn melody used in the orchestral introduction. The composer accepted and wrote the aria that has since become famous, "Avant de quitter ces lieux."

And when, due to one of the Théâtre Lyrique's recurring financial breakdowns, the performance rights for *Faust* passed to the Académie, a ballet had to be added (since there is no opera performed there without a ballet, as Wagner had learned from painful experience). Gounod, who at that time was very much engrossed in liturgical music, was disinclined to do the work. He wrote a note to young Saint-Saëns asking him to compose this music. Saint-Saëns hurried to Saint-Cloud and found Gounod at home, playing cards with the local parish priest.

Saint-Saëns pleaded and said it could not be done; Gounod looked at him and, shaking his head, said, "All right, all right." Gounod agreed to provide the music after all.

From a purely business point of view, *Faust* was Gounod's biggest failure. A few weeks after the premiere, Gounod and his librettists struck a deal with the Choudens publishing house in which he relinquished all the rights to the opera to Choudens in return for fifteen thousand francs. Choudens then started a successful campaign to stage the work throughout France; this brought him a fortune. Sometime later, Choudens crossed Gounod by chance in the street. "Why are you wearing such an old and worn-out hat?" asked Choudens.

"Quite simple, my friend," replied Gounod. "This is my *Faust* hat."

Both men remembered this incident very well. Many years later, Gounod managed to sell Choudens the rights for *Le tribut de Zamora* with very advantageous clauses for himself in the contract. The opera was an utter failure, but the composer managed to bring it to the fiftieth performance in order to milk it to the last ounce of profit. "What is this worn-out overcoat you are wearing?" he asked Choudens at their next meeting.

As expected, Choudens answered, "This is my *Zamora* coat."

It must have been four years since I last saw Gounod, so I thought that the Légion d'honneur was a good pretext to visit him and have a nice afternoon reminiscing about memories so dear to our hearts. He greeted me:

At long last, dear Hippolyte. How long have I been awaiting this visit? If I'm not mistaken, since our beloved friend left us for a better world, we have not met for a serious heart-to-heart talk. We needed the Légion d'honneur to bring us together again. Come, my dear friend; let me embrace you and thank you for the warm blessing you sent me.

There was a time when I hoped I would slowly ascend the rungs of a different hierarchy, the one headed by our Holy Father in Rome. But as we say, "L'homme propose et Dieu dispose." And if this award that has been bestowed on me brings you to my house, it has done a good thing.

This is your first visit to my new dwelling, here on the Place Malesherbes. My brother-in-law, the architect, lives on the floor below mine. He is the one who drew up the plans for this house, and supervised its building. Look through the window, my friend, and you will be able to see the great stone monument to the Dumas family—the monument for the grandfather, the general; the other one for Alexandre the elder; and next to it you can see the palace of our friend Alexandre the younger.

I live here amidst my family: on the ground floor, my daughter Jeanne; on the second floor, my brother-in-law and my sister-in-law; and my son Jean lives on the top floor. My beloved wife and I, we dwell here on the third floor. The paintings depicting scenes from my operas that adorn the staircase were painted by my nephew Guillaume Duboeuf. You can see Sapho playing her harp, Marguerite sitting at her spinning wheel, and Juliet watching Romeo escape into the garden at dawn after climbing down from the balcony.

I was dumbfounded and surprised at what I found there. Is this really the place where Gounod lives, or is it some freakish temple? The dome-like ceiling, the tinted windows through which light trickles parsimoniously, the majestic organ on a pedestal, all those little wooden statues representing Jesus suffering on his final voyage to Calvary; all those give the place a churchlike atmosphere. Only the

Pleyel grand piano in the middle of the spacious room, the writing table with the adjacent silent keyboard, and the cozy corner strewn with comfortable armchairs, sofas, and Persian rugs carried me back to reality and reminded me that this was the dwelling of a gifted and hardworking musician, a man of fine tastes who can also appreciate the benefits of luxury.

We were sitting there in the diffuse light, slowly sipping the excellent Armagnac he had poured us. He said to me,

> You know, Hippolyte, you are barely six years older than me, and today it seems to us that we have reached the same age, so I dare to be quite candid with you. Outwardly I may look a tiny bit worn-out at seventy, but *inside* the twenty-year-old lad has not aged. The house grows old but the tenant doesn't change. Sometimes I feel like I'm overflowing with energy. I get enthusiastic over any kind of job thrown at me, but in the end I scatter my energy over inconsequential things. Do you know what I'm doing these days? You won't believe it. I'm writing an article about breast-feeding—yes. And believe me, I'm working on it much harder than on The Wedding March for Three Trombones and an Organ, which I just finished composing as a commission for the Duke of Albany. But there is one thing I'm not going to do anymore—I'll never write another opera.
>
> Do you remember, some years ago you asked me which one of my operas I liked most, or something similar? I have written sixteen operas in twenty-seven years, and only two of them have caught the fancy of the public, Faust and Romeo and Juliet. You don't ask a father which one of his children is his favorite. But come closer, my friend, and I'll whisper in your ear this shameful secret: more than any other, I love Mireille. This is the apple of my eye.
>
> When I let Mistral know that I would love to turn his great Provençal epic poem into an opera he wrote me a letter saying, "I'm very happy that you like my little girl, but until now you have met her

only in the poem. Come to Arles, to Avignon, to Saint-Rémy. Watch her walk in the fields, dance the farandole with the young country boys, exit the church through the big portal after vespers." It took me no time at all to go south. I took lodging at a small inn not far from Mistral's home. I rose before daybreak and went wandering aimlessly in the fields, listening to a pageant of bird songs and breathing in the fragrance of lavender, thyme, and God knows what other smells were mixing in the morning air. From time to time, a youngster crossed my path and greeted me with a fresh, "Bonjour, m'sieu," with that unmistakable Provençal accent and the broadest of smiles. I was suffused with happiness. Musical ideas where flying around me like a swarm of butterflies; all I had to do was pluck them one after the other.

Mistral took me to the ruins of the old village up on the cliff, from which we had a panoramic view of the Crau desert in whose pebble-strewn aridity Mireille stumbled, with the last reserve of energy remaining in her poor, exhausted body, toward her wounded lover, to die in his arms. When we got home from that walk I played for the poet excerpts that I had already composed for the opera on an old, dusty harmonium. His emotion was such that he was unable to hold back his tears.

It just so happens that at that moment Marie Miolan-Carvalho, who was to sing the title role, was traveling with her husband, the theater director, on the train from Marseilles—where she had just made a series of appearances—back to Paris. I went to Tarascon, where the train made a short stop, to pay my respects to the couple. I also wanted to share the enthusiasm my work on Mireille inspired in me with those who would soon become active partners in bringing my heroine to life. I told them in a torrential flow of words of my happiness, my boundless inspiration, and the feverish state in which composition immersed me. Mme Carvalho tilted her head slightly through the open window of the train car and said, "Never mind all that, just let it be brilliant. Make it sparkling, yes, sparkling." And Carvalho added, his voice coming from the depths of the car, "And even that is not brilliant enough."

I thought to myself, brilliant, sparkling? Why? What is brilliant in this poignant story? There is nothing brilliant in the arid and scorched Crau desert, nothing sparkling in the pure, blue Provençal sky.

But that did not help me, and the next six months became a bitter struggle between my artistic integrity and their down-to-earth pragmatism. After endless and useless discussion I was compelled to make changes to my opera, to dilute it with sweetened rose water, to bring it down to the taste of the lowest common denominator, to shorten here and to lengthen there and to supply Mme Carvalho with her beloved vocalizations. I added, the valse-ariette "O légère hirondelle"; I had to change the recitatives, which are so very much woven into the texture of the opera and full of expression, into insipid dialogues. Needless to say, Mireille must stay alive at the end of the opera at the Théâtre Lyrique—the audience would rather have the composer dead than mourn the loss of his heroine. In some mysterious and unexplained way her life force is suddenly restored, and she can join her beloved in a triumphant final duet. How did I accept becoming an accomplice to this crime against my own work? Why did I give in to coercion and submit to the decisions and poor taste of my sponsors? It is because I wanted my opera to be performed and to please everyone. Not everyone has the inner strength to resist temptation; people built of the stuff of martyrs are very rare. Had I been Bizet, Don José and Carmen might have fallen into each other's arms at the end of act 4 and lived happily together to this day. But then I would not have been obliged to jump into a frozen river while suffering from a dangerous illness.

But please, my dear friend, don't think it doesn't cost me dearly. It tears me to shreds and gnaws at my entrails. I have experienced this innumerable times. With every new work there comes a new evil, a new crucifixion. I had to abandon the creatures that my brain had created, that most intimate part of myself, into the hands of Philistines, the hands of those who earn their living by castrating, falsifying, bleeding them dry, and turning them into grotesque caricatures. This is what befell me every time I had to face those monsters, the theater directors. They are just miserable assassins, heartless torturers. Take me, beat me, tear away my beard; never mind, I'm just unimportant, worthless. But my creations, my brainchildren...let them be, let them go on their respectable way. Who is going to say to the public, "Ladies and gentlemen, what you see here is not what I meant you to see. This is not my work! I do not recognize that creature!"?

Now please tell me, Hippolyte, is it so strange that I have had to be confined to Dr. Blanche's convalescence home again and again? Can a man who is being drawn to crucifixion each evening maintain his sanity?

When I returned home, it suddenly dawned on me that Gounod, in spite of being surrounded by a swarm of admirers, was very lonely, and I thought to myself: Dear friend, how lonely you are in this big house of yours, with all your family and relatives around you. I suddenly grasped the whole story; you crave a real friend, someone able to appreciate you for your true value. I suddenly understood what you silently meant to say to me. I'm not sure I can provide all this, but I promise, from now on I will come to visit you more often and offer the only thing that matters to you these days: honest and true friendship.

13

DAS EWIG-WEIBLICHE ZIEHT UNS HINAN[17]

My friend Eugène Delacroix painted the great masterpiece he called *La Liberté guidant le peuple* (Liberty Leading the People). In this painting the mythical, patriotic figure Marianne leads a revolutionary party in the 1830 uprising in Paris. This representation of a heroine drawing her followers into combat, infusing them with courage and enthusiasm, is not a mere allegory; it is a role great women have always assumed throughout history, sometimes behind the scenes or in the intimacy of bedrooms, and sometimes in open rebellion against accepted traditions and customary behavior.

In our beautiful French language, the nouns beauty, republic, reason, self-control, discipline, influence, will, poetry, music, inspiration, and form all belong to the feminine gender. But we probably do not pay enough heed to the leading role and influence women of outstanding strength of character have had on male leaders in all fields, and on creative artists in particular.

---

17 The Eternal Feminine draws us on (from Goethe's *Faust*).

It is almost a cliché to call George Sand the *femme fatale par excellence*, and to picture her liaisons with Alfred de Musset and Frédéric Chopin as the quintessence of Romanticism. The truth is that whether appearing in male attire or parading in the outfit of an eastern princess, and even when she aimed her big, dark eyes at the current object of her adulation as if to suck his bone marrow dry, George Sand was never a romantic figure. As a matter of fact, she was a wise and practical woman who never threw herself into love affairs on passionate and sensual impulse, but rather in response to a methodical search for true love.

George Sand said,

> As often as I have loved in my life, so have I been unfaithful. But there is not the faintest trace of repentance in my heart. All those spells of cheating were the direct consequence of my craving for some ideal that drove me to relinquish the routine, the imperfect, striving to attain flawless perfection.

Every new experience would bring the raw material for a new novel. Only her devotion to her son Maurice took precedence over her writing.

Prosper Mérimée, who was also one of her lovers, would burst into a fit of rage when he would wake up in the middle of the night and find himself alone in bed instead of clasping her in his arms. He would find her sitting beside the cold hearth, shivering in spite of the blanket covering her shoulders, making good use of his slumber to resume her literary activities.

She was born Amantine Aurore Lucile Dupin, and her mother's maiden name was Delaborde. I was just recently made aware of this fact. That's not such a common name—I must remember to ask young

Élie-Miriam Delaborde if this is just a coincidence or whether they are related in some way.

George Sand married Baron Casimir Dudevant in 1822 when she was eighteen. They separated in 1831 and she never remarried. She picked her pen name when she made her literary first steps in collaboration with Jules Sandeau (who was also one of her first lovers), when they published a few stories under the name Sand.

I clearly remember the first time we met in 1835 at a political meeting organized by my cousin Olinde Rodrigues. In 1825, Saint-Simon, on his deathbed, had appointed Olinde head of the movement he had founded. This utopic movement preaches social equality and theorizes that the modern industrial upsurge will be the main tool to attain its goals.

I was immediately puzzled by this woman. I was shocked by her opinionated and provocative attitude, her self-confidence, and mainly because she dressed in a man's attire, and ostensibly smoked cigars. Curiously, those were also the main reasons that brought me to reverse my judgment about her a little later. She earned my unqualified admiration when I started, during later meetings, to understand the honesty of her feelings, her enmity of hypocrisy, her struggle for gender equality, and the complexity of her fascinating personality.

Though she never became a militant member of the Saint-Simon movement, she always openly displayed her sympathy for its cause. All her life she fought ardently for the improvement of the economic standing of underprivileged classes. Deeply engaged ideologically, she nevertheless avoided direct participation in street uprisings. Although I personally do not share her political outlook, I still admire the way she fought to support her opinions. I met her quite often, mostly at Pauline Viardot's salon. On one of those occasions she told me, "The world will know and understand me someday. But if that day does not arrive, it does not matter greatly. I shall have opened the way for women."

She had a very rigid, private ethical code, a definite sense of justice, and a code of behavior. She was one of the last women in Paris who believed in the principles of morality. She took the young poet Alfred de Musset on a trip to Venice, fully intending to heal him of his addiction to alcohol, drugs, and women, and hoping they would reach the pinnacle of ideal love together. When she understood that she had failed to attain that goal, she sought solace in the arms of the handsome Italian doctor under whose care Musset found himself during the serious illness caused by his excesses. She even expected the patient to extend his blessing to this strange situation and to find his place in the new arrangement, in the platonic role of a brother, a son, or a friend, whatever his choice or personal preference was. How strange it is that this woman, the subject of so many exalted men's daydreams, was completely devoid of a sense of humor.

She planned her liaison with Chopin in the midst of her love affair with Félicien Mallefille, a young writer she employed as a private teacher for her son Maurice. She made sure of all the angles beforehand, and even turned to a specialist for advice. The letter she wrote to Albert Grzymala, Chopin's friend and patron, is a stunning document. It is the negation of Romanticism dressed up as pure Romanticism.

> My dear friend, I need you. I got entangled in an embarrassing, even maddening situation, and I can get out of it only with your help. You've probably guessed it: it's about Chopin. I can't properly explain the impression this small creature has made on me. I'm not in the habit of falling in love with men, unless they have first fallen in love with me. The hesitant manner in which he avoids me tries my patience and drives me to the brink of despondency. It is utterly in

contradiction with whatever I have been told about him. Could it be possible that some religious misconceptions are standing between him and love? You must free him from these doubts at all costs; you must make clear to him that true love, being the source of everything that is good and sublime, not only estranged us from God, but, on the contrary, it brings us nearer to Him. I don't expect any sacrifice from him that deviates from his beliefs; all I want is to bring him happiness. Neither do I intend to bind him in any kind of ties or to hinder his imagination in any way. I will be satisfied if we could find together, from time to time, a few hours of pure dedication and sweet poetry. We would both live our lives separately, but when the spirit pushes us into each other's arms, we would be lifted in a fantastic voyage toward the stars, and we would be consumed together in the sacred flame. Tell him all this, my friend, and even more.

I hope to see you soon in Nohant. As for the little one, he can come whenever he likes, provided he lets me know in time, so that I may send Mallefille to Paris, or even better, to Geneva.

Sand got what she was after. But with the health of her lover deteriorating, all her well-laid plans went haywire. Her passion had to be converted into motherly care. This change in her feelings and attitude shattered Chopin to the roots of his manliness. But he would not let go and kept being drawn to her—for quite a long time. She was his home, his bastion, his refuge. One day, this burden became too heavy for her to carry and with Grzymala's help she regained her freedom. She said,

The illness gnawing and consuming this poor man succeeded in devastating me, too. I would never have sent him away but for the fact that I knew I couldn't help him anymore. His unhappiness stems from jealousy, suspicion, and the safeguarding of his love for me, and for those ills I have no remedy.

In a moment of weakness, she turned her back on her duty and abandoned the dying artist to his fate. But what seems to me unforgivable is that his moral and physical suffering did not stop her from publishing the story of their love in her new novel *Lucrezia Floriani*. There, she unveils Chopin's complex personality and quite a few intimate details of his life. She was very surprised when several of her best friends like Liszt and Heine severely admonished her as a result.

Heine said,

George Sand, this high priest of women's rights, tired of her role as a nurse. Since my compulsory taking to bed, she has completely ignored me. She has treated my ill friend, Chopin, even worse; she has tortured him in the cruelest way in a shameless novel—albeit written in a heavenly way.

Liszt said,

George catches her butterfly and tames it, feeding it with plenty of honey and flowers. This is the period of love. When the butterfly shows signs of struggle, she pierces it with her needle. This is the death throe. Later, she dissects the butterfly, soaks it in some preserving solution, and adds it the collection of her novel's personae.

Chopin has read *Lucrezia Floriani*, but has not voiced his opinion on it. To his last breath, he wished and hoped that Sand would take her leave of him. She has accused some ill-intentioned people of being instrumental in the ending of their relationship. She even maintained that she was unaware of his ardent wish to see her, until everything was over.

Sand said, "People with good intentions thought that for my own good I shouldn't be told that he wants to see me; they were also convinced that for *his* peace of mind it was much better to conceal from him the fact that I was willing to run to visit him at any moment."

But she was well aware of the fact that her ending their relationship at this crucial time, at the hour he needed her support and physical nearness most, was an indelible blemish on her personality and on the picture of herself she wished to pass on to the next generation. This filled her with remorse. I even suspect that the love she later bestowed on the lonely and aging Flaubert was in some manner motivated by the need she had to repent for her inexcusable conduct toward Chopin.

It goes without saying that this autumnal love affair also found its way into a novel, *Le dernier amour* published in 1866, which is dedicated to Flaubert.

In *Consuelo*, one of her most beloved books, Sand describes her friend Pauline Viardot. Pauline is a friend to everyone who is lucky enough to know her.

Sometime after Chopin's funeral, Viardot wrote to Sand,

A long time has passed since I let you have news of me, but it is even longer that you haven't written to me. As for myself, my dear one, I felt such sorrow over the death of poor Chopin that I did not know how to begin my letter. I am sure you, too, must have been stricken and that, had you known that his end was so near, you would have come to clasp his hand for the last time. I do not know on what date he returned to Paris, or what agonies he suffered. I was apprised of his death by strangers, who came and with great ceremony asked me whether I would take part in a requiem that was to be held at La Madeleine. It was at that moment that I realized how much love I had for him.

Sure enough, she sang the "Tuba Mirum" from Mozart's Requiem at that ceremony. She and the soprano had to be hidden behind a curtain because women were banned from singing in the church.

Viardot left the stage years ago, but everyone knows that she was one of the great singers of her day, a gifted pianist, composer, poet, painter, philologist, and excelled at several other topics she put her mind to study and practice. But she mainly had, and still has, a magnetic personality, exuding love and understanding all around her. Her ability to combine her different talents and to leave the imprint of her unique talent (with a hint of a feminine touch and imagination as well) has made her one of the central figures of the cultural landscape of our century. Many people say she's ugly. I can understand that. I remember that I also thought so when I first met her. But I have to make a genuine effort to recall that impression, because I have known her so well for…for how long? I don't remember exactly, but it is certainly more than forty years. And thinking of or even remotely relating her to any physical appearance sounds preposterous to me. Her intellectual glamor is such that you forget when in her presence that she even *has* a physical appearance at all. Still, she has managed to kindle many an amorous flame in several men, men who were her intellectual equals. I will cite only Musset, Gounod, and Turgenev.

She is the daughter of the famous Spanish tenor Manuel del Popolo Vicente Garcia and his wife Joaquina Sitchez, who was also a singer. Her godfather was the composer Ferdinando Paer, and her godmother was Princess Pauline Galitsin—hence her two middle names. Her elder brother, Patricio Rodriguez Garcia, was also a renowned singer and is still a respected teacher and has successfully researched the human voice. Her late sister, Maria Felicita, thirteen years her senior, was the legendary Maria Malibran, who died so tragically in England just a few months after marrying the violinist Charles de Bériot. At the age of six, she had already studied the piano with no less a giant than young Liszt and composition with Anton Reicha. She fully intended to pursue a career as a pianist. But after her father's death in 1832, she submitted to her mother's will and directed the majority of her talented effort to her voice. Still, the quality of her piano playing was such that she played piano duets with such great artists as Chopin and Clara Schumann.

It is hard to give a comprehensive list of her achievements in music, but to name a few, she was the first and unforgettable personification of Fidès, and no one will ever really know how much help Meyerbeer got from her during the composition of *Le prophète*. She sang Brahms's *Rhapsody for Contralto, Male Choir, and Orchestra* at its premiere in Jena, in March 1870. The Schumann song cycle *Liederkreis*, op. 24, composed in 1840 to poems by Heine, is dedicated to her. So is Saint-Saëns's opera *Samson et Dalila*. She declined to sing the title role, claiming she was too old to personify this bewitching enchantress. Too old! Almost all singers we see on stage today are way too old for the roles they sing. What a pity! What a loss! But at least I have the personal consolation to have heard her sing two of Dalila's arias from the opera, with Saint-Saëns accompanying her on the organ, at one of her regular Thursday evenings.

As far as I know she has to this day composed three operas (all of them to librettos by Turgenev), numerous songs (amongst them the twelve mazurkas by Chopin for voice and piano), and quite a lot of instrumental music, mainly for piano or for violin and piano.

Many courted her, among them Musset, who asked her to marry him when she was eighteen. Her friend George Sand dissuaded her and arranged for her to meet Louis Viardot, who was a small-time author, a critic, and the current manager of the Théâtre Italien. He was twenty years her senior, but Sand convinced her that he would be able to look after her needs in a much more reliable manner than the poet. So she became Mme Pauline Viardot; she was nineteen when she married.

Louis Viardot relinquished the directorship of the Théâtre Italien in order to devote all his time and energy to promoting her career—he became, in fact, her impresario and followed her during her travels all over Europe. One of those trips brought her to Saint Petersburg, where she sang in *The Barber of Seville*. This was one of her favorites, as Rossini actually wrote the Figaro role for her late father. Ivan Sergeyev Turgenev saw her that evening and fell in love with her on the spot. This passion for her would last to the end of his life. From that point forward, he divided his time between Russia and France, and her complaisant husband had no option but to accept this strange situation and share the diva in a perfect love triangle.

Turgenev would take Viardot to literary gatherings, where they would meet with Flaubert, Gautier, Renan, Daudet, or the Goncourt brothers. She was the only woman admitted to those meetings. Still, when she would voice her opinion on this or that topic, everyone in this most select group would drink in her words with religious fervor.

From time to time she would ask Turgenev to leave her home for some time so she could accommodate a new lover. Poor Turgenev had to find lodging on the rue de Rivoli, which was actually near the place where Tolstoy lived those very days when he stayed in Paris. Turgenev suffered, but he waited patiently, knowing perfectly well that in the end her door would always reopen for him.

One of those temporary lovers who brought Turgenev so much misery was the young and charming Gounod. George Sand is the one who let me in on this affair:

> It happened in 1849, the year she reaped one of her greatest successes as Fidès in Meyerbeer's Le prophète. No one could refuse her anything thereafter. We were neighbors then; we lived in the d'Orléans Square. One day she came to me enthralled, excited, and agitated: "I just met a genius, a real genius! He is thirty-one, as handsome as Adonis, as talented as Mozart, and as inspired as Gluck. His name is Charles Gounod. I've already succeeded in con-

vincing Nestor Roqueplan to commission a new opera from him in which I will sing the main role. We even found a librettist for it, Émile Augier, with whom Gounod played in the Luxembourg Gardens as a child. The action will be centered on the Greek poetess Sapho. Sapho and the deceitful courtesan Glycère are both in love with Phaon. To save Phaon's life, Sapho gives in to her rival. But Phaon thinks that Sapho has betrayed him and he curses her. Sapho throws herself into the sea."

When I asked where Gounod was just now, Pauline very candidly told me that he was busy composing the opera at her country home. "All by himself?" I asked

"No, Louis and Ivan are there with him."

"So the triangle has developed into a rectangle?" I suggested. Pauline smiled and shook her head. I understood immediately; there was no foursome and no triangle there—just [Louis] Viardot and Turgenev torn in the grip of jealousy, and Pauline with Gounod in a blooming festival of love and creativity.

Days and even months went by. *Sapho* was eventually completed and staged in the Salle Le Peletier on April 4, 1851, with Pauline Viardot in the title role, and with Anne Poinsot as Glycère, and Louis Guémard and Hippolyte Brémont singing Phaon and Pythéas. It was a *succès d'estime*, mainly due to Viardot's masterly performance.

Gounod in the meantime had joined the intimate circle of the elderly Pierre Zimmermann, his former piano teacher at the Conservatoire. In a swift and slick maneuver Zimmermann's wife contrived to have the eldest of their four daughters, Anna, betrothed to the composer, the new comet in the sky of French opera. The betrothal took Viardot completely by surprise. She did not attend the wedding, but not because her pride was hurt or anything like that. She had simply not been invited. A golden bracelet she sent the bride as a wedding present was returned without any kind of explanation. Anna Zimmermann-Gounod never left the slightest doubt as to her animosity toward her groom's benefactress. I must admit with a little sense of shame and unhappiness that Gounod seconded his wife's move and completely severed any bond between himself and Viardot. But he lost at that gambit, because he swapped a brilliant and formidable friend for a pusillanimous, vindictive, insignificant, and bitter little wife.

I was a regular guest at the parties Viardot held on Thursday evenings at her apartment in Montmartre, near the building where Georges Bizet and Ludovic Halévy lived with their wives, Geneviève and Valentine. On these evenings she generally did not perform herself, neither as a pianist nor as a singer. She preferred to give the stage to her guests, especially to those young, budding talents she and her close friends went out scouting to discover in the beehive that was Paris. But even then, when she was only a spectator, she still remained the hub, the inspiring center of the event.

Everyone hung on her words, awaiting her judgment, which was always fair and pertinent. She would always find the right compliment, and if the performance left something to be desired she would find a word of encouragement. But she would rather keep silent than utter a falsehood. Someone told me that she went with the British soprano Adelaide Kemble to the farewell concert given by Giuditta Pasta in London in 1850. When Kemble asked Viardot about Pasta's voice, the answer was typical: "Ah! It is a ruin, but so is Leonardo's *Last Supper*."

Sometimes she would even give in to her guests' request and join in the music making. She would take all her guests down to the ground floor, to the picture gallery where the organ was. One of the guests would sit at the organ, and she would sing for us music that was rarely performed in France: Handel's and Mendelssohn's arias, amongst others. She always said that she loved music more than she loved her voice, and since she used to sing everything—from Bach to Wagner—the inevitable result was that she ruined her voice. Today she teaches singing at the Conservatoire, doing her best to leave a legacy to a handful of lucky students.

She had a special gift of inspiring great, creative minds. She worked, together with Chopin, to dress up several of his mazurkas with words, making it possible for her to perform them at her recitals, giving this music widespread recognition.

She has been a close friend and favorite singer of Berlioz since her appearance in his historical revivals of Gluck's *Orphée* and *Alceste*. He said that her performance lifted him to seventh heaven. As an unparalleled token of friendship, she prepared the voice and piano reduction of *Les Troyens* for him.

After young Massenet, totally unknown at the time, performed excerpts from his oratorio *Maria Magdalena* in her salon, she adopted the young composer and his work, bringing them to the forefront of public attention by singing the title role in a festive concert conducted by Édouard Colonne.

If I'm not mistaken, the first performance of act 2 of *Tristan und Isolde* was held at her place. Only two people were invited to witness it: Hector Berlioz and Countess Marie von Muchanoff- Kalergis, who had donated ten thousand francs in a futile effort to try to extricate Wagner from his debts. Wagner himself sang Tristan and naturally Viardot was Isolde. Karl Klindworth had been specially invited to come over from London to accompany them on the piano. After the performance the two guests looked perplexed, but Viardot was enthusiastic, ecstatic, and taken over completely.

Another unconditional supporter of Wagner was Judith Gautier. On the evening of the infamous *Tannhäuser* scandal in 1861, I stepped out of the Salle Le Peletier during the first intermission to breathe some fresh air. Before the main entrance stood Berlioz, debating vehemently with Théophile Gautier. Next to Gautier stood his beautiful daughter Judith; she was not yet sixteen at that time. I approached the little group to listen to what they had to say. They were discussing *Tannhäuser*, naturally. Gautier was taking Wagner's side, which Berlioz criticized. Judith, her eyes flashing with excitement, suddenly intervened and with no consideration for the venerable and respected Berlioz, burst into this angry, almost insolent attack: "It's so obvious that you're talking about a colleague of yours. What you say is purely a composer's jealousy. I want you to know that *Tannhäuser* is a masterpiece whether you like it or not."

Judith is the daughter of Ernesta Grisi and Théophile Gautier. Ernesta is the sister of the celebrated ballerina Carlotta Grisi and they are cousins of the famous singers Giuditta and Giulia Grisi. Gautier is a fanatic balletomane and fell in love with Carlotta Grisi. He has written for her (in collaboration with Vernoy de Saint-Georges) the book for the ballet *Giselle*. Given Carlotta's unavailability—she was the mistress of the great choreographer Jules Perrot—Gautier married her sister Ernesta.

Fifteen years later, the first Wagner Festival took place in Bayreuth. Judith Gautier was among the pilgrims pouring in from every corner of the world. Since the *Tannhäuser* evening she had managed to make a name for herself as a writer, a fighter for the feminist cause, and a fierce defender of Wagner's works. She has met the composer several times and supported Franz Liszt's daughter, Cosima, in her struggle to get a divorce from her former husband, the renowned pianist and conductor Hans von Bülow. Judith herself had recently divorced her husband, the writer Catulle Mendès.

Judith was still breathtakingly beautiful and people all around were staring at her as if she were some freak of nature. In Bayreuth she took a house next to the Villa Wahnfried. In her small living room Wagner was sprawled across the carpet at her feet, drowned in her beauty, intoxicated by the smell of her Parisian perfume, sucking from her lips the strength he needed to compose *Parsifal*.

He was her guide when she visited the theater, holding her hand while they climbed over the backstage scenery for the *Ring der Nibelungen*. He told her that her kisses were "the magnificent drunkenness of my life, the summit and pride of my existence." She returned to Paris. He moaned and cried out in despair, "Oh, you are the essence of my life, sweet friend; I have to see you again, because I love you!" He asked her to send him souvenirs and presents: golden satin, like the color of her skin; the perfume that had bewitched him; a cover for the couch that he would name after her; rose water, silk, amber, Turkish slippers. "I embrace you, my beautiful one, I love you, my dear soul, my adored little child, my Judith."

Suddenly there was nothing—complete silence. And somewhat later, a short note explaining that from that point forward, Cosima would be in charge of communication between them: "Don't you worry about me. I'll soon overcome this. Be nice to Cosima and write her long letters. All my love."

Judith Gautier's task was complete. The opera *Parsifal* was finished and the ironfisted wife was back in the saddle, in control. It was as things should be.

There is another love story that I would like to add to this collection, a most unusual story Berlioz told us, Stephen Heller and me, one evening in August 1868 when we were sipping our Armagnac after a delicious supper at my place. No, it's not the story of his stormy love for Henriette Smithson. Every music lover familiar with the *Symphonie fantastique* knows its origin. This story might go by the title "First and Last Love."

Berlioz said,

My maternal grandfather lived in Meylan, a village not far from Grenoble. As a child I used to spend a few weeks there every year, at the end of the summer, with my mother and my sisters. On the outskirts of the village, in a big white villa, lived a lady with her two granddaughters; the younger one was called Estelle. The first time I met her she wore pink half boots. Can you imagine that? Pink! I had never seen such a thing before. I was twelve years old at the time, and she was eighteen. I vividly remember her tall, elegant figure, and her large, dark eyes. The very moment I saw her I felt as if an electric current had passed through me. My heart began to beat faster, and I think I broke into a heavy sweat. I had been struck by that very rare thing: love at first sight. From that moment my life was hell. No—it was heaven. I'm sorry, I think it was simultaneously hell and heaven combined. My behavior during the next few days must have been quite erratic, because everyone around us became aware at once of that puppy love that devoured me. Naturally, the first person to be aware of it was Estelle herself. I think she was rather amused by it at that time, in a kind of playful and cruel way. And that, as you can guess, only increased my suffering.

I clearly remember the pangs of jealousy that gnawed at my very soul when I saw her dancing, light as a feather in the wind, in the arms of my cousin, a petty cavalry officer in the army, wearing a glittering uniform. I can feel those pangs of jealousy to this very day. There is a popular saying, time heals all wounds. Believe me, time has not cured me of this first and shattering experience.

I stopped seeing her when I was thirteen. Still, that did not alter my feelings in the least. I was thirty when I crossed the Alps on my way back from my sojourn at the Villa Medici. On the way to Paris, I saw Meylan and the white villa from afar. Tears filled my eyes.

"That is quite a story," said Heller. "You never spoke of her to me. Do you know what became of her?"

"Wait," said Berlioz. "This is only the prologue. Let's go out and breathe some air, and I'll finish my tale when we return—if you can say that an unfinished story has an end."

We went out into the cool, crisp night and strolled in the park.

Berlioz had returned from Russia a short while before our meeting. The eight concerts he conducted there had been a huge success. But Berlioz looked worn and tired. I don't recall ever seeing him look so dejected. And last week he had just come back from Grenoble, where he had presided over a jury for a male voice choral competition. I felt that in spite of his weariness he had an urgent need to unburden himself of this story. He continued: "Exactly twenty years ago, in mid-August 1848, my father died. I was in London at the time and on my return to France I hurried to La Côte Saint-André to join my two sisters. Before setting out to return to Paris, a sudden and irresistible longing drove me to go and revisit Meylan. *Agnosco veteris vestigia flammae.*"

"Could you please translate that?" I asked. "I'm sorry to say, but I never bothered to learn Latin. As a toddler in Bordeaux I learned the rudiments of Hebrew, and I can read Hebrew quite passably. At M. Morhange's school on the rue des Blancs-Manteaux, we were too busy with solfeggio and French grammar to bother about Latin. At home in Bordeaux we spoke Ladino,[18] and I also have a basic knowledge of Yiddish, German, and English because my professional activities—a lifetime ago—required these languages to communicate with foreign contacts. But, you see, I always felt that not knowing Latin was an

---

18 Ladino, or Judeo-Spanish, is a language derived from Old Spanish and spoken by Sephardic Jews scattered around the world after their expulsion from Spain in 1492.

enormous gap in my general education. By the way, I have many more of these kinds of holes in my cultural cloak."[19]

"Who doesn't?" retorted Berlioz. "The only proper way to judge a person is according to whatever it is that *surrounds* those holes. And believe me, Hippolyte, my friend, you have no cause to complain. The stuff your cloak is made of is rich and glittering, so the holes in it are hardly perceptible. As for that that bit of Latin, it means, 'I recognize the remnants of my first flame.' It's from Virgil's *Aeneid*. Dido confesses to her sister that she recognizes in her inner feelings for Aeneas the same kind of passion she felt for her late husband. But let me now turn back to my tale."

Berlioz continued his story:

After paying my respects to the house that had once belonged to my grandfather and where I had spent so many summer vacations, I hesitantly set out toward the white villa on the outskirts of the village, on the slight hilly slope where the mountain starts its climb into the clouds. I had glimpsed that same house from a distance as I came back from Rome, sixteen years earlier. I first saw Estelle in this house. My heart was playing tympani at an incredible and irregular rate in my chest. I won't bother you with the details. Just let me tell you that I felt exactly like the teenager struck by the lightning of love thirty-five years ago. The next day I was in Grenoble, with my cousins and their mother. The emotional toll of the day before must have left its impact on me and I probably looked a bit groggy. My cousin Victor was somewhat concerned about my well-being and asked me what was the matter. I told him I had been to Meylan the day before. He became curious, and without even a moment of hesitation I unfolded the whole story for him, probably so I could share

---

19 I have since remedied this shortcoming, as I needed Latin for my research concerning the last days of Jesus and the early Christian sects (J.H.R.).

the oppression I felt in my heart with someone nearby. He laughed at me good-naturedly.

"Don't be ridiculous, Hector. Do you realize that Estelle is fifty-one now? Her eldest son, who is twenty-two, is studying law with me."

"So you must certainly know where she lives now," I stammered.

"Since her husband died she has lived in Vif. That is some ten kilometers from here."

"I must go there and pay her my respects."

"Are you out of your mind? You would be making a fool of yourself and you'd only manage to embarrass her. I beg you to reconsider."

"At least let me write a letter to her."

Victor agreed to this, though without expressing too much enthusiasm. So I sat down and wrote to her a very long letter, hinting at my feelings. This is how I ended this letter:

> I'm going back to my hectic existence. You will probably never see me, nor know who I am, but you will, I trust, forgive the strange liberty I am taking in writing to you now. For my part, I forgive you in advance for laughing at the nostalgia of the man as you once laughed at the adoration of the child.

"It's getting a little bit chilly, so I suggest we go home now," I said. "You can finish telling your extraordinary story next to the cozy fireplace, with another glass of that great Armagnac my son Edgar has sent me from Bordeaux."

So we sat down comfortably to listen to the unfolding of this unusual confession.

> You have no idea how lonely I feel. Marie died six years ago; my son Louis, with whom, after years of estrangement, I had finally managed

to slowly build a closer relationship of confidence and understanding, died of yellow fever in Havana just over a year ago, in June. He was thirty-three. So many visits to graveyards—yes, I still put flowers on Henriette's grave—are terribly depressing. I sometimes feel like this is the final rehearsal for my own funeral

I think it is this loneliness that rekindled the old flame that was never really extinguished. It is now consuming me and burns up the last ounces of energy I have left, while also surprisingly keeping me on my feet.

In September of '64, I was overcome by an overwhelming wave of nostalgia, an irresistible need to return to the root of events that had shaped my whole life. I resolved to make one last trip to Meylan. When I arrived in Grenoble my brother-in-law, Marc Suat, the husband of my late sister Adèle, was waiting for me at the train station with his two daughters. No more hesitation, no more groping this time. I had asked him to make some inquiries to find out about Estelle's whereabouts. Sure enough, he had located her in Lyons. And so my odyssey began with this ultimate visit to Meylan, where my senses had been aroused for the first time and where I placed the beginning of my sensibility, and hence the birth of my career as an artist. That same evening, I was in Lyons; I wrote her this letter, a copy of which I religiously keep among my private documents:

September 23, 1864

Madame,

I come once again from Meylan, a second pilgrimage to the haunts of my childhood fancies, more painful still than the one I made sixteen years ago. On that occasion I ventured to write to you at Vif, where you were then living. This time I do more: I ask you to receive me. Oh, don't be afraid, I shall control myself; I shall not get carried away. My heart is numbed by the cold grip of one inexorable reality. Grant me a few moments—let me see you again, I beg of you.

And yes, she agreed to see me the next day. I was on fire again—like the first day I saw her, half a century ago. But now, this had nothing to do with her stunning looks. Forty-nine years. We have all undergone the inexorable physical metamorphosis nature brings on us with age. Still, she had kept her proud allure, and that graceful carriage of her head. But this was only a slight reminder; I did not really need it. In my heart it was the seed sown so long ago that had suddenly sprouted into full maturity. I had to make a superhuman effort to keep control and conduct myself in a proper and suitable manner. She understood perfectly what happened and in her well-groomed and ladylike manner she managed to keep me at a distance with a mixture of coolness and sympathy. This time there was no amusement, nor cruelty in her grasping the situation. I felt a wave of warmth and compassion. I had to forcibly tear myself away to end this meeting, a meeting that only a few months ago I had not dared to hope would ever materialize.

And here my friend Hector Berlioz gave a big sigh and went silent for a few minutes. Heller and I kept silent too. And then it seemed that all his inner turmoil calmed, and he went on with his tale, immensely relieved.

Since that day, four years ago, we have kept in touch with a more or less regular exchange of correspondence. Her first letter concludes with those few sentences:

To my mind, the time to begin a relationship is not when one already feels the weight of years and has lived long enough to have had one's fill of life's disappointments. I admit to you that I have reached that point. The time left to me is short and grows shorter every day. What is the use of forming a relationship that today springs up and tomorrow may be cut down? It would only be to accumulate fresh sorrows.

You must not think that in all that I have just said there is any intention on my part to hurt you by disparaging the memories you have of me. I respect them and I am touched by their persistence. You're still quite young at heart. With me it is not so. I'm really and truly old, no longer fit for anything but to keep—as, believe me, I shall—a large place for you in my memory. It will always give me pleasure to hear of the triumphs that you are destined to win.

Goodbye, and once again let me assure you of my kindest regards.

Estelle

And in another letter she wrote that she will always be truly grateful for the feelings I have toward her.

She is now living with one of her sons in Geneva. Since then, I have visited her every summer. This, I think, sums up the situation. Very uncharacteristic of my normal behavior, and contrary to my natural disposition, I have been very discreet about this entire affair. But now that I have opened the gates to this tumultuous torrent and emptied this overflowing cup, I can say thank you, my friends, for your help and understanding. Now I can take my bow and leave the stage.

14

CAMILLE SAINT-SAËNS

October 1872

I was invited to one of the famous Monday evening parties at Saint-Saëns's place on the rue du Faubourg Saint-Honoré. The young Spanish violinist Pablo de Sarasate was the star of the evening. He played a piece Saint-Saëns had just finished writing especially for him: *Introduction et rondo capriccio*. That daredevil has belittled all violinists within earshot by his brilliant, faultless, and daring virtuosity. I must add that Saint-Saëns's work, though probably claiming no place among the recognized "backbone pieces" in the repertoire for the instrument, is a sparkling work, full of charm, nicely balanced and enjoyable. It is mostly written in a way that has allowed the young master to show off his technical prowess in the most spectacular fashion.

The enthusiastic reception his new work was given by all present encouraged our host to produce a series of exhibitory feats that left us all speechless. He had instructed Delibes and Bizet to stretch out a big screen like those used in a shadow puppet show. And he, Saint-Saëns, clad in a big gown and with a pair of long braids cascading from his head on both sides of his black beard, sat behind that curtain next to what looked like a spinning wheel. He intoned, in what sounded to me like a fully trained falsetto voice, Marguerite's spinning song and Jewel's aria from Gounod's *Faust*. He parodied Mme Miolan-Carvalho's mannerisms in the most astonishing fashion, including her trills and that detestable habit she has of singing her high notes a tiny bit higher than the proper pitch. This was really some feat, as in my opinion it is easier to teach a tone-deaf person to sing accurately than to get a trained musician to sing out of tune at will. Saint-Saëns's feat got its rightful reward with thunderous applause. Next on the program came a witty parody on themes from Wagner's *Ring des Nibelungen* played four-hands by Saint-Saëns and his pupil and friend, young Gabriel Fauré, a very gifted but extremely shy musician. As Saint-Saëns is well-known for his staunch support of Wagner's music, there was no recrimination from the handful of Wagnerites present. Even *they* understood that what they had just heard was a good-humored prank with no malice and no criticism, a skillful concoction meant to entertain and nothing else. So they joined in the general outburst of laughter and cheers. That was the moment our host chose to have us take a break from the stream of music.

His apartment is located on the top floor of the building, right under the roof. From the staircase, looking toward the inner courtyard, there is a door leading to an open space, level with the roof. In the middle of this small balcony stood a telescope. It was manufactured especially for Saint-Saëns according to his specific instructions as to how the instrument should be built. Saint-Saëns's obsession with astronomy is more than a mere hobby—it is an addiction. Only his insufficient knowledge of mathematics has kept him from achieving a professional level in that field. But I have been told that he also occupies himself with two other extra-musical fields: geology and zoology. With regards to the latter, I heard that he has made significant contributions to the research on butterflies.

We were all invited to take turns looking through the lens at the star-strewn skies. We were lucky: the sky was clear and the spectacle was breathtaking. Our host was enthusiastically lecturing on Cassiopeia, Andromeda, and Orion, but the coolness of the autumn night chased me back into the large and warm living room. The two landladies, Saint-Saëns's mother Clémence and her elderly aunt Charlotte Masson, were busy unloading trays filled to the brim with fruit and pastries. Saint-Saëns calls them his two mothers. Both women were widowed in the same year, 1836. They resolved to tackle the arduous but rewarding task of raising young Camille Saint-Saëns (who was not yet a year old at the time) together.

When he was only two years old he was already capable of calling every sound he heard by its proper name according to the musical scale. At three he could read and write freely. He composed gallops and waltzes (at the writing desk, mind you, not at the piano) and made appearances as a pianist at private parties. At five he played *Don Giovanni* on the piano, transposing from the full orchestral score on the spot. He also presented a formal analysis of the opera. When he was seven he read books in the original Latin, was engaged in botanical research, in paleontology, and in entomology. This is when his great love for astronomy began. He spent countless hours watching the astral bodies and drew his own independent conclusions about men and the universe.

He was eleven when he gave his first public concert as a solo pianist. He was accompanied by a group of musicians from the Théâtre Italien and they introduced Parisian music lovers to the complete cycle of Mozart's piano concertos. I was there on the evening he played Concerto no. 15 in B-flat Major at the Salle Pleyel. As an encore he volunteered to play by heart any of Beethoven's thirty-two piano sonatas. Out of pure curiosity (and maybe some inner disbelief or challenge) I raised my hand and asked for the B-flat Major Sonata, the one known as the *Hammerklavier*. The boy was somewhat surprised and looked at me perplexedly—we were not yet acquainted at the time—perhaps wondering who this man was who even *knew* of this rare pearl. But he sat at the piano and played this excruciatingly hard work without a hitch. After this concert, at which he also played some of Bach's preludes and fugues, a piano sonata by Hummel, and Beethoven's Piano Concerto no. 3, a flabbergasted listener in the audience asked his mother, "Madame Saint-Saëns, what music will the boy play when he grows up?" She responded, "He will play his *own* music, of course."

Mme Charlotte Masson, Saint-Saëns's great-aunt, told me some refreshing stories from her ward's childhood.

He was ever looking out for new listening experiences. He would often play at opening and closing doors to hear the creaking and ascertain their changing pitch. He would run from clock to clock to listen to the mechanical noise of their inner machinery and wait with delight for their chime, expressing his joy noisily. The crescendo whistle of the boiling teapot had a magical effect on him. Recently he said to me that he was convinced that Berlioz must have also gone through a similar experience as a child, and that this left its imprint on "Infernal Ride" from *La damnation de Faust*.

> The very first time I opened the old upright piano that had been standing in its corner for years without being used, he didn't smash both hands on the keyboard as most children I know would do. He touched the keys one by one, listening to the sound they produced,

and only after the sound had died away completely did he touch the next key. I taught him the name of the notes and they immediately became his dear friends, each sound with its individual identity.

With piano lessons, things were more difficult. He would protest those exercises all beginners have to go through and say, "The bass doesn't sing."

He was five years old when he was asked to accompany two amateur lady singers at a private party. One of them sang too fast, the other too slowly. Little Camille stopped playing and asked his mother, "Maman, which one of the ladies am I supposed to accompany?"

When he was seven I judged it was time for him to get professional guidance and I put him in the hands of Camille-Marie Stamaty.[20]

Saint-Saëns himself told me about the lessons with Stamaty.

He advocated Kalkbrenner's methods of teaching, which centered on developing wrist, hand, and finger control. The arm and body took as little a part in the performance as possible. To achieve this as fast as possible, he had installed a kind of contraption, a stand, next to the keyboard, at keyboard height. During the entire lesson my arms rested on that contraption and it was as though they were paralyzed; I was only able to practice from the wrist down. How I hated that method! But I can't deny that I owe this exercise most of my technical ability: my sturdy fingers, the elasticity of my wrist, and the softness of my touch. Around the same time I also received my

---

20 I knew Stamaty only perfunctorily. He had been one of Friedrich Kalkbrenner's star pupils and he also went to Leipzig to train under Mendelssohn. His remarkable career as a pianist was cut short when he suffered some kind of malady (I think of a rheumatic nature) that hindered his physical abilities. He had to leave the concert hall and turned to composition and mainly to teaching, a field in which he excelled. He died two years ago. He was not yet sixty (J.H.R.).

first lessons in musical composition from Pierre Maleden. [And with a big smile he added:] This was way before I'd gotten a real formation in the class of your brother-in-law, Halévy.

In 1848, I was admitted to François Benoist's organ class at the Conservatoire. I was not yet thirteen. Our teacher, François Benoist, who was fifty-four at the time, was a small man who was always impeccably dressed. He gave three lessons a week, and he could later boast that in over fifty years of teaching—he started in 1819 and retired a few months ago—he never once missed a lesson.

During the class, while the students were playing the organ, he was busy orchestrating on behalf of the opera in order to increase his income. But this did not take his mind in the least from the task at hand: listening with the most intense attention to his pupils play.

He himself was only a mediocre player but he excelled as a teacher. The list of his pupils includes Georges Bizet, Adolphe Adam, Louis Lefébure-Wély, Charles Lecocq, and César Franck. On my first day I was asked to play on the Conservatoire's antique organ. I immediately became the laughingstock of my classmates. As you can well imagine, my pride was hurt to such an extent that I didn't dare show my face in the street. I resolved on the spot that I had to teach all those "old hands" a resounding lesson. I went daily to the Saint-Germain l'Auxerrois Church and started practicing on the organ there for hours. A few months later I was asked again to display my ability to master the instrument; there was no more laughter, nor were there sneers to be heard in the class. Even less so when, at the end of the year, I was awarded second prize for organ playing. In my second year I reaped first prize.

Immediately after that, I was allowed to join Fromental Halévy's much-vaunted composition class. I was fifteen years old.

Halévy had only one major fault: he would make his appearance in the class only when he had no other urgent business to attend to. I owe my extensive knowledge of music literature to his repeated lack of attendance. All those hours that should have been spent in the composition class, I spent in the music library studying the masterpieces of past and present musical geniuses. To sum it up, I could say that if we—my classmates and I—have become musicians, it is in no way thanks to what we learned within this absurd but much-cherished and touching institution, the Conservatoire; we simply were already musicians when entering it. We just needed time to grow and ripen in our trade. Time, practice, persistence, dedication, and love of our art made us what we are today.

I entered the competition for the Prix de Rome twice. My first try was in 1852; the second came twelve years later—as you know, to no avail. But even though this failure has in some ways hindered the advancement of my career—the directors at the opera house refuse to consider me a serious composer—it never broke my spirit nor altered my determination to achieve my artistic goals. I don't need a bunch of engravers, painters, and sculptors to evaluate my potential and tell me who and what I really am.

Now I would like to go back to Charlotte Masson's confidences, this time concerning her nephew as a grownup and responsible man. "God did not bestow physical beauty on our Camille," she said to me.

"Yes," I replied, "but you can't expect *everything* in a single person, unless he is a god himself."

Mme Masson went on:

Still, I think that insolent viola player from the Armingaud Quartet, Édouard Lalo, went too far in comparing his face to a parrot's head. Not everyone is born an Apollo. Still, my grandnephew's face faithfully reflects his superior intelligence and the boundless warmth of his personality. Even if his caustic tongue has sometimes gotten the best of him and sounds offensive to some, he still overflows with a wealth of friendship and true dedication. You should hear about that from your own nephew, Georges Bizet, who is his dear friend and confidant. Or that unfortunate young man walking on crutches, Charles Lecocq, who probably wouldn't have achieved anything without Camille's help.

His detractors say that his playing is cold and dry. Nonsense! He just refuses to strut around. Being one of the great and true artists of the piano, he despises all the mannerisms that go with the virtuoso display. For him restraint, clarity, perspicuity, and fidelity to the texts are the main qualities required of a good performing musician. As for his compositions, I just want to quote what Berlioz said about him: "He knows everything, but the trouble is that he lacks inexperience." What he really meant is that Camille doesn't grope to try to find his way; he doesn't vacillate, and he is not tormented by doubts while composing. Is this a bad thing?

He was once asked about his composition process and he answered very simply that "it comes to me naturally, like an apple tree bearing apples."

In Paris the words "music" and "opera" are synonymous, and have been for many years. Camille writes symphonies and symphonic poems, concertos and sonatas, trios, quartets, quintets...because that is what he is inclined to write. That kind of work brings neither money nor glory to the composer. Rather, it is a kind of service, an offering to music, done with no intention of a reward. Twice he was refused the Prix de Rome, which, in addition to laurels and an enhanced reputation, would have given him a generous grant. So he has to work hard to earn a living. Since he has been nominated to play the organ at La Madeleine, the high mass on Sundays at that church has become a public attraction even more than the shows at the Opéra-Comique. Liszt voiced the opinion that my nephew is the world's greatest organist.

The four years he taught at the École Niedermeyer are noteworthy. The aim of this boarding school on the rue Neuve-Fontaine is to train the next generation of youngsters aiming for a career as professional musicians in the bosom of the Catholic Church in France. They study religious music, with special emphasis on the art of playing the organ. In addition to studying the ancient church traditions of plain song and Gregorian music, they also get sound basic training toward becoming capable choir masters. The composer Louis Niedermeyer opened the school in 1853. He died in '61 and his son, who succeeded him in running the school, asked Camille to take over his father's place as piano teacher. But Camille was not satisfied with mere piano teaching, and he introduced his students to the best of old as well as modern music, from Bach to Schumann, Liszt, and Wagner. And to make sure that his pupils get as broad an education as possible, he would add to his lessons dissertations about trees, flowers, stones, bees, and butterflies, and naturally about the stars and planets in the skies. Gabriel Fauré, André Messager, and Eugène Gigout were his pupils there. All three of them were gifted youngsters who have since been among his closest friends.

By the way, did you know that the main theme of the first movement of Camille's Piano Concerto in G Minor is borrowed from a Tantum ergo written by Fauré as an exercise in his class? Can you imagine a nicer tribute from a teacher to his pupil?

I want to take a moment here to draw a brief sketch of Gabriel Fauré, this pupil and lifelong friend of Saint-Saëns.

At one of the Monday musical parties that Saint-Saëns held at his home years ago, a lady sang Gounod's song "Venise." A young man with a swarthy face played the piano. He looked like an Arab prince and his mane seemed to undulate as if with the gondolas of an invisible lagoon. He played the accompaniment by heart with an enticing beauty, his eyes half closed, his hands caressing the keys with a refined nonchalance. I sat there breathless. Saint-Saëns introduced him to me: "Gabriel Fauré, a student of mine at the École Niedermeyer for religious music." Saint-Saëns's voice, which usually had some sharp and strident overtones, had a strange softness to it. I looked at him and I understood at once: my host loved this youngster.

Pauline Viardot, who knows him very well—for a time he had been engaged to her youngest daughter, Marianne—told me:

> He was like a member of the family and would visit almost daily our apartment on the rue de Douai in winter and our residence in Bougival in summer. We would spend hours playing charades and others witty games. It happened quite often that our quiet and shy Gabriel would beat us all with his shrewd repartees. Even Ivan Turgenev, who was well-known for his sharp and brilliant wit, was no match for young Gabriel when he was in full form. We still quote the lines he invented in a game of verses we played:
>
> > *Je regardais passer l'omnibus sur le pont*
> > *avec cet air pensif que les omnibus ont.*
> > *I watched the local train running on the bridge*
> > *with that thoughtful countenance trains always have.*
>
> The youngest of my three daughters, Marianne, excelled in singing his songs. He always asked her to sing one of his first songs, the one about the flower asking the butterfly not to fly away. As he accompanied her in this song, with the devotion of a lovesick youngster, we all knew who was the flower here, and who the butterfly. My favorite songs at that time were the fragrant "Chant d'automne" set to words by Charles Baudelaire, and naturally the song "Barcarolle," which was dedicated to me. By the way, Gabriel also dedicated one

of his most vibrant works, the 1876 Violin Sonata in A, to my son Paul! It was played at the Paris Exhibition of 1878.

He was nine years old when his father brought him from his sunny town in the Ariège region to the École Niedermeyer. Little Gabriel suddenly found himself in an unfriendly environment; a gray school, with a gray courtyard and gray skies overhead. He was left there with no parents, no siblings, and no friends. His new schoolfellows treated him poorly and he was unable to defend himself. He very often went hungry and was always cold. He learned rather quickly that music can feed you and keep you warm. As a pupil he was nothing—last in the class in all subjects—but in music he bloomed and excelled. He revered Niedermeyer, the headmaster who taught piano and basic composition. When Niedermeyer died in early '61, Saint-Saëns was asked to take his place, and though his official role was piano teacher, he introduced his pupils to such a broad range of extra-musical subjects that I am at a loss to enumerate them all.

The École Niedermeyer was established for the education of musicians in the service of the church, and I must point out that the musical knowledge imparted to the students there far exceeded that taught at the Conservatoire. While Fauré was introduced to Palestrina and Orlando di Lasso, to Frescobaldi, Sweelinck, and Buxtehude, the organ students at the Conservatoire were not yet familiar with the works of Johann Sebastian Bach. As Fauré was already swimming freely in the sea of Beethoven's and Schumann's works, at the Conservatoire they played fantasies by Kalkbrenner and variations by Hertz! There was only one rehearsal room at 10, rue Neuve-Fontaine, and fifteen pianos were crowded into it. Fifteen pupils played at the same time, but naturally not together, as each of them had his own personal agenda! What a cacophony, and what an exceptional way to gain a unique ability to concentrate and acquire the knack of detaching oneself from one's environment.

Fauré once told me about that unforgettable experience he shared with his friend Eugène Gigout. They had saved penny by penny (actually centime by centime) to buy tickets to the topmost gallery at the Opéra to watch Gounod's Faust. After the performance they walked back to their boarding school, in the cold and wet winter night. When they got there the doors of the school were already locked. They walked until daybreak through the streets, chilled to the bone, but intoxicated by the music they had just heard and that was still alive and resounding in their memories. At first light they found shelter in a church that had opened its gates at dawn.

Fauré was twenty when he graduated from Niedermeyer with highest honors in 1865. All the tools a professional musician needs were at his fingertips; he was an accomplished organist, a fine pianist, and had a broad knowledge of musical literature, both that of the past as well as our contemporary music. He was free to choose his way according to his personal inclinations. He chose to become a composer. No, that is not accurate: he was born to be a composer, thus he really had no choice! And in that field his humble and modest personality brought him to tackle more intimate forms in which to mold his creations: the art song, the piano piece, and the chamber music! By shunning more ambitious works, and especially the Opéra, he doomed himself to forego all hopes of public recognition, success, fame, and financial independent. To tell the truth, he really had no option; he knew only one way: his own!

His first professional engagement was at the Saint-Sauveur Church in Rennes. He did not like it there and the priest in charge of that church had doubts about the sincerity of his religious convictions. On Sundays when monsieur le curé was giving his weekly sermon, Fauré slipped away for a smoke. One Sunday morning in early 1870, after having spent the whole night at a ball, he presented himself for duty still wearing his evening dress. He was asked on the spot to hand in his resignation. He was very happy to return to Paris, and almost immediately was engaged as assistant organist at Notre-Dame de Clignancourt. His career there was cut short by the outbreak of the war. He volunteered for military service and took part in three battles: Le Bourget, Champigny, and Créteil.

He got engaged to my daughter Marianne in '77 (after four years of procrastination). I have tried to persuade him again and again to turn his talents toward opera, mainly because I knew that my daughter needed the glamour of superficial success in order to strengthen her feelings toward him. She never returned the love he craved and that he was worthy of. When she realized that there was no chance for a breakthrough, she broke off the engagement. He suffered terribly and it showed. It took him ten years to tell me, "In the end, all turned out for the best. I'm sure that if the marriage with Marianne had gone through, she would sooner or later have diverted me from my way." By then he was married for four years to Marie, daughter of the sculptor Emmanuel Frémiet.

I have lived in Versailles since '92 and I am avoiding trips to Paris as much as possible, especially those that necessitate staying the night. But when Fauré forwarded an invitation to attend the playing of his requiem, on January 21, 1893, I was so happy that even the thought of the unpleasant train ride could not frighten me. In January 1888 I was at La Madeleine when Fauré conducted the first performance of his requiem, and I was bewitched by the beauty of that composition. In his invitation for this "second" performance, Fauré added a few words explaining that this would be a premiere because he had made some radical changes to the work and had expanded it by adding music that had not been included in the first version. I must confess that I feared that these changes might somehow tarnish the beauty of the pearl he presented us in 1888. But I should have known better. As I still remembered the work quite well, this was a most welcome reunion, and the changes only enhanced my pleasure. La Madeleine was overcrowded, but no one seemed to complain. Fauré's conducting was as assured as that of a seasoned

professional. To say that it was a success would be an understate-
ment. After the performance, Fauré told me:

> Everything I have managed to retain by way of religious
> illusion I put into my requiem. It is dominated by a very
> human feeling of faith in eternal rest. I fully acknowledge
> the fact that I have tried to avoid what people normally
> think is appropriate for funeral music; after all those years
> of playing the organ at burials, I can say without being
> pretentious that I know all of it by heart. I wanted to write
> something different.

> In 1885 after many years I went back to Pamiers, the sunny
> little town at the foot of the Pyreneans where I was born, to
> attend the burial of my father. During the funeral procession
> I had to support my mother, who was very weak, and she
> said to me, "He will like resting here; there is so much sun!"
> Somehow I knew that it would only be a matter of months
> until she joined him. When I returned to Paris I decided to
> start composing this requiem. The open grave of my father
> and my mother's happy and radiant face were before my
> eyes the whole time. To be quite honest, I must say that I
> don't believe in hell or in Judgment Day. Here on earth is
> where hell is, and Judgment Day is with us every day. And if
> there is expiation, it is required from us daily, right here on
> earth. That is one of the reasons that there is no Dies Irae in
> my requiem.

> If I hope and look for a long life it is not because I am afraid
> to die; it's because I know there is still so much for me to
> achieve, that I still need years in order to learn to transform
> my ideas into musical works. I aspire to the ultimate
> simplicity, to the utter saving of means, to the rejection of
> everything that is not an integral part of the basic texture of

the living organism. I want to achieve purity of expression, refined spirituality. I so passionately crave to be granted that purity that I am willing, this very moment, to get on my knees before God, even though I don't know whether He exists, and ask for His blessing. And if on my last day on earth I am able to say that I have succeeded in advancing the refinement of French music one inch further, then I can go with joy, in peace, and with a clear conscience.

May 1880

Like all French composers, Saint-Saëns wanted to have a work of his staged in one of the opera houses of Paris. But as he so justly pointed out, his failure to win the Prix de Rome very much stood in his way. That is why he tried to have Princess Mathilde, the niece of Napoleon III and a great patron of the arts, intercede in his favor with the management of those houses. He played the piano quite regularly in her salon. She said to him, "Young man, you play the organ at La Madeleine and the piano in my salon. What more do you want?"

He had to look elsewhere for help and he turned to Auber, who interceded with Carvalho, the director of the Théâtre Lyrique, to supply him with a libretto. That was in 1864. Saint-Saëns was very much surprised to get a positive response. But the reason was quite simple: Carvalho had a libretto that had been sitting in his lap for quite a long time, and he had been unable to get any composer interested in it. That was *Le timbre d'argent* (The Silvery Sound), a libretto by Jules Barbier and Michel Carré. The action of this opera was so ludicrous, so incredibly absurd, that no one would touch it. Almost the same thing had happened to Bizet the year before with *Les pêcheurs de perles*.

Saint-Saëns told me the whole story.

I could not afford to be choosy, so I accepted the task, even with a kind of gratitude. I composed the opera in two months and had to wait three years until Carvalho found the time to listen to it, and then another ten years for the work to be staged. That was in February '77 at the Théâtre Lyrique, five years after my second opera La princesse jaune [The Yellow Princess] was performed at the Opéra-Comique.

That opera at first wandered between four opera houses; it changed its appearance according to the whims of different directors; it survived two bankruptcies and two wars, a minor war between the librettists Barbier and Carré and the much bigger and more serious war between France and Prussia.

Shortly after completing Le timbre d'argent I was intrigued by the idea of writing an oratorio in the tradition of Handel and Mendelssohn on a biblical subject. I chose the story of the rise and fall of Samson as told in Judges. I was no doubt influenced by the libretto Voltaire had written for Rameau 150 years ago. I asked Ferdinand Lemaire, a gifted young man who just married a distant relative of mine, to work with me in preparing the text for that oratorio. "An oratorio?" he said. "No, let's make it an opera!"

So I outlined my plan for the opera and Lemaire put it into verse. The first act would show the Israelites enslaved by the Philistines and Samson leading an uprising and defeating the oppressor. At the end of that act, Delilah starts her attempt to seduce Samson. The second act is the center of the action and that is why I started working on it before composing the first act: Delilah succeeds in rekindling Samson's lust for her and through cunning, deceit, and trickery she extirpates from him the secret of his strength. In the third act the imprisoned Samson, blinded and his head completely shaved, asks God for forgiveness. The Philistines celebrate their victory in an untamed bacchanalia in the temple of their god Dagon. They bring in the shackled Samson and both the high priest and Delilah mock him. Samson prays to God to be given, if only just for a moment, his strength back. Standing between two pillars he pulls them down and the temple collapses, burying all present, Samson as well as the Philistines.

I wrote the role of Delilah for our great mutual friend Pauline Viardot, and the opera is dedicated to her. After completing most of act 2 I had a private performance of it in my home in 1870. The reaction to it was so cold that I stopped working on the opera altogether. Only two years later, when I met Liszt in Weimar, he convinced me to complete it and promised to have it staged in Weimar. So I worked on it sporadically until '75. That is when I had act 1 performed at the Théâtre du Châtelet. This received the cold shoulder too. Shortly after that Pauline organized a performance, this time of act 2. She sang Delilah, Henri Regnault sang Samson, and Bussine was the high priest of Dagon. I played the piano. She had hoped to convince Halanzier to stage to work at the Académie. But no opera director showed any interest in Samson et Dalila. True to his promise, Liszt had his successor in Weimar, Eduard Lassen, stage the work, translated into German, in December 1877. Pauline was fifty-six and though I begged her to take the role, she declined, saying that she was too old to play the role of a young seductress. A German lady, Auguste von Müller, sang Delilah and the performance was a resounding success. In my unbiased opinion, it is the best work my pen has produced to this day. But as to when it will be performed here in France, "O König, das kann ich dir nicht sagen," as Tristan tells King Marke.

During the war I served in the National Guard together with our departed friend, Georges Bizet. During the Reign of Terror of the Paris Commune he retired to his summer residence in Le Vésinet and I started on the first of my many trips to London. In that city I found a much friendlier atmosphere and a more positive understanding for serious music than in my native town.

In 1871, in the aftermath of the downfall of the Second Empire, the French humiliation, and the bloodbath of the Paris Commune, Saint-Saëns, together with Romain Bussine and Henri Duparc, founded the Société nationale de musique. Bussine is a poet, a professional singer, and a teacher at the Conservatoire. He sang the role of the high priest with Pauline Viardot when she organized the private hearing of act 2 of *Samson et Dalila* in Croissy. Duparc, who was twenty-three years old at the time, is a promising young composer. The motto of this organization was *"Ars gallica"* and its aim was to promote French instrumental music. Amongst supporters of this initiative were Franck, Chausson, Fauré, Massenet, Guiraud, and many others. They had no concert hall in which to perform, no funds, and no orchestra. But the Société nationale de musique perpetrated a revolution in the habits of Parisian concertgoers and enhanced the prestige of French composers.

Saint-Saëns explained:

When my symphonic poem Le rouet d'Omphale, a work inspired by my favorite poet Victor Hugo, was played at one of the concerts of the Société nationale de musique, the old dispute about the nature of—and justification for—programmatic music flared up again. I voiced my unshakable belief that this polemic was utterly pointless: if the music is good, the program won't hurt it. If it's mediocre, the program will not redeem it. This is also the spirit in which I present for posterity's judgment my three other symphonic poems: Phaëton, The Youth of Hercules, and the Danse Macabre. This last work, which is based on a song I had composed a few years earlier based on a poem by Henri Cazalis, was greeted with such an avalanche of shrieking and hissing at its premiere in 1874 that my mother, who was in the audience, was aghast and fainted in her seat.

July 1886

After fifteen years at the helm of the Société nationale de musique, after having invested so much talent, know-how, and dedication to making it the central hub of the musical life of Paris, both Bussine and Saint-Saëns had been compelled to tender their resignations. At the outset, the aim of the organization had been to counter the preference given to vocal, and especially operatic, works over instrumental music in France. The other cornerstones of the Société nationale de musique were its firm stand in favoring French music and to an even greater degree the promotion of works by young and unknown French composers. This prejudiced approach was no doubt a reaction to the shame and national resentment felt in France after the defeat and humiliation of 1870. It also reflects one of the facets of the cultural struggle between the French and German basic ways of thinking. As early as the seventies, some non-French works found their way into programs of the Société nationale de musique, and this tendency had started to take on worrisome proportions. Saint-Saëns, who from the outset had been against this trend and insisted on the purity and respect of the original charter, did everything in his power to counter this trend. But he and his ally Bussine were no match for the scheming new secretary, Vincent d'Indy, who was backed by the influential crowd of César Franck's followers.

The election of Saint-Saëns to the Institut de France in '81 was a long-expected event and in some ways the redress of an injustice. Being elected to this venerable institution carries unequalled prestige and respect. During the previous vacancy, in '78, everyone expected Saint-Saëns to be chosen to fill the empty place, but Massenet was elected as a result of some sleight-of-hand maneuver by Ambroise Thomas, Massenet's mentor. Massenet was thirty-six, seven years Saint-Saëns's junior, and the youngest member ever to be elected to the Académie.

July 1890

Because it had such an impact on his creative career, I can't avoid touching on a more intimate subject: Saint-Saëns's private life. There have always been rumors circulating about him, mainly on two subjects: his allegedly Jewish origins and his sexual affinities.

He has always denied being of Jewish descent, pointing out that with a name like Saint-Saëns no one could seriously consider truth behind it. But in my opinion, this is no proof at all. There is a small town in Normandy called Saint-Saëns, and it is a well-known fact that when Napoleon urged all Jews to change their patronymic, many of them chose the name of the locality where they lived as their new surname. I was also told that when her husband died and young Camille was three months old, Clémence Saint-Saëns reverted to her maiden name. But all this actually proves nothing. And when someone points out that one of Saint-Saëns's uncles is a priest I can only bring up the example of Alphonse and Théodore Ratisbonne. They are the sons of Auguste Ratisbonne, who was president of the Consistoire of Alsace, and after converting to Catholicism they are today among the most militant Catholic missionaries. (By the way, Ratisbonne is also the name of a town; it is the French name for the city of Regensburg in Bavaria.) D'Indy put it very bluntly: "His being a Saint makes no sense—he is Jewish."

The second rumor seems to suggest that he is more attracted to people of his own gender than to members of the gentler sex. Nonetheless, there are a few things that tend to point the other way, such as his long and unsuccessful courtship of Augusta Holmès, that blonde-haired beauty who sang Delilah in the very first hearing of act 2 at Saint-Saëns's home in 1872.

On top of being a first-class mezzo-soprano, Holmès is an excellent pianist and a budding composer. I heard Pasdeloup conducting her *Les Argonautes* at the Concerts populaires in April '81. Holmès's father was Irish and her mother English, but she was born in Paris in 1847. Some say that her biological father was the poet Alfred de Vigny (who in any case was her godfather) and others spread the rumor that they were lovers. Elite Parisian painters, writers, and musicians crowded her salon on the rue Mansard and could not get enough of her singing Gluck's arias and Schumann's songs. Saint-Saëns also contributed more than a few songs to her repertoire, and during those evenings in her salon when she sang them, Saint-Saëns would accompany her on the piano with a very atypically loose and erupting performance. He dedicated his symphonic poem *Le rouet d'Omphale* to her. He has also written two sonnets for her: in the first, she is compared to Astarte, and in the second to Sappho. He proposed to her more than once but was always gently but firmly rejected. Still, she agreed to join him on his trip to Munich for the premiere of Wagner's *Das Rheingold* in September '69. Catulle Mendès (the young Jewish poet of the so-called Parnassus group) and his beautiful wife Judith (Théophile Gautier's daughter) also came along. This is where the well-known love affair between Wagner and Judith started. Mendès found solace in Holmès's arms, and, though they never married, they have lived as a stable couple since then. Saint-Saëns was left with the Rhine maidens and the goddesses from Valhalla. That certainly did not add to Saint-Saëns's wholehearted skepticism concerning bliss in married life.

It is hard to understand what induced him, on the spur of the moment, to get married in 1875 to Marie Laure Truffot, the young sister of one of his pupils. I really don't understand what got into him. He may have thought that his social standing compelled him to settle down, start a family, and become a respected citizen like everyone else. Marie was nineteen and he was nearing forty. It was a marriage with no courtship and no honeymoon. Immediately after the wedding the newlyweds settled in the old apartment on the rue du Faubourg Saint-Honoré. Charlotte Masson, Saint-Saëns's mother's aunt, had been dead for a few years. She had always been a much nicer and more generous person than her niece Clémence, who did not like her daughter-in-law.

I met Marie a few months ago, after a performance of Saint-Saëns's opera *Ascanio* at the Palais Garnier. She spoke to me very frankly and her grief was deep and sincere.

> His behavior was very difficult and gruff, but nevertheless he also had some good traits. Where music was concerned we were always in complete agreement. He would play for me his new compositions and ask my opinion. He offered to dedicate the symphonic poem La jeunesse d'Hercule, which he was composing at that time, to me. But as I was not really enthusiastic about that specific work, I asked him to instead dedicate to me the oratorio Le déluge. But he didn't.

> He loved our two little sons, André and Jean-François, with boundless tenderness, but he was too busy, and was also probably unfit, to take any part in their upbringing. Our home on the rue du Faubourg Saint-Honoré was getting too small for the five of us—Clémence, his mother, lived with us and ruled the household like a sergeant

major—so we moved to a larger apartment on the rue Monsieur le Prince on the Left Bank. Now Camille could have more privacy and the quiet he needed for his work. Our apartment was on the fourth floor of a high but narrow building. Its windows faced the gray, bare walls of the medical school.

It was there, on May 28, 1878, that the disaster that ruined our life struck. Camille had just finished composing his requiem, a work for tenor, chorus and orchestra, which took him only eight days to compose in a frenzy of inspiration. It was three o'clock in the afternoon and I was about to take the children for a walk in the park. I went to my room to make myself up. My mother-in-law was dozing in the dining room. The maidservant had opened the window in the small washhouse next to the kitchen to ventilate the room and let the steam out. No one saw that two-year-old André had climbed onto the window sill. He probably heard some voices from the apartment below ours; little friends of his lived there. When we heard the horrified screams of passersby in the street below, it was already too late.

Camille came home one hour later. The neighbors told him what had happened; he rushed home and threw himself on his little son's lifeless body in a fit of pain and despair. Later he blamed me for what he said was criminal negligence. He never forgave me.

Six weeks later our little baby, Jean-François, came down with scarlet fever and the doctors were unable to save him. We buried him next to his brother in the Montmartre Cemetery.

Sometime after the death of our children, we went to a health resort in the south. We were there for two days when suddenly my husband disappeared. The staff from our hotel organized a search in the region, but to no avail.

I waited for him for three days, lonely and dejected. Duparc, who was staying at the same hotel, brought me back to Paris. When I got home, my mother-in-law told me that Camille wanted me to leave without delay. I packed my belongings and went back to live with my parents. I haven't seen my husband since then.

Saint-Saëns's mother died two years ago, in 1888. He has left Paris, I think permanently, as he has sold the apartment. He lives now in the Canary Islands, and I hear that he travels a lot, mostly in North Africa. He comes to Paris from time to time, but avoids getting in touch with friends and acquaintances from old.

Paris, November 13, 1892

Dear old friend,

It has been quite some time since we last met; I know, only I am to blame.

Now I am in Paris for a few weeks on the blessed occasion (I'm sure you've heard) of the staging of Samson et Dalila at the Opéra. It took them fifteen years. And that only after it got such an enthusiastic welcome two years ago in Rouen and at the Théâtre Eden here in Paris.

I visited our mutual friend Pauline in Bougival yesterday. As you may know, this opera was dedicated to her, and I had (in vain, I am sorry to say) hoped she would sing the leading role at the premiere in Weimar. She will be seventy next year. And she told me that you have recently celebrated your eightieth birthday! Congratulations, young man!

I have invited her to the opening night, on November 23, and she insisted that you escort her there. So, Hippolyte, for old times' sake, would you be so kind...?

Très amicalement,

Camille Saint-Saëns

15

A STAR-STUDDED FIRMAMENT

October 28, 1883

Eight and a half years have passed since the press and the Parisian public rejected *Carmen*. Eight years have elapsed since it started on its way to worldwide recognition with its staging in Vienna, in October '75, four months too late for Bizet to reap the fruits of his life's labor.

Last night *Carmen* came home to Paris; Célestine Galli-Marié has brought her back in an unforgettable performance, and was called again and again to take bow after bow by an ecstatic crowd shouting, "Bravo! Bravo!" and stamping their feet in frenzy. I don't remember a similar ovation at the Salle Favart.

Yesterday in the early afternoon, on the very day of the revival of *Carmen* at the Opéra-Comique, I was invited to a small party, actually a friendly gathering, at Pauline Viardot's home in Bougival. Normally whenever she entertains, the elite of the Parisian intellectual leadership crowds the place. But Pauline Viardot is still mourning the death, here in Bougival just over a month ago, of her lifelong friend and lover, Ivan Turgenev. Only four guests were asked to this intimate afternoon gathering, a commemoration more than a party: Pauline's seventy-eight-year-old brother, Manuel Garcia, was there; Célestine Galli-Marié, looking forward to breathing new life into the imminent reopening of *Carmen,* was the guest of honor; Ernest Legouvé, the poet and dramatist who is recognized as the spearhead of the fight for women's rights; and me, probably because I am the uncle of Bizet's widow, but perhaps also in view of the friendly relations Pauline and I have entertained all those years.

I said "commemoration" because this meeting was meant as a gesture of respectful admiration to the memory of Pauline and Manuel's sister, Maria Garcia-Malibran, to pay tribute to the memory of Turgenev, and, last but not least, to send Galli-Marié to the stage that night with our warmest blessings.

This meeting having taken place only yesterday, it is still fresh in my memory and I think I can give almost an exact rendering of it; anyhow, it is as near the real thing as can be. The five of us sat in Pauline's spacious drawing-room, next to the large veranda overlooking the gentle waters of the Seine flowing at our feet, sipping the excellent Burgundy wine Pauline had chosen from her cellar for the occasion.

Garcia started by reading all twenty-seven stanzas of the poem Musset wrote in memory of Maria Malibran.

IX

N'était-ce pas hier, fille joyeuse et folle,
Que ta verve railleuse animait Corilla,
Et que tu nous lançais avec la Rosina

La roulade amoureuse et l'œillade espagnole?
Ces pleurs sur tes bras nus, quand tu chantais le Saule,
N'était-ce pas hier, pâle Desdemona?

Through some unexplained magic, his rich and caressing baritone had retrieved all the vitality of his youth; his face was transformed and his eyes were shining. Almost fifty years have elapsed since that fateful day when Maria Malibran fell from her galloping horse in Manchester. Outwardly she seemed to have escaped without a scratch and she refused to see a doctor. But only a trained physician could have detected, and maybe even healed, the internal damage. She continued to perform in London where she had been living for the previous two years. A few months later, she was dead. The voice that had enthralled countless audiences, this gift of heaven, was silenced for eternity.

"It was our father who forced her by bitter and stubborn training to expand her natural contralto range," Pauline said, "and transformed it into the vibrant soprano voice that so perfectly matched her personality. Yes, our father was the teacher of the three of us—a great teacher, an outstanding tenor and an accomplished actor who, when on the stage, swept up all around him in a whirlpool of frenzied action. I was only eleven when he died. That was fifty-one years ago but I still remember vividly the singing lessons I took from the age of five. I even remember overhearing from the next room in our house some stormy exchanges between Maria and him whenever he gave *her* lessons. I think that almost every such session was a violent clash of wills between those two indomitable personalities."

"Yes, he was a tyrant. But he got results," Garcia added.

"I have a personal recollection on this topic," Legouvé said. "It must have been in the late twenties. I was walking with Berlioz—who was still a young medical student, but knew more about opera than about anatomy—next to the Garcia's house, when suddenly we heard bloodcurdling screams emanating from one of the windows. I stopped in my tracks and took Berlioz's arm. 'Should we get help?' I asked. 'It's nothing,' replied Berlioz. 'It's just Garcia hammering trills into his daughter's vocal cords.'"

Garcia concurred, "His determination to drive Maria to the very limits of endurance on her way to achieve perfection in the art of singing and acting could no doubt be dubbed cruelty in many enlightened circles. But I must point out with some amount of pride that his methods were pretty effective. On the night they first sang Desdemona and Otello in Rossini's opera, Maria suddenly realized that the knife Father aimed at her chest was the sharp-edged, curved dagger he had bought just a few days before from a Turkish merchant. Like hunted prey she escaped to the far side of the stage and, almost crazed with fear, she shrieked in our native Spanish, '*Papa, Papa, per l'amor de Dios*, don't kill me!' And as the deadly weapon came closer without wavering, with raging despair she threw herself at him and savagely bit his hand. Now it was Father's turn to let out a cry and retreat. The unsuspecting audience was stunned by the realistic acting they had just witnessed and broke out in an avalanche of applause."

"I cannot but compliment her on her courageous action," Galli-Marié said. "If I had reacted the same way last year when I sang *Carmen* in Genoa, I would not have this small scar on my left cheek." Her hand touched a pale, tiny, barely perceptible scar on her face. "That idiotic tenor they gave me as Don José was so clumsy that I would be wary of letting him go down a flight of stairs behind me, for fear he would trip over his own feet and push me down. Since that memorable evening they have used a knife with a dull blade that retracts into the handle at the slightest pressure. But back to your family—I was told that your father organized you all into some kind of Garcia Opera Company..."

"That was for our American tour in 1826," Garcia explained. "I was twenty-one, Maria was eighteen, and you, Pauline, you were five years old, if I am not mistaken. The central work of our repertoire on the tour was Rossini's *Il barbiere di Seviglia*—the composer wrote Lindoro's role especially for my father. Our family is of genuine Sevillian stock, in spite of the fact that my sisters were born in Paris, so it is only natural that we should feel that this opera is 'our' opera."

"And since Carmen is also a Sevillian, I believe I am entitled to consider myself a member of the family," Galli-Marié said.

"And so is Fidelio," Legouvé added. "Jean Nicolas Bouilly, who wrote the play on which the libretto is based, was my tutor. In addition, I'm known as the flag bearer for women's rights, so I am certainly related to Beethoven's Leonora, and I also demand admission into this noble Sevillian clan."

"To the best of my knowledge," Garcia continued, "ours was the first American production of *The Barber of Seville*. Father was Lindoro-Almaviva, Maria was Rosina, Mother sang Bertha's role, and I was honored to be Figaro."

"I was too young to join this brilliant team," Pauline lamented.

"Lorenzo da Ponte came to one of our performances," her brother added.

"The famous da Ponte?" I exclaimed. "The one who wrote the librettos for *Cosi fan tutti*, *Le nozze di Figaro*, and *Don Giovanni* for Mozart? What the devil was he doing in America?"

Garcia answered, "I heard he had to flee Vienna as a consequence of some scandalous rumors he was linked to. As I understood from what he told our parents, his situation was quite precarious and he made a living teaching Italian. In his honor, Father decided to stage a performance of *Don Giovanni* that had not been included on our original schedule. This was an excellent idea, as this brought us one of our major successes of the tour."

Pauline added, "I was only five years old then, but I remember Father's uncontrolled fit of rage when Maria secretly married that scoundrel Malibran and left our family troupe. Naturally I was unable to grasp what all the fuss was about, but I clearly remember Father's loud shouts that lasted for what seemed to me days without end."

"The pressure on Maria seems to have been too heavy," Garcia elaborated. "She had to break away. And we had no choice but to continue our tour without her. At least she was spared that frightening incident in Mexico when, on our way to Vera Cruz, a gang of brigands attacked us and robbed us of all our earnings from the previous two years: £6,000 in gold coins. We came back to Paris with nothing but the clothes on our backs. The 'Mexican adventure' of the Garcia family was the talk of all of Paris, and no one could imagine then that a few decades hence all of France would be thrown into a 'Mexican adventure' far more serious than the one we had just experienced."

"That one should have been called the *Max*ican," I suggested.[21]

"One year later Maria joined us in Paris," Pauline continued. "Her husband, a banker, had gone bankrupt and proved to be a real villain— he had tried to exploit her in the most shameless manner."

"Why didn't Maria revert to her maiden name?" Galli-Marié inquired. "It is unfit that such a man's name should be remembered for all time in the annals of music, let alone thanks to the woman he treated so badly."

---

21 Reference to the wretched tragicomedy that ended with the retreat of the French armed forces from Mexico and the execution of the French protégé "Emperor" Maximilian in 1867.

Garcia explained, "The name was an emblem, a symbol for her; it was a sign of her independence. From the day of her marriage she felt that she had broken away from the ties that impeded her artistic freedom. She had matured from the phase of a student to that of a full-fledged artist. This experience, as nasty and painful as it was, was real life, not acting on the stage or some kind of make believe. It added a tremendous measure of depth and insight to whatever she was to undertake for the rest of her short life."

"But luckily," Pauline added, "in the end she found happiness with the man she had been waiting for, the great violinist Charles de Bériot."

"When he finally gave up his unsuccessful attempts to court Henriette Sontag," Galli-Marié quipped.

Pauline asked with surprise, "Where did you get that information, little chick? You were not even born at the time."

"I've got a real knack for gossip," Galli-Marié replied with a smile.

Pauline laughed.

"She had to wait six years to get a divorce from Malibran so she could marry Bériot and legalize the status of their son," Garcia said.

"I was a guest at their wedding," Legouvé reminisced. "Sigismond Thalberg, who was considered to be one of the leading piano virtuosos at the time, was also present. Maria asked him to play, and with his characteristic gallantry he replied, 'After you, madame.' Marie said that after all the day's ordeals she was too tired and that she was 'not in voice,' but when Thalberg insisted she gave in. I had no idea that Maria could sing so badly. But Thalberg put everything in its right place and played with his usual brio. She warmed up and suddenly sang as though she had been transformed. The demon of music took hold of her. When he finished playing she jumped up and said, 'And now—it's my turn!' As if struck by a magic wand, her weariness disappeared and she sang divinely. At this point Thalberg, very much unlike his usual self, got caught up in the game. When she finished singing, he called, 'And now—me!' And so they went on taking turns, with mounting inspiration, until the wee hours of the morning."

"What a very characteristic story this is," Garcia smiled. "I can still see her now, her face flushed with the excitement of the competition. Competition was a lifeline for her; it lifted her to greatness."

"I owe her so much that I can hardly describe it," Legouvé said. "To me, music was just a homely art entirely based on niceties and esprit—until I saw her on stage. Thereafter music was transformed into the most tempestuous expression of pure poetics. It became for me an art capable of expressing all the hues of love and suffering to their fullest capacity, while at the same time sharing to some extent those feelings with the listener. Maria opened a magical new world for me."

Galli-Marié added, "People complained that she did not always respect the rules of *bon gout*, that she was often taken to exaggeration in her acting and leaned on cheap theatrics."

"I've heard those accusations firsthand," I agreed. "They originated with my friend, the painter Delacroix. But I think he was mistaken in his judgment; as far as she was concerned, artificial effects did not exist. She put her soul into every character she brought to the stage."

"Anyhow, Delacroix is voicing the opinion of a tiny minority," Garcia went on. "In the opposite corner stand a host of fervent admirers: Chopin, Mendelssohn, Liszt, Rossini, Donizetti, Bellini, and Moscheles."

Legouvé added, "Mendelssohn was entirely captivated by her when he met her in London in 1830. He always fell prey to feminine charm combined with musical capacity on the highest level. Later he fell in love with Jenny Lind."

"Jenny Lind?" Galli-Marié asked. "Feminine charm, you said?"

"In that particular field, my dear," Garcia teased, "it would be better for you to rely on a man's judgment. I knew the Swedish Nightingale pretty well. She came to Paris for the sole purpose of taking lessons from me. She might not have been beautiful in the traditional sense of the word, and she was not endowed with a convivial character either, but attractive she was, to the highest degree."

"As far as I am concerned," I said, "the most attractive among the coloratura nightingales was Henriette Sontag. She had a mane of blonde hair framing the face of a maiden—shining blue eyes like limpid springs, and a tiny smiling mouth that produced sounds as clear as crystal bells and as sweet as trilling birds."

"I'm sure that an impressive number of prima donnas gave a big sigh of relief when she decided to leave the stage at the age of twenty-four," Legouvé agreed, "so that she wouldn't jeopardize the diplomatic career of the Italian Count Rossi, whom she had secretly married."

Pauline added, "My sister had only kind words for her. 'How can anyone sing so beautifully?' she would say. I'm sure she did not feel threatened by her—not on a professional level, that is. They were so different, like fire and crystal."

"What was there to be afraid of considering the crowd of admirers she had?" Garcia asked. "When Bellini heard Maria singing, '*Ah! Non credea mirarti,*' in the last act of his opera *La sonnambula*, he completely forgot himself. It was as if she had said, 'For someone who could create such music, for him I will go through water and fire.' They became friends. When she was told that he had died, on September 23, 1835, at the age of thirty-four, she froze for a moment; then, waving her hand across her forehead as if to chase away some malignant cloud, she muttered, 'I know that very soon, I will follow him.' And exactly one year later, on September 23, 1836, as a result of that fatal fall, she followed him as she had predicted. She was twenty-eight."

"There were other great singers besides my sister," Pauline admitted, "but none of them was able to fill the void she left behind. Musset said in the last stanza of the poem he wrote in memory of her:

XXVII

Meurs donc! ta mort est douce, et ta tâche est remplie.
Ce que l'homme ici-bas appelle le génie,
C'est le besoin d'aimer; hors de là tout est vain.
Et, puisque tôt ou tard l'amour humain s'oublie,
Il est d'une grande âme et d'un heureux destin
D'expirer comme toi pour un amour divin!"

Galli-Marié interjected, "But my dear Madame Viardot, if I may, let me tell you how mistaken you are when you say that there was no one there to fill the void Mme Malibran left. Two years after her death, a fourteen-year-old child appeared on the stage and struck the world in awe. Her name was Pauline Garcia, the little sister of the deceased. You, my dear Pauline, are Maria's successor, you and no one else!"

"Compared to her I was the ugly little duckling…"

"The little duckling that transformed into a magnificent white swan in due time," I added. "I still remember Musset writing in the *Revue des deux Mondes,* 'With the very first sounds, her sister's admirers were stunned. This was the same timbre, pleasant and powerful, the very same rugged and sweet Spanish magic, tasting like fruit ripened in the wilderness. And not only was the great voice of Maria Malibran given back to us thanks to this child, but also her very soul. She knows the secret of the great masters; she will never express something that she has not previously experienced in the depth of the abyss.'"

"You uncover forgotten treasures, my dear friend," Pauline said. "It is possible that the burden of the years has not altered my feelings, but my ability to express them—the instrument that brought them to life, my voice—alas, it is gone. Not even a memory; it is a ruin."

"That is because you never bothered to spare your strength," explained Galli-Marié. "You gave precedence to your mission over wisdom. You harnessed your voice in the service of music—old and new, deep or shallow, poetic and dramatic—until you brought it down in shambles. But at least there is some consolation: when you left the stage, the Conservatoire was blessed with a new and peerless teacher, the best it's ever had."

Garcia added, "Naturally, there is nothing tangible in this theory about continuation, about following in the footsteps of a former generation. It is nice to talk about it and to fantasize a little bit on the subject, but the truth is that Maria was born for the operas of Rossini, Donizetti, and Bellini, while you, Pauline, your composers were Halévy and Meyerbeer. When you appeared in the role of Fidès in *Le prophète* you created a new type of prima donna, the star in the mezzo-soprano range. And you brought another novelty with you: the type of singer who is an artist first and a virtuoso second."

"If I may add, you are not only a master of singing but an artist at the piano, as a composer, in painting, and in literature," I said.

"Enough, Hippolyte. All those compliments embarrass me and make me blush," Pauline said.

A steward came in and interrupted our conversation; he whispered something in Pauline's ear. She said that the refreshments were served in the next room. We entered the drawing room where we were greeted by a big table overflowing with the best of French and Viennese pastries. In the middle of the table was a big bowl full of fresh fruit, and in the corner of the room there was a smaller table with an assortment of drinks.

We were all enjoying ourselves tremendously as our palates appreciated the delicacies of Pauline's lavish entertainment. But after a while I suddenly realized that Galli-Marié was content with sipping her lemonade without touching the succulent food. I went to ask her why, and she explained that she never ate anything before a performance because her voice and her general well-being were at their best on an empty stomach.

When we went back to the veranda we picked up the conversation where we had left it. We reviewed the great stars who had shaped the cultural landscape of the first half of our century. Some of them, like Nourrit, for instance, died before Célestine Galli-Marié was even born. And some of them are still alive today. But Galli-Marié was too young to have heard most of them and her curiosity knew no bounds; she wanted to hear all the gossip she could possibly glean from us. In her eyes we represented the heart of the "Old Guard."

Garcia told about that many-sided, talented man, Adolphe Nourrit, who had been a great actor, a first-class painter, a gifted writer, and above all a tenor with one of the most beautiful and vibrant voices in the history of French opera. Nourrit had been a pupil of the elder Manuel Garcia, the father of Pauline Viardot and Manuel Garcia who were sitting with us on this this beautiful afternoon. Meyerbeer valued his talent as a librettist more than that of Scribe. Halévy is indebted to him for the idea and for the text of the most celebrated aria he ever wrote, Eléazar's aria "Rachel, quand du Seigneur" from *La juive*. He also wrote the scenario for Marie Taglione's greatest success, the ballet for which she will always be remembered: *La Sylphide*. With that he introduced poetry into the world of operatic ballet. His competence can be judged by the number of roles that composers wrote especially for him, including Néoclès in *Le siège de Corinthe*, Aménophis in *Moïse et Pharaon*, Arnold in *Guillaume Tell*, and the title role in *Le comte Ory*, all given to him by Rossini; from Auber, he got Masaniello in *La muette de Portici* and Gustav in *Gustav III*; from Meyerbeer, he got Robert in *Robert le diable* and Raoul in *Les Huguenots*. As for my brother-in-law Halévy, as I already mentioned, he changed Eléazar in *La juive*, who was originally to be sung by a bass, into a tenor at Nourrit's request and tailored the role to his range. Nourrit also brought Schubert's songs to France. He himself provided them with a French translation.

When Duponchel invited Gilbert Duprez to join the team, Nourrit saw dark days looming on the horizon. He said, "He has a tremendous advantage over me: he is *new*. The public already knows me by heart." Duprez had built his reputation on his suave, veiled voice and he produced the high C with a chest voice. When he first sang it for the public, in Arnold's aria from *Guillaume Tell*, one of Nourrit's famous favorites, it fell on the audience like a thunderbolt.

At that point Legouvé interrupted Garcia's laudatory flow of words to tell us this amusing anecdote:

In that very same aria, Duprez had the incongruous habit of singing F where Rossini had written a G-flat. This F would drive Berlioz almost to insanity. Once he accosted Duprez after a performance and asked him why he constantly did that. "I don't know," answered Duprez, "that note simply kills me. But if you come to tomorrow's performance, I promise you I'll sing G-flat, as it is written, as a special service to M. Berlioz." But the next day, when Berlioz expected with mounting excitement the infinite pleasure this much-anticipated note was meant to bring, the singer's throat again emitted that accursed F. He didn't even *try* to mend his ways. And Berlioz went home boiling with impotent rage.

Incidentally, Rossini detested Duprez's high C. The first time he heard it was at a musical gathering at his home. Panic stricken, he ran to check if his beloved collection of rare Venetian crystal remained intact. He said to Duprez, "You sound like a castrated rooster that is about to be decapitated. Nourrit sings this C with a head voice, and that is also the way I want to hear it from you." But Duprez and the public felt otherwise, and they won. And by this they conspired in bringing Nourrit to his death—he jumped from the window of his hotel room in Naples. Only then did the public wake up and accuse Duponchel of opening the window. But it was too late.

All those reminiscences took us back to the early days of the Grand Opéra when Malibran and Giuditta Pasta were twin suns on the stage. Malibran started her career as a soloist in London. She was seventeen and sang as a member of the choir, when she was asked to replace, at the last minute, the indisposed Giuditta Negri in the role of Rosina in Rossini's *Barbiere*. Giuditta Negri was a Jewish doctor's daughter, from a small village near Milan. She conquered the world under the name the public gave her, La Pasta. Comparing Pasta's performance with that of Malibran became a kind of common social game. Take, for instance, the difference between them enacting Desdemona in the murder scene. Malibran ran from the dagger, looking in despair for a way to escape, fighting the closed doors and windows. As for Pasta, she walked calmly toward the murderous blade with equanimity, with a proud bearing, and with a noble and serene acceptance of her fate. Preference is a matter of taste, but there is no doubt that both of them were supreme actors. Pasta gave the impression that she strode directly out of a Racine or a Corneille tragedy, exactly like the great actress Rachel.

And Garcia added this professional appraisal:

At the outset of Giuditta Pasta's career her voice was full of defects, both technical defects and faults inherent to her natural timbre, the tone of her voice. But she mastered her craft and got full control of her voice through sheer willpower and determination, in a way I have never seen in my life. She brought her voice to a degree of perfection I have rarely encountered. Her range was from the deep A to the high D-sharp, all of it blended in a homogeneous texture and without any stitch or seam. She was able to produce an infinite number of nuances and played with them at will. By the simple process of changing color she could plead, caress, command, threaten, or cry, and when she cried, the whole audience cried with her.

Rossini didn't like her and refused to write for her. When Bellini discovered her and wrote Norma and La sonnambula for her she was already past her peak. And that was a real tragedy. When, at long last, she found the music that was really tailored to fit her, she was faced with the new challenge of her voice starting to lose the flawless perfection she had worked so hard to impart to it. But her magnetic appearance had such an impact that the public never became aware of the defects in her voice. Even the so-called "experts" would swear that the singing they heard was the pinnacle of perfection.

And Legouvé remarked,

Her period of glory actually did not last more than ten years. What a pity that she didn't have the wisdom to retire when she was at her peak. She dragged on for another twenty years in an endless parade of pathetic "farewell appearances."

The trouble with Pasta was that she could not afford to go easy on her strength and spare her potential. The competition was too keen and she had to deal with the formidable challenge of Malibran and Giulia Grisi.

Grisi! What a string of reminiscences this name inspires.
It actually has something to do with Théophile Gautier. Gautier

and I became friends in the wake of the *Hernani* uproar. He liked to tease me by calling me Jacob. Endeavoring to return the compliment, I had already made up my mind to call him Amadeus, but on second thought I decided that I couldn't call a poet by the name of the greatest of all musicians. So I settled for Gottlieb, which is German for Amadeus, like Amadeus is the Latin form of Théophile. Gautier was not overjoyed, but accepted the jest in the spirit it was intended.

During those days I was considered by my entourage to be a kind of matchmaker. I also used to volunteer for the task when my friends were in need of a shoulder to cry on. So when Gautier fell hopelessly in love with Carlotta Grisi, a love that lasted all his life, he turned to me for support and advice. Grisi was in love with the great Jules Perrot, her dancing partner and coach. The advice I gave Gautier was to try to openly and ostensibly court a good friend of Grisi's, or maybe even her younger sister Ernesta, in an effort to make Grisi jealous. The courtship with Ernesta had unexpected results: Gautier and Ernesta Grisi married and had two beautiful daughters, Estelle and Judith, whom Gautier adored. And, naturally, I was considered in the Gautier household to be almost a member of the family.

But back to the conversation.

"Another Italian gift to our French culture," Legouvé continued. "There were four of them: the first Grisi was Giuditta. In 1830 Bellini wrote the role of Romeo in *I Capuletti e i Montecchi* for her. And her sister Giulia, who was six years younger, sang Juliet in that production. Giulia was soon to outshine her. Giuditta and Giulia had two cousins, Ernesta and Carlotta. Both were brought up to become singers; Carlotta Grisi switched to ballet and became, as you know, one of the foremost dancers of our time. She was the original Giselle. She left the stage in '53, and as far as I know she is still leading a happy life somewhere near Geneva.

"And though her name was not Grisi, the great contralto Josephina Grassini, who was for so many years one of the leading stars at the Théâtre Italien, was the four Grisi girls' maternal aunt."

I added, "Giulia Grisi sang Adalgisa to Pasta's Norma at the premiere in Milan in 1831. She was unhappy with the conditions at La Scala, but they refused to let her go. Her contract was binding by the laws then in force in Italy, and to break it was a criminal offense, so she fled to Paris where her aunt Josephina Grassini and her sister Giuditta welcomed her. She joined them in the ranks of the Théâtre Italien where she immediately asserted herself as the best. She had already starred in Bellini's premieres in Italy (*I Capuletti e i Montecchi* and *Norma*), where she appeared in the role of the second lady. It was time now for her to premiere as a Bellini prima donna alongside Rubini in *I puritani* in '35. In '43 she starred in her greatest role, Norina in Donizetti's *Don Pasquale.* The tenor who sang Ernesto went by the name of Mario and was to become her husband. Mario was the scion of a family of the Italian nobility whose real name was Marchese Giovanni Matteo de Candia. But when he decided on a career in the theater it was evident that he had to choose a stage name: hence, Mario."

"I must add that there never was a more glamorous couple in the annals of opera than Giulia Grisi and her Mario," Pauline said.

"They were rather good," Garcia conceded, "but they lacked incandescence, some stormy outbursts, and they had no originality either. Grisi followed in Pasta's footsteps and Mario tried to imitate Duprez, and the impervious public never saw the difference. Grisi's big error was that she also tried to fill Pauline's shoes, but they were way too big for her. Meyerbeer's operas simply were not made for her."

Pauline added, "And when she realized that, she tried a new tactic: she tried to mess up my performances. It ended up becoming a habit of hers, that whenever I was to appear with Mario, he suddenly 'took ill' at the last moment with some mysterious ailment. When this systematic method became obvious to me I prepared a replacement in due time. Only poor Mario paid the price."

"Yes, but they had the good fortune of teaming up with Tamburini and Lablache to form a legendary quartet," Legouvé said. "They were not a quartet in the usual meaning of the term—soprano, tenor, and two basses don't make up a traditional foursome. This was the setup Bellini chose for his *I puritani*. In '35, at the premiere, Rubini was still the tenor. In the wake of the exceptional success of this quartet, Donizetti composed a second warhorse for this particular combination, the quartet in *Don Pasquale*. The life and soul of this ensemble was naturally the one and only Lablache."

"Luigi Lablache, the greatest of them all!" I readily agreed. "As big as his voice was, his physical dimensions were great as well; he was a giant of a man, and a wonderful, wise, and warm person."

Garcia added, "Jenny Lind never uttered a good word about any of her colleagues, but after she attended one of Lablache's performances, she exclaimed, 'What an artist! What a voice! And what acting! Oh, God! This is a genius! A real genius!'"

"He was certainly the most accomplished musician amongst the singers," Legouvé agreed. "At the Naples Conservatory where he studied, he played the violin and the cello. Once, a double bass was urgently needed and he was asked to fill in; he trained for a few hours and performed admirably. When Haydn died, they held a memorial service at the Naples Cathedral. They sang Mozart's Requiem. Lablache, who was fifteen at the time, sang as a contralto in the choir. Four contraltos against twelve tenors, twelve counter-tenors, and sixteen basses. The contraltos were asked to sing at the top of their lungs. Young Lablache sang with such enthusiasm and power that he succeeded in establishing a balance between the voice groups, but by the end of the service he was left voiceless; absolutely no sound came from his throat. He could not even speak anymore. The doctor who examined him gave a grim prognosis: his vocal cords had been damaged beyond repair and he would probably remain mute for the rest of his life. Two months later he woke up in the morning with a fit of coughing. After the coughing subsided he found that his voice had returned—not *his* voice, but a completely new voice. Now he talked and sang with a deep and clear bass voice, a wonderful bass voice that later enthralled all of Europe to the day of his death."

"The lintels trembled when he belted," I added. "And he was a mighty actor, playing serious as well as comedic roles. As a youngster he was tall and lean, but at some point he started putting on weight at an alarming rate and he developed an enormous belly. As he was unusually tall, he looked like a real giant, but despite his dimensions he was incredibly nimble. Gautier dubbed him 'the butterflying elephant.'"

"Wagner thought he would be an ideal Don Giovanni," Pauline said, "but this was before he grew to such alarming physical proportions."

Garcia said, "He was a great Leporello, a great Bartolo, and a great Figaro, but his most memorable role was Don Pasquale, a role Donizetti created for him. I remember how he tried in vain to close the green jacket with the golden buttons with which he had hoped to impress the beautiful Norina, and how he strode with ridiculous dancing steps toward the young woman, like a giant beetle vainly trying to spread its wings. It made us laugh until we cried, but it was also heartbreaking."

"As big as his body was, his heart was even bigger," Pauline continued. "The second time he sang Mozart's Requiem was in 1827, at Beethoven's funeral in Vienna. He insisted on paying all the singers from his own pocket. He was chosen to be a pallbearer and he remembered this occasion as being the highest honor bestowed on him in all his life.

"He sang in Mozart's Requiem on three more occasions: when Napoleon's remains were brought from St. Helena, at Bellini's funeral service, and at La Madeleine, when I participated from behind a curtain at Chopin's burial ceremony."

Galli-Marié jumped in to say, "How sorry I am that I have to cut short these thrilling stories, but it is time for me to go back to town and get ready for tonight's performance of *Carmen*."

I offered to join her. "Nothing can make me miss this evening," I said. "Carvalho has personally invited Geneviève Halévy to come to the opening of the revival, but she was not really up to going. I managed to persuade her by promising that I would be at her side the entire time, and if needed I would take her home whenever she asked. I've waited far too long to see a worthwhile production of this opera. I thank you all for this exciting voyage down memory lane."

Pauline said, "But please keep in mind that still better than the reminiscences of the past is the creative making of the present. Bless you, my dear Carmen, and give my warmest regards to all those surrounding you who are helping you in your endeavor. We all pray for a big success. Good luck."

"If I succeed in making my Carmen tonight a tiny bit better, it will be thanks to the inspiration I gathered in the presence of these ghosts of the past," Galli-Marié replied.

Garcia sang,

> *And let it be tonight, happy daughter of the muses,*
> *that your radiant Carmen shall stir up our senses*
> *with the voluptuous fire of intoxicating Spain.*
> *This is the fate you read in the cards.*
> *And let it be tonight, you mortal gypsy girl.*

After the second act, we went to the bar opposite the theater on the Place Boïeldieu for light refreshments. Henri Meilhac and Ludovic Halévy joined our table, and a few minutes later Adolphe Bizet, poor Georges Bizet's father, came to sit with us as well.

A swarm of enthusiastic friends came to pay their respects. I shall mention only a few of them: Gounod was leading the crowd and beaming with joy. Carvalho, who had always liked Georges Bizet but was rather reticent about his music, had suddenly become a staunch supporter. Pasdeloup, to whom Bizet had dedicated the score, and Choudens, who had published it, looked very satisfied. Delibes had always openly shown his admiration for Bizet's music. After having made a name for himself with three great scores for the ballet, he had finally also gained recognition as an opera composer with *Lakmé*, which has been very much appreciated by the public since its premiere here at the Opéra-Comique a few months ago. Thomas, Massenet, and Lecocq, as well as a host of newspapermen, all showered compliments and praise in the warmest of terms for what one of them called "the new pearl of French lyric art."

But I had a strange feeling. I could tell that Geneviève was shaken, and I was somehow unsure of her state of mind. I dreaded some unexpected reaction. I whispered in her ear, "*Bébé*, was it too much for you? Do you want me to take you home?" (After all those years, in the intimacy of our family circle, I still call her *bébé*.) She vehemently shook her head and answered with this cryptic sentence, "No, Uncle Hippo. This cup I must drain to the last drop!"

Don José's last sentence, "*Vous pouvez m'arrêter…c'est moi qui l'ai tuée! Ah! Carmen! Ma Carmen adorée!*" and the last two F-sharp empty octaves of the orchestra were drowned in an explosion of applause. Geneviève took my hand and literally drew me out of the hall. The cabriolet I had hired in advance was waiting for us, as agreed, at the corner of the rue de Marivaux and the rue Grétry. As we sat down and the horse started to move, Geneviève broke into hysterical tears. She clung to me and buried her face in my overcoat. Then she looked at me with a wildly shattered face and said, "*Ce n'est pas moi qui l'ai tué!*" (It is not me who killed him!), as if the last words of the opera had opened a dam and an irresistible torrent threatened her sanity. I drew her closer to me, and suddenly remembered the day she ran away from home and came looking for shelter and warmth with me. She sobbed, "I loved him. I still do! But I was so lonely."

The horse's hooves chimed their hollow staccato on the cobbled street.

The drive to 22, rue de Douai was rather short considering Parisian distances. I gave the coachman a substantial tip and asked him to come back and pick me up in one hour. I had to support Geneviève when we climbed the stairs to her door. Faithful Marie opened the door and I asked her to pour us a glass of cognac. But she said she had prepared a warm Alsatian punch, *glühwein* they call it. The drink was well met and it cheered us up. Geneviève had started to calm down and little Jacques, whom the commotion had awakened, ran from his room to hug his mother. Then for the first time in years Geneviève opened her heart to me. It was for her like a very much-needed confession.

Since my earliest childhood I have always been jealous of music. Father was so immersed in it that he was almost never able to spend any time with us. So my love of music was always tempered by the uncanny feeling that it was robbing me of some of the affection to which I felt I was entitled.

With Georges, things became even more terrifying…he always fell in love with the ladies he composed. Before our marriage it was the fair maiden of Perth. After we married, he was infatuated with Djamileh (actually Musset's Namouna), and then mesmerized by the mysterious Arlésienne, who never appears on stage in Daudet's play. And when Carmen came around, he forsook me completely. Even when he was with me, his mind was far away. Day and night it was Carmen—Carmen, who had bewitched him as she had bewitched Don José. Naturally, I was jealous.

And now, thinking of it from the perspective of a few years' distance, I am sure that my somewhat frivolous behavior, my tendency to flirt by not keeping enough distance, up to a certain point, from men's attentions—it was some kind of reaction to this jealousy. On one hand it must have been a kind of protest, and on the other a kind of wish for retribution. Maybe I wanted Georges to be jealous in order to rekindle his love.

My heart goes out to you, my dear niece, my darling Geneviève. It is hard for us common mortals to understand the needs of creative geniuses, the way they instinctively totally identify with the character they create or fall in love with it. Pygmalion and Galatea. And if it takes a huge effort to understand such an outstanding artist, it is incalculably harder to become a real source of support for such a genius.

16

CÉSAR FRANCK AND HIS GANG

In April 1886 I combined a business trip to Brussels with a visit to the beautiful opera house they have there, the Théâtre de la Monnaie. Emmanuel Chabrier had told me that they would produce his new opera *Gwendoline* there, so I decided that this would be a golden opportunity to revisit this town and hear its first-class music making again.

I normally refrain from giving my personal opinion on musical works. I like to be lenient, especially with the younger composers, and to look in their work for what I can enjoy more than for what annoys me. I leave to the professional critics the task of voicing their opinion in public. But here I would like to put my principles aside for a moment and say a few words in praise of *Gwendoline*. Though I think that some of the music was far too advanced for me, I enjoyed the whole evening tremendously. I also want to add that there were several places where the music really was so enjoyable that I eagerly looked forward to a second hearing. I must ask Chabrier for a copy of the score.

On the train on my way back to Paris a very pleasant surprise awaited me: in my compartment, I found myself sitting opposite Catulle Mendès and Augusta Holmès. Mendès is a very old acquaintance of mine; his family left Bordeaux and came to Paris when Mendès was sixteen or seventeen years old, I think.

Mendès wrote the libretto for Chabrier's *Gwendoline*. Chabrier himself has remained in Brussels to supervise some further productions of the opera. Augusta Holmès, who for years had been Mendès's companion and is the mother of his four children, is a highly gifted composer, pianist, and singer who had been a pupil of César Franck until 1876.

We naturally talked about *Gwendoline*, about the libretto, and about opera in general. At a certain point our conversation turned toward César Franck and his gang.

Augusta Holmès said:

I think that of our entire gang, Henri Duparc was the closest to him. Franck considered him to be his true heir. Like Franck, Duparc also aimed to endow his works with an elusive spiritual greatness with roots in the deep religious faith shared by both men, and the daily torments of a layman behaving like a monk. It goes without saying that Duparc's cultural baggage was so much richer than Franck's; he drew and painted in a very pleasant style, he was a refined poet, and he was, generally speaking, endowed with a discerning sensibility regarding everything concerning beauty. Even after he was struck by his mysterious illness and almost completely lost his eyesight, he went on impregnating himself with beauty through his remaining senses and trying to find some relief from his suffering in the world of aesthetics.

In complete contrast to Duparc, Franck's taste in literature and art was unstable and inconsistent. He was prone to strange and sometimes embarrassing utterances. He was completely devoid of luster or sophisticated refinement and didn't seem to care very much about either. But his attachment to Duparc was rooted elsewhere. Both of their lives were nurtured by their deep craving for the world of mysteries. For Duparc, who had received his basic education at a Jesuit school, this search was rewarded on the occasion of a pilgrimage to Lourdes where he was enlightened by a vision of the Holy Spirit. "Enveloped by a halo like the moon on a silvery, cloudless winter night," is the description Duparc gives of this unique experience.

I still seem to see César Franck hurrying down the street, small but squat, with his bushy side whiskers, his waistcoat too large, and his trousers too short for him. Nothing in his outward appearance would remotely suggest that here was a creative artist of stupendous stature and a revered teacher adored by his pupils. He never walked like the common mortal; he always hurried wherever he was going with running steps. On the threshold of his sixtieth birthday he still spent most of his time giving music lessons at countless private homes and boarding schools, running from one place to the other. His day invariably began in the same way: He never rose later than 5:30 in the morning, and he began his daily routine with two hours of writing music. Then, with a sigh of resignation, he left home to run errands. On Sundays and Fridays, as well as on festive days, his agenda changed and you would find him sitting high over the flock of churchgoers, at the keyboard of the organ at Sainte-Clotide.

Franck had many pupils, but only a handful of them were considered his "gang," his faithful followers, the intimate members of his inner circle. These few acted as the apostles of his musical creed. One of them—who, by the way, was the only Jew in this nest of fanatically devout Catholics, some of who were even avowed Jew-haters—was young Albert Cahen.

Cahen belongs to a wealthy banker's family of Antwerp with which I had extended business relations. After I published my first book, *Les trois filles de la Bible*, in '67, Cahen came to visit me and we had several lively exchanges of views centering on the subject of religion. His most important work to this day is a biblical drama, *Jean le Précurseur* (about John the Baptist, naturally), which was performed at the Concert National in 1874.

One morning Cahen took me to the recently built Sainte-Clotilde church in Saint-Germain-des-Prés on the rue Las Cases. Its impressive twin spires, almost seventy meters high, can be seen from far away. I think the building of the church was started in the late twenties or early thirties; anyway, it officially opened at the end of 1857, and right from the start César Franck was chosen as its incumbent organist. Its organ is a modern instrument with an unbelievable sound; it can go from the dimmest pianissimo to a thunderous fortissimo without transition, its legato is seamless, and it has a wealth of registers that were unheard of until now. Franck has called it "my orchestra." It was built by Aristide Cavaillé-Coll, the greatest organ builder in France, and in spite of his being still rather young, about my age, his reputation has spread well beyond the boundaries of our country.

The church was almost empty when we got there; an elderly lady was prostrate in one of the first rows near the altar, and a younger woman with her teenaged son was kneeling in one of the last rows in the left-wing nave. Unlike most churches I have seen, the interior was rather well lit; the light filtered diffusely but unhindered through the many stained-glass windows and the great rose that had been handcrafted by Thibaut. But the main feature of the church was the resounding sound, the cascade of chords running along the arcades. The entire interior of the church reverberated with the mighty sound of hundreds of pipes singing a hymn of praise to Almighty God in a universal language of adulation and servitude. I was not given time to admire the paintings by Lenepveu or the many sculptures by Pradier, Duret, and Guillaume—all four of who have won the Prix de Rome in their respective arts.

Cahen took me up the narrow, spiraling staircase leading to a secluded alcove that is the realm of the organist. There, in the mysterious, windowless half-darkness, his hands running across the keyboards and his feet pumping the pedals, oblivious to his surroundings, his face radiant with an angelic smile, sat César Franck, sending his musical prayer toward heaven. Some say this is not the music of a believer, but of a man struggling with his faith, an eternal repentant. Those who cling to this belief should someday climb these stairs and see the maestro in this intimate cubicle; they may change their minds.

The Catholic clergy looks with suspicion at Franck. I even heard that a high-ranking ecclesiastical personality said that *Les Béatitudes*, which Frank has been working on for ten years, a work he himself considers to be his highest achievement, borders on heresy. How the monsignor arrived at this conclusion is beyond my reckoning. The only performance of this work was, as far as I know, at Franck's home on the boulevard Saint-Michel, with piano accompaniment replacing the orchestra. After the prologue, most of those in attendance left, and at the end of the first of eight parts, only two people remained: the composers Victorin de Joncières and Édouard Lalo. The unenviable task of comforting the bereaved was left to them.

César Franck, whose invaluable contribution to the shaping of French music in the second half of this century is staggering, is actually not a Frenchman at all. He was born in 1822 in Liège. I've heard that his family has been making church windows for generations. His father, Nicolas, was a petty clerk in a bank. When he found that his eldest son possessed outstanding musical gifts he resolved to exploit them to the hilt. He decided that César-Auguste's talent (those are the pretentious names he had given his son at birth) was going to sustain his entire family. He organized tour after tour through Belgium and France and exhibited young César-Auguste again and again. The public soon tired of this circus and the anticipated benefits dragged into deficit. Instead of bringing laurels and glory, he brought a kind of boring gloom. The boy really was an accomplished master of the piano and a born musician, but he was missing the charm that is one of the main features of a wunderkind. His appearance was that of a squat, blushing, shy teenager, too old to be a wunderkind but still too young to be taken seriously. He was easy prey for critics in search of a target for their acerbic tongues and sharpened pens. Faced with those disappointing results, the ambitious father tried another avenue: the Conservatoire. The studies there were free of tuition, and the more gifted amongst the students could earn stipends that, when well-managed, could support a whole family. Young César took Zimmermann's piano class, Benoist's organ class, and the composition class of Leborne, a fellow Belgian. I never thought of it before, but Franck's connection to Belgian artists seems to me to be quite extensive.

Two of his pupils come from Belgium—Cahen was born in Antwerp and Lekeu was born in Verviers. Vieuxtemps was also born in Verviers, a town only a few miles away from Liège where Franck himself was born and where the young violinist Eugène Ysaïe, to whom the wonderful violin sonata is dedicated, was also born. And I haven't even mentioned Fétis and Sax.

My friend Charles Alkan, who was head of the jury at the 1838 piano competition, told me this very interesting story:

> There sat that little guy who looked as if he didn't know how to count to three. And suddenly out of nowhere he gave a performance of one of Hummel's piano concertos like a true virtuoso. Now came his turn at sight-reading: a complex E-flat major étude. And what do you think the lad did? With unexpected nonchalance and gall, in complete contrast with his outer appearance, he transposed the piece a third down on the spot and gave us a first-class performance in C major. All of us, the members of the jury, were convinced that this exhibition of full control entitled him to first prize. But Cherubini, the director, was of a different mind. "This youngster has broken the rules of this competition. He has gained an unfair advantage over his fellow competitors. He merits no reward," he said. This argument seemed far-fetched to us and we loudly voiced our protest. In the end we settled for a compromise: first prize was awarded to another student and for Franck they invented an honorary title, le Grand Prix d'honneur. This was awarded for the first and last time at the Conservatoire.

But that was not the end of the adventures of this very odd boy. During the organ examinations, students were required to improvise a fugue and a sonata movement on themes that were given to them. Young César Franck combined into the counterpoint of his fugue the subject of the sonata. Unluckily for him, the judges were devoid of the musical perception necessary to appreciate the true value of this feat, and Franck did not even receive an honorary mention. When Benoist, the director of the organ class, took it upon himself to open the eyes of the examiners to the brilliant display of technical knowledge and unusual talent that their obtuseness had missed, they had no other option, for fear of their ignorance being displayed and made public, but to revise their verdict and grant this very unpalatable pupil second prize. For Nicolas, Franck's father, this was too much to swallow. He needed his son's know-how and talent to be transformed into good cash to support his family. If the lad was unable to bring home the coveted prizes of the Conservatoire, he would have to go back to the life of the ambulant music prodigy—and so ended his formal studies.

Here is where his dual career as a teacher and as a composer actually began. Those two occupations, which would fill his entire life, where actually forced on him by a father looking for material benefits.

This is also when he concocted the original scheme of selling his works even before they were composed by issuing a series of subscriptions amongst a wide circle of musicians and music lovers. Like many others, I took part, in early 1841, in buying a series of trios by the young "César-Auguste Franck from Liège." I paid a down payment of twelve francs and added my name to the list that already included such illustrious names as Meyerbeer, Spontini, Donizetti, Auber, Halévy, Liszt, Schumann, Mendelssohn, and Chopin.

A few weeks later I received in the mail the first of these compositions: Trio in F-sharp Minor, op. 1 no. 1. I wasted no time and took the notes, still smelling nicely of printing ink, and sat at the piano to get my first impression. A few minutes later I knew beyond a shadow of a doubt that this clumsy Belgian youth was going to bring major change, a new era in the development of French music.

I still blush remembering an incident that happened more than thirty-five years later, on the occasion of the first hearing of his symphonic poem *Les Éolides*. I went to congratulate him and said to him, "What can I do, Monsieur Franck? For me you will forever remain the composer of those trios." How could I have been so stupid? Did I really say that?

But this unpretentious man looked at me with a shy smile and simply muttered, "To my great satisfaction, I dare say that since then I have done much better work."

I didn't know how or where I could find a hiding place for my embarrassment. What is it that drove me to remind the composer of the oratorios *Ruth, La Tour de Babel, Rédemption,* and countless other compositions of these youthful eruptions? Sheepishly I kept silent. He was right, of course. Still, I won't take back my opinion; in each new work of Franck's, I look for that stimulating blending of dim chromatic hues with strict counterpoint, of lusciousness mixed with abstinence, of asceticism combined with ecstasy, that unique assortment through which I attained, more than thirty years ago, such elation, such an unforgettable experience. Still, I'm happy to say that in several of his works of recent years I was able to find traces of those anticipated traits. I want to mention particularly the marvelous string quartet in which the composer seems to have attained the highest degree of self-expression, thus bringing us, the listeners, to awaken our own inner voices.

On February 17, 1889, I attended the subscription concert at the Conservatoire. On the program was César Franck's new symphonic work. He simply calls it Symphony in D Minor. The conductor was Jules Garcin—whose real name is Salomon; Garcin is his mother's maiden name—who has been chief conductor here for three or four years. He is a staunch advocate of German music and strives to introduce into his programs the works of Wagner and Brahms. The musicians of the orchestra, backed by the active help of the management, did everything in their power to undermine the performance. But Garcin stood his ground solidly and gave a mastery reading of this new work. I really can't understand how the audience was able to seal its ears and hearts to the beauty of that composition. But there seems to be no end to the stupidity and narrow-mindedness bred by ill will.

"Is that a symphony?" shouted one of the Conservatoire professors. "Who has ever heard of a symphony parading an English horn? Show me a Haydn or a Beethoven symphony with an English horn in the score. That is what I said. Call this music anything you like—but it is surely no symphony!"

And near another door stood my friend Gounod surrounded by his usual retinue of admirers. He pronounced his verdict in the very same manner that he liked to throw his witty (or so they say) pearls of wisdom, the ones the press so loves to quote: "This symphony is an expression of impotence under the disguise of a Credo."

January 1891

The Société nationale de musique was founded by Saint-Saëns and Bussine to promote French music, and they had welcomed Franck to join the society as its oldest member. The debut concert held on November 17, 1871, opened with Franck's Trio in B-flat Major, op. 1 no. 2. But almost from the beginning there were undercurrents of rivalry; the faction headed by Franck and his followers (foremost amongst them Vincent d'Indy, who was the leader of the French

Wagnerites and who strongly advocated the adoption of German profundity into the French musical language) were intent on accepting manuscripts by non-French composers. This was against the professed policy of the society and negated its motto, "*Ars gallica.*" It would lead to a confrontation that ultimately forced the resignations of Bussine and Saint-Saëns in 1886. César Franck was elected president with d'Indy and Chausson as secretaries. The secretaries dictated the policies of the institution. Now, after César Franck's death, they have elected d'Indy to the presidency.

As I wanted to know what this meant for the future of French music, I asked my friend Albert Cahen, who had been Franck's pupil and was also an intimate of the family, to spend a weekend with me at Fromont so I could extract from him all the information I wanted. True to his nature, Cahen gave me a comprehensive and colorful picture of the situation.

The park outside was covered with snow and the weather was bitterly cold. It has been years since we have had such a severe winter here. But in the spacious dining room it was warm and cozy. The fire in the fireplace was singing a very happy tune and we had a pleasant atmosphere around the table. Six of us were gathered around the table: Besides me there was Albert Cahen and his twenty-year-old daughter Josephine. Then there was twelve-year-old Magali Viera-Molina. She called me Uncle Hippo, but she's actually the great-granddaughter of my late sister Nancy. Magali has been a regular guest for years, coming to stay with me while her parents go on their skiing holidays. Karolina Bernhardt, who sang the role of Nelly in the private hearing of my opera *David Rizzio* in 1873, was virtually a member of the family. A singing teacher, she came to visit me regularly. She was thirty-seven and divorced. And there was also Jacques Bizet, the nineteen-year-old son of my niece Geneviève and our dearly missed Georges. My faithful Jeanette, who has been with me for over twenty-five years, has never accepted an invitation to sit at our table despite my repeated pleas. She always insists on continuing to serve us while she takes her meals in the kitchen.

After the tournedos, Rossini, and the *profiterolles au chocolat*, we sipped with great pleasure an excellent cognac while enjoying conversation.

Cahen said:

In 1846 when Nicolas Franck, César's father, found among his son's compositions the song L'ange et l'enfant [The Angel and the Child] with the dedication 'To Mlle Desmousseaux, in remembrance of sweet moments,' he tore up the sheet of music in front of the young composer. He could not let César become involved in an amorous adventure, let alone, God forbid, consider the possibility of a wedding. That would mean the end of the financial support that was the main income for the family. Moreover, bringing an actress into his respectable family was unthinkable.

Mlle Desmousseaux, whose real name was Eugénie-Félicité Saillot, was the daughter of a couple of actors, members of the Comédie-Française, who had chosen the name Desmousseaux as their professional stage name. Their daughter Félicité was also meant for a career on the stage, and piano lessons were deemed to be part of the general education needed to become an accomplished actress.

When his father tore the song with the dedication, César left home without hesitation, went to the home of his beloved, and asked for asylum. He told the Desmousseauxs that his intention was to marry their daughter; naturally on condition that she would accept him and that her parents had no objection. He also reminded them that for a man who had not yet reached his twenty-fifth birthday, the law required parental consent for him to get married—so he would have to wait for almost two years, during which time he would go on courting his future bride under the attentive supervision of her parents. He was immediately accepted with open arms and treated as a son. On the spot he reconstructed from memory the song his father had destroyed. From that day, he stopped using the name by which he had been known until then, César-Auguste. As a gesture symbolizing his break with the past and to affirm his full independence, he would be known from that day forward as César Franck.

They were married on February 22, 1848, the very day the revolution started in the streets of Paris. On nearing the Notre-Dame-de-Lorette Church, the church where he had been appointed assistant organist in 1847 and where the religious ceremony was due to take place, they were stopped by an unforeseen obstacle: a barricade blocked the entire width of the street. The insurgents defending the stronghold met the young couple with cries of "Vivat! Vivat!" and enthusiastically heaved them over of the heap of cobblestones, taking great care to protect their festive garb from getting crumpled.

When Berlioz heard about this incident, he said, probably with a note of irony in his voice, "Normally this kind of burlesque adventure happens only to me."

Typically it was Lina who asked about the dynamics of a husband and wife. Cahen continued:

Looking back, it is hard not to draw the conclusion that Franck swapped the tyranny of his father for that of his wife (and years later, for that of his sons). This may be on account of his submissive character, a trait that always attracted to him bullies and people with a domineering nature.

The atmosphere in the Franck household deteriorated due to his wife's persistent demand that he stick to his calling as the high priest of music and that he should strive toward obtaining eternal life in the bosom of the Catholic Church. The obvious display of sensuality, nay, of eroticism, in most of his recent secular compositions, annoyed her beyond words. She suspected him of being secretly in love with his pupil, the young composer Augusta Holmès, and credited this sentiment to be the main reason for this new trend in his musical expression. She was persuaded that Holmès was the source of the inspiration for the F Minor Quintet for Piano and Strings. The work was dedicated to Saint-Saëns. It was played at a concert of the Société nationale de musique in '79 and Saint-Saëns played the piano part at first sight (what we call prima vista). After the performance Saint-Saëns, who appeared to be very agitated, stormed out of the hall without shaking the composer's hand, without even waiting for the applause to subside. Some people say that this is because he had been personally, emotionally involved with Holmès and her image seemed to be clearly woven into the fabric of the quintet.

Here I interrupted Cahen's flow of words in order to voice my own opinion about this incident that I had also witnessed. "I think they are mistaken; Saint-Saëns's courtship of Holmès had taken place nearly a decade earlier," I said. "It is true that he proposed to her and was rejected—that was before he got married, needless to say. Still, they have remained very good friends to this very day.

"By 1879 it was a well-known fact that Holmès had been living with Catulle Mendès for the past ten years and that the couple, though they were not married, had already had three children. My personal opinion is that Saint-Saëns, whose music is so essentially French, never really came to terms with Franck's idiom. Franck's music has deep roots in German culture, though it has an unmistakable superficial Gallic shine. But I think this glaring fit of temper was mainly related to the struggle within the Société nationale de musique."

Jacques, who had been listening eagerly but had hardly uttered a word all evening, then said, "I would very much like to know what kind of a teacher he was and whether his influence left a lasting impression on his pupils' artistic output."

Cahen answered at length:

Franck's nomination to head the organ class when Benoist retired came as a complete surprise to everyone. The selection of teachers at the Conservatoire was, almost as a matter of tradition, made by pulling strings behind the scenes, intrigues, blackmail, and a "you scratch my back and I'll scratch yours" policy. The fact that this institution had accepted into its ranks a new teacher by only relying on his achievements as a recognized master at his craft, strengthened the hope that a new age was dawning with the creation of the Société nationale de musique. Still, it would be preposterous to think that the new teacher would be fancied by his colleagues. The fact that Franck used his position as professor of the organ class to introduce his pupils to the science—or, I should say, the art—of composition greatly annoyed many of the other teachers and even some of the students in the composition class. Nobody was willing to admit that this was not a presumptuous intrusion into a field that was not his own, but simply a matter of a fundamental principle according to which musical performance is much more than mere technical control and know-how; it requires a profound understanding of music in general and ability of free action in all of its domains.

The rumor about this very unusual teacher, so humble and naïve—we called him Pater Seraphicus—surrounded by a group of gifted youngsters that rejected the customary competitive spirit of this institution and considered themselves to be the apostles of pure music, spread rapidly. I'm very proud of having had the privilege of belonging to this group. I can't say whether it was by mere chance that almost all of Franck's pupils came from the higher social strata, from ancient nobility like Castillon and d'Indy, or from financial nobility like Chausson, Duparc, and myself. Compared to this homogeneous faction, which I admit was not free of condescension, the other students appeared to be rabble. Not without envy they called us "Franck's gang." And we were rather proud of this distinction.

We used to meet at Franck's place on the boulevard Saint-Michel, in a room with windows facing a shaded green garden. There we would discuss literature and art in general and exchange views about God and men. We played for one another our most recent work and listened with full attention to encouragement or criticism coming from our friends as well as from our venerated teacher. The highest praise he could give was saying, "J'aime ça" [I like this], and the harshest criticism he would utter was the negative of the same statement, "Je n'aime pas ça." Everything with him was driven through the channel of love, and he loved us too, all of us together as a group, and each of us separately as an individual entity. And his holy mission was to help this entity find its personal musical path. He never tried to force us to choose a certain way or to accept a given solution. He only directed us in the gentlest manner in the right direction, toward the place where we could find the solution on our own.

He himself regarded our collective opinion more than he minded the criticism of the greatest experts; not one of his new works was ever to reach the public without us first approving of it.

Did he shape us, or did we shape him? I think it was a reciprocal process. The trust we put in his leadership made every one of us a leader; the trust he put in our creative powers has made us creators.

"This only partly satisfies my curiosity about your group," I said. "What became of the entire bunch? I remember that a few years ago, I think it was in '74, they performed your *Jean le Précurseur* at the Société Nationale. I also remember hearing some music by Castillon. But apart from d'Indy, who is making such fuss, I really have no idea what the rest are up to."

Cahen continued:

I've been asking myself for some time if there is some kind of curse hanging over our heads, the heads of those in Franck's gang. The first to be cut down was our friend Alexis de Castillon. He was the secretary of the Société nationale de musique and one of the great hopes of French music in the second half of our century. He was a handsome young man, the scion of an old family of Languedoc nobility. As an officer in the cavalry he was called to duty at the most creative stage of his artistic life. He was caught with his battalion in a snowstorm, fell ill with pneumonia, and in March of '73 we all went to the family's estate near Chartres to accompany him on his last journey. His mother said to us with an edge of hostility in her voice, "I didn't know that my son had so many friends among the musicians," as if to accuse us of having brought this disaster on their family. When we invited her to be the guest of honor at the memorial concert we had organized in memory of Alexis, with a program wholly and solely comprising his works, she politely but firmly declined.

The jewel of our group, the wondrous, talented youngster Guillaume Lekeu, walked among us for only a very few years. Franck was stunned by his unusual, instinctive virtuosity in counterpoint, far beyond the mastery he himself could muster. Lekeu's eyes were always glowing like burning coals and his tongue was as sharp as a whip, the tongue of a youth who would never accept anything less than the absolute best. He was a protégé of Stéphane Mallarmé and a brilliant philosophy student at the University of Paris. He was a sensitive and stormy youth. During a performance of Tristan in Bayreuth, which we attended together, he fainted out of sheer emotional overload. We had to carry him out of the hall.

He had his personal and unconventional views about almost everything, but especially concerning musical form. According to him, form was subordinate to content, in such a way that the substance of a work should actually dictate the form the work should assume. He always kept a copy of Beethoven's String Quartet in A Minor, op. 132, at hand. He considered this work to be the highest summit ever attained in music. To my great sorrow, we never played for him the third movement from this quartet, the one Beethoven subtitled "Heiliger Dankgesang eines Genesenen an die Gottheit, in der lydischen Tonart" [A Convalescent's Holy Song of Thanksgiving to the Divinity, in the Lydian Mode], the movement he dearly loved. A few days after drinking a glass of fruit juice contaminated with bacteria, he died of typhoid fever. He was not yet twenty-four years old.

At that point Karolina Bernhardt said, "In my last concert I sang two of Henri Duparc's songs. But I have since heard that he has stopped composing altogether."

"Yes," I said, "I have had the pleasure and privilege of being acquainted with him. He's also one of those ill-fated pupils of César Franck. Six years ago he complained of acute headaches, fatigue, and anxiety. His doctors call it 'neurasthenia.' He has left Paris and settled in Switzerland, I think somewhere near Lake Leman. I have periodically asked his friends about his health and occupation. They are unanimous in their assessments that he has definitely abandoned musical composition. What a loss. What a promising career he had. But we still have his seventeen melodies written between '68 and '84, each one of them a full-fledged work of art, a unique occurrence in the literature of music. That's right, I didn't say in French art or in French music—I really think of this in terms of universal values. I believe that in the years to come these songs will be recognized worldwide as a significant contribution to our human cultural heritage."

"I didn't really catch his name," said Jacques. "Could you please repeat it for me and tell me more about him?"

"Yes," said Cahen. "His name is Henri Duparc. He was also a prominent member of our circle, one of César Franck's favorite pupils. He was actually 'converted' to music by Franck, who was his piano teacher when he was a student at the Jesuit College in Vaugirard. He was twenty-two when the war broke out and he was drafted into the army. Shortly after the war, in November of '71, he married a young Scotswoman named Helen Mac Swinney. At that time he joined Bussine and Saint-Saëns in the creation of the Société nationale de musique. Duparc was an extremely self-critical composer. He has destroyed works that have been performed and met with public approval like his cello sonata, the *Poème nocturne*, and *Ländler*. This is due to an exaggerated pursuit of perfection—some even say misplaced criticism.

"In some ways I could say that I, too, have been the victim of some kind of 'accident,' on account of me being the only one in the gang who has abandoned our master's ideals. After the cool reception given to my biblical poem *Jean le Précurseur* in 1874, I have drifted and became a composer of fashionable music, whose intrinsic worth is approaching nothingness, and whose success is even less."

"My dear Albert," I said, "I think your modesty is exaggerated. You are getting to be self-critical too. I hope you're not planning to destroy your compositions—I know that they staged your *Belle au bois dormant* [Sleeping Beauty] in '86 in Geneva. And if my memory isn't playing tricks on me, last year your opera *Le Vénitien* was performed in Rouen. I should say that this is quite well done—you're not yet forty-five years old!"

"Well, actually I *am* forty-five years old; I celebrated my birthday two weeks ago," Cahen said. "I must admit that even my ballet *Fleur de neige* will be performed in a few months in Brussels. But Paris is out of reach for me. And I really believe that I'm far from the level of, say, Chausson. Ah, Ernest Chausson, what a pure soul—a composer who writes according to his conscience. I have always had a feeling that his music speaks the language of César Franck with a purer accent and stricter syntax than that of the master himself.

"That leaves us with Vincent d'Indy, the man with iron principles, the active promoter of education, the man who became president of the Société nationale de musique after he ousted Saint-Saëns and Bussine. He has become addicted to the cult of Franck and the worship of Wagner. In spite of his dogmatic anti-Jewish sentiments, he has always had courteous, dare I say friendly, relations with me. His music is solidly anchored in the Franckist tradition and displays a wealth of know-how. Thanks to his activities, he has singlehandedly given the ill-fated Franck gang a semblance of assurance and continuity."

In July 1890, Franck was hurrying in his usual way to arrive on time to a private hearing of the *Variations symphoniques* at the home of the pianist Paul Brandt. He was crossing the Pont Royal when a horse-drawn omnibus hit him and threw him, writhing in pain, to the pavement. How he managed to get to Brandt's house remains a mystery, but even though he was in agony, he insisted on keeping to the scheduled program. He played the second piano part (the reduction made from the orchestral accompaniment). After the performance, he fainted; it was the beginning of the end. Over the following months he strived to go on fulfilling both his duties as a teacher and as the organ player at Sainte-Clotilde. With the coming of the cooler days of autumn he developed a high fever. The doctor diagnosed him with pleurisy and declared that he was beyond help. During those final days Franck had been haunted by the theme for a fugue that he was unable to compose. On his deathbed, he muttered, "Oh, my poor children! Oh, my poor children!" No one knew for sure whether he meant his sons, his pupils, or those works that were still simmering in his mind and had found no way to be brought to fruition.

We buried him on November 10, on a cold and gray day, at the Montrouge Cemetery. The Académie des beaux-arts did not send a representative. The director of the Conservatoire, Ambroise Thomas, was conspicuously absent. He sent Delibes to fill in.

In his funeral oration, Emmanuel Chabrier, one of Franck's closest friends, said:

Farewell, dear master. On parting from you we part from one of this century's great artists and from the wonderful teacher who raised a full generation of powerful musicians, profound thinkers, and impregnated them with faith. We say goodbye to an honest and guileless man who has always been generous with truthful advice, and all his toil was never in expectation of a reward. Adieu, dear *maître*, and may you rest in peace.

17

THE ERA OF THE VIRTUOSO

March 1831, from the *Gazette Musicale*

In the last few months the sensational events of musical life here in Paris seem to come one after another in quick succession. We have hardly recovered from the excitement of the performance of young Berlioz's *Symphonie fantastique* last December, and here we are once again submitted to new amazements at the sight of the tall, gaunt figure, like an ambulant skeleton, of the violin wizard Paganini. This artist, with his ghostly face and his long black hair cascading down to his shoulders in a disorderly manner, who has become a household name, is walking our streets accompanied by his young son Achilles and his dwarfish secretary.

The newest fashion amongst dandies is walking in boots à la Paganini, smelling à la Paganini perfumes, and enjoying delicious dishes that have been served at the table of our famous Italian guest. The truth is, the illustrious man does not eat very much, as he is suffering from some gastric ailment that brings him much misery. This is the reason for his emaciation, his yellowish complexion, and his frequent disappearances that are so shrouded in mystery.

Paganini became a legend during his lifetime. I clearly remember that even before he gave his first concert in Paris in 1831—this was shortly after I finished my studies at the Lycée Voltaire—his name was on everyone's lips in the fashionable Paris salons.

In '33 he decided to settle in Paris and I had the opportunity to meet him at several social parties. But his arrival at those parties was always unexpected. Whenever some host asked him if he would come to a party or social gathering, his invariable answer was, "Maybe," and in most cases he wouldn't show up. But on those rare occasions when he chose to surprise everyone and make an appearance at such a party, his mere presence caused general excitement and a whirlpool of people would surround him.

Strange rumors circulated about this magician of the violin. One of them was that he had sold his immortal soul to Satan in order to obtain the incredible control he has over his instrument. Until further notice, the devil has imprisoned it in an old suitcase that he deposited in a junkyard in Hamburg. Another story going around is that he came to possess his legendary technical skill by practicing day and night while he was in jail, imprisoned for allegedly murdering his mistress (and, according to other sources, his mistress's lover). And because his jailers refused to supply him with replacement strings for his violin, he had no option but to perform his daily practice sessions on the only string he had left, the G string. In this manner he was forced to master the technique that enables him to play entire works on this lone string, even when that work requires great technical skill when all four strings were available.

Paganini's opening concert at the Théâtre Italien exceeded all expectations. This eccentric emissary of the devil (or of God?), with his pallid face and contorted body, kept us gasping for breath from the moment he jumped on the stage from a hidden door to the final weary bow he took, which was met with thunderous applause, looking very much like a puppet whose operator had stopped pulling the strings. His violin, which could reach the resonance of a full organ, groaned and sobbed, screamed and begged, soared to cantilenas so sweet that they intoxicated our senses and brought us to the verge of swooning. And in between these displays of sentimentality, he showered us with a deluge of dizzying passages, of tremolos in two or three voices, of staccatos, pizzicatos, spiccatos, glissandos, flageolets, and double-stringed chords the likes of which we had never heard before. Then the strings started breaking one after the other and we were granted the famous display of prowess on the G string. The audience was ecstatic. And even if it is true that the artist uses faulty strings on purpose so they will break during the performance, what is wrong with that? This surely was part of the show.

Paganini was born to a poor family, and many are the tales about the misery of his childhood. One day, at the outset of his career, he lost all his money in a card game and was left with no option but to pawn his violin. Thus he arrived in Leghorn, where he had a concert scheduled for the evening, but had no instrument. By a stroke of incredible luck (some would call it divine Providence) a French merchant named Livron was in town and had tickets for the concert. In his possession was a very valuable violin, made by Giuseppe Guarneri, one of the greatest artists of the Cremona school. He had taken the instrument with him, intending to show it to the promising young violinist.

Paganini told him about the difficult straits he was in and begged the merchant to lend him the Guarneri for the evening. The Frenchman was happy to oblige, and Paganini had found an instrument equal to his talent. After the concert nothing Paganini could do or say would convince Livron to take back his violin. "No one can give a soul to this beautiful piece of wood, but you did!" he said. "It is yours by right. You have earned it!"

At a later stage of his life Paganini would win a Stradivarius in a wager against the painter Pasini, but the Guarneri would always remain his favorite instrument.

In 1836 he invested huge sums of money in the Casino Paganini, the gambling house that was to open in Paris. But when the government refused to grant the licenses required for opening the casino, this "bargain" cost him fifty thousand francs. With this in mind, the story Berlioz told is hard to believe; I won't tell it verbatim since it appears in Berlioz's much-advertised memoirs. Here is a short report of the facts.

In 1833, after a performance of the *Symphonie fantastique*, Paganini went to Berlioz to become acquainted with him and to praise his symphony. He told Berlioz that he had recently bought a Stradivari viola and that he knew of no composition that could do justice to the instrument. He suggested that Berlioz write a large-scale work for it. At first, Berlioz recoiled, saying that only Paganini himself could undertake such a task, but on Paganini's insistence, Berlioz set out to compose *Harold in Italy*.

When the first movement was completed, Paganini insisted on seeing it. On the spot he voiced his disappointment. "This is not what I had in mind," he said. "The viola has too many silent spells. I must be playing all the time!" A few days later Paganini left Paris and did not come back for three years. Berlioz finished *Harold in Italy* with no more concern about Paganini. It had its first performance in November

1834. The great violinist, who actually initiated the composition of the work, was in Nice at the time.

In December '38, when Berlioz conducted both the *Fantastique* and *Harold* at the Conservatoire, Paganini was in the audience and, for the first time, heard the work he had instigated. His health had very much degraded, and the terrible throat affliction that was to cause his untimely death made it impossible for him to talk. The concert had barely ended; Berlioz was still perspiring and shaking from effort and excitement when he was met on his way to his dressing room by Paganini and his son Achilles. Little Achillino served his father as an interpreter. He was the only person who could make sense of his father's unintelligible whisper. Paganini would whisper in his son's ear and Achillino would relay his message. He told Berlioz that his father wanted him to know that he had never been so deeply impressed at a concert and, when Berlioz tried to make little of it, Paganini literally dragged him back to the stage and, in front of the orchestra and the amazed audience, knelt down and kissed Berlioz's hand!

Two days later Achillino arrived at Berlioz's house with a letter from his father, in which Paganini expressed his admiration for the young French composer, telling him that he was the real heir to Beethoven, and begging him to accept, as a token of friendship, the munificent sum of twenty thousand francs. This gift enabled Berlioz to work undisturbed for most of 1839 on his great dramatic symphony *Roméo et Juliette*, which he dedicated to Paganini.

Paganini's concert heralded the beginning of what I call "the era of the virtuoso" in Paris. The challenge of perfection in performance and external brilliancy has always been an integral part of the art of music. The greatest and mightiest of the geniuses of past generations have been unable to resist the temptation of exhibiting their talent and stand in competition with well-known performing virtuosos. The best-known examples are naturally Bach measuring up against Marchand in Dresden and Mozart's contest with Clementi. Yes there have been a multitude of great virtuosos in the past: I know of Bach and Handel, the kings of the organ; of Tartini and Viotti, the masters of the violin; of Mozart and Beethoven, the indisputable rulers of the piano, and there were probably, in the distant past, many more musicians of this magnitude who had attained absolute control of their instruments. But all those great performers, and their less prominent colleagues, had made their art an instrument in the service of music; they never viewed their technical skill as a goal in itself. In our century, the virtuoso has become a professional who knows all the secrets of his instrument and is able to stun the public with his fireworks, but he doesn't bother about such trivial things as expressivity or depth of feeling. The important words of modern times are speed, agility, power, and volume, while words like profound, emotional, and poetic have become obsolete.

Many of my friends started their musical career as virtuosos: Heller, Alkan, Kalkbrenner, Moscheles, Hiller, Rubinstein,[22] Bizet, Saint-Saëns, and even Chopin at the outset of his career. Schumann himself, had it not been for the unfortunate accident that permanently damaged his hand in an exaggerated effort to increase its agility by using a mechanical device, saw in a career of wandering musician a means of spreading music and giving vent to his creative urges. Today it is his widow, the eminent pianist Clara Schumann, who is the spokesman and herald of the opposite camp. She advocates—like her

---

22 This is a reference to Anton Rubinstein, not Anton's brother Nikolai, the famous teacher from Moscow.

friend Joachim in the ranks of violinists—restrained musicianship, free of all kind of fireworks, a meaningful and expressive playing of the instrument. My friend Alkan would certainly have given her a piece of his mind on the topic of feminine pianistic interpretation, but Alkan, as everyone knows, was a staunch misogynist.

The virtuoso who puts all his technical capacities at the service of exhibitionism is the creation of our modern society. And so is the public who has forgotten the tiny difference between true art and the circus of sleight of hand.

There was much of the acrobat in Paganini, but he was a supremely gifted acrobat—so very gifted indeed that even his acrobatics (let alone his true moments of inspiration) were always imprinted with the seal of genius. To our great misfortune, acrobats are much more commonplace in our world than geniuses. So, not surprisingly, Paganini's many imitators centered mainly on his exterior mannerisms, his superficial appearance. This new fashion is not restricted solely to the concert hall. Every family in our city (and not only in *our* city) has become a potential hotbed for little Paganinis-to-be—and not only on the surly and difficult violin. It occurs mainly on the most submissive and indulgent of all musical instruments, the ever-befitting piano. Our shrewd friend Heinrich Heine says on this topic:

> No one ever defines the boredom spreading from the French classical tragedy better than this housewife from Louis XV's time who said, "Don't you envy the nobility and forgive their arrogance; as a punishment from heaven they are compelled to sit every evening at the Théâtre Français and get bored to death!"

> Even worse is the fate of the ruling middle class today; for them, heaven invented an artistic enjoyment tenfold more horrific: the pianoforte! Its voice is heard in every home, at every social gathering, day and night without respite. Sure enough, pianoforte is the name

of the new instrument of torture that brings so much misery to the privileged class, punishing them with whips and scorpions for the cheating and exploitation that has elevated them to their dominating position. If only it were possible for the innocent bystander not to suffer with them. Poor me! At this very moment my neighbor's daughters and the maid living beyond the wall, all hammer on the keyboard a fantasy for four left hands.

This increasing spread of piano playing, and with it the triumphal expeditions of the virtuosos in virgin territories, is characteristic of our days and serves as a kind of witness to the victory of machine over spirit. The mechanical command, the accuracy of an automaton, the identification with the resounding board, men becoming a musical instrument, this is what is crowned today with the highest praise and glory. Like locusts swarm, piano virtuosos invade Paris every winter, not to earn some money here, but to build up a reputation. Their ultimate goal is to reap in other countries a harvest of coins tenfold greater. Paris serves them as an advertisement where their praise can be read in giant capital letters. And I say "their praise can be read," because the Parisian press spreads their praise throughout the whole world. And indeed, these pianists have proved themselves to be virtuosos in the art of using the press and journalists.

There is much talk here about the corruption that has crept into the realm of the press. But this is not the case here. Corruption you will find with the virtuosos themselves when they strive to gain a foothold in the press at any price. The knavishness with which they crowd the newspapers' editorial offices in an effort to awake pity and to beg for the printing of a few words of praise is almost unbelievable.

The matadors for this season are Camillo Sivori and Alexander Dreyschock. The first one is a violinist, and that alone is already a good reason for me to place him above the other one, the one who knocks terribly on the piano keys. Indeed, with the violinists the virtuosity does not express itself through finger agility or mere technique alone, as with the pianists. The violin is an instrument prone to moods, almost like a human being. There is a latent spiritual affinity between it and its player. The violin is attuned to the smallest inconvenience, to every trace of emotional stress, to the tiniest flutter of its tamer's heart—this naturally being dependent on the tamer harboring a sensitive heart. As much more as a violinist is shrewder and heartless, so the level of his playing will be steadier. If he stays wide awake he will be able at any time to rely on his violin to obey him blindly. But this meritorious security is a consequence of a spiritual limitation, and in fact it is the greatest of the masters who have been those given to spells of moodiness and to outer or inner influences. I never heard better playing, nor did I ever hear worse playing, than the playing of Paganini (whose pupil M. Sivori pretends to be). As they were both born in Genoa, there is a distinct possibility that Sivori has crossed paths with Paganini on the street as a child, as the narrow streets of this city hardly allow for two people walking in opposite directions to pass each other without brushing elbows. But a pupil of Paganini he never was, as Paganini, to the best of my knowledge, had no pupils.

The germ of virtuosity has also spread to the ranks of the pianists: a host of child prodigies capable of performing hair-raising acrobatics has suddenly swarmed over Paris. Most of them are ephemeral apparitions, like shooting stars passing in the sky and vanishing without leaving any substantial trace or memory. The real stars, the ones who sparkle and light the skies of the musical world, are those who have shed the skin of virtuosity. They have relinquished cheap juggling and superficial brilliance in order to harness the knowledge and command that a faultless basic technique has earned them in the service of rendering and recreating immortal musical gems. First and foremost among them stands Franz Liszt. He is Paganini's equal in the realm of the piano. In spite of the fact that he has, for a long time already, stubbornly refused to play in public, he still carries the crown and title of king of pianists. He now devotes his time and energy mainly to composing, conducting, and, what seems to be even more important to him, spreading modern music and advancing young, promising composers who have not yet made their mark.

If Wagner considers himself to be the prophet of the "music of the future," Liszt is without a doubt its high priest and most ardent missionary. But this fact does not prevent him from also extending help to young musicians who have chosen not to follow the path opened by the Wizard of Bayreuth.

For some years now Liszt has lived in Weimar, and under his aegis this city has become the focus of spirited musical activity and the Mecca of young musicians in search of an opportunity to express their talent and to get started on their way to fame.

So Paganini had no pupils worth mentioning; and if he had heirs—or, to be nearer the truth, if he ever had an heir— to his art, it isn't amongst the violinists that we will find him. Charles de Bériot, the founder of the Belgian school of violinists, learned his trade by following in the footsteps of Viotti (Heine says about Bériot's playing that his late wife's soul, the celebrated Maria Malibran, sings through his violin.) Henri Vieuxtemps, Émile Sauret, Hubert Léonard, and Eugène Ysaÿe have made Bériot their standard bearer. As for Wieniawski and Sarasate, child prodigies from Poland and Spain, they grew up in the Paris Conservatoire under the guidance of Massart and Alard. Every one of those great artists struck out on a very individual path of his own, and except for a technical trick here and there, they have borrowed from Paganini only the new, general trend of ever-growing expectations and challenges. In contrast with the violinists, the pianists were devoid of any kind of restraint in their endeavors to transpose the heroic feats of the famous bow on the strings of the Stradivarius into a language that has grown more and more sophisticated with the ever-greater improvements made by Pleyel and Erard on their pianos. No more serene and elegant sitting over the instrument—from now on we'll have dramatic swinging and fearful contortions of the body. Gone are the days of the gracious ballet of fingers linked to the black and white keys—from now on there will be strikes of the forearms, the elbows, the shoulders, the whole body. And instead of the brilliant strings of pearls singing their melodies, we now have salvos, volleys, explosions, and foaming cascades running down as the pianist's hand, lifted high, dashes onto the keys like a hawk onto its prey. Should we be surprised now that a musician like Ignaz Moscheles, a representative of the old school, has met with ignominious failure here? And even those lions of the fashionable salons like Kalkbrenner and Herz are pushed aside and lose their luster. One day after a performance of the young bohemian Alexander Dreyschock, this knight of lightning and thunder (the same one Heine writes about), I saw Pleyel looking into the tormented instrument left on the stage. Dreyschock asked, "What you are looking for, my friend?" "I'm counting the wounded and killed," answered Pleyel with a deep sigh.

So who is this heir of Paganini I have been hinting at? That is not even a riddle, as you know the answer to it as well as I do. I'm talking about Liszt Ferenc—or Franz Liszt, as he has been calling himself for years.

Like Paganini, Liszt was endowed with abilities to play music that far surpass the natural and normal average. Like Paganini, he has the magical aura that has brought the public to ecstasy. Like Paganini, he has the gift of a dual personality, that of a genius and that of a wizard, of an untamed savage possessing the soul of a romantic bard. This is what they have in common. But the difference between them is also abysmal: the magnetic attractiveness of one comes from his satanic ugliness, while the other gets his invincible charm from his radiant handsomeness. Paganini never swerved from his path; from his first appearance before the public until he left the stage, he never looked right or left. Liszt never tires in his search for new horizons and is always conscious of his surroundings and supremely self-critical. Paganini was the phenomenon begetting imitation. Liszt is the teacher and educator of the next generation and the next generation after that. One was a great performer and a mediocre composer; the other created new musical expressions looking toward the future.

The first time I heard Franz Liszt in the concert hall at the Conservatoire, he was still far from the black cassock the Catholic Church would offer him in his later years. The role of high priest of modern music that he would fulfill in due time in Weimar was a dream that had only just begun to sprout. What I saw that evening was a strange blending of Apollo and Lord Byron, of Don Juan and Mephistopheles. Two Erard grand pianos were at his disposal on the stage and he strolled from one to the other with utter nonchalance, sometimes even in the middle of playing a composition. When the Princess of Belgiojoso gave him as an honorary present a choice set of silverware, the man seated next to me said with a touch of bitterness that in return for ruining the two first-rate instruments standing before us, this chap ought to have been rewarded with a good beating instead of an expensive gift. I think his judgment was biased by jealousy; we men, with all our admiration for the feats of virtuosity of an artist, cannot keep from the being somewhat uneasy and even angry at witnessing the hysteric behavior of some of the ladies in the audience. In the row in front of us, one woman swooned, and another had a fit of convulsions. Another admirer tore off her pearl necklace and threw it at the piano. Two countesses had a brawl in their efforts to get hold of the pair of green gloves the godly youngster had left on the piano. And he himself fit perfectly in the general picture; at a certain moment (perhaps it was planned that way?) he fainted into the arms of an attendant and was carried, unconscious, from the stage. Fortunately he regained his senses in no time and the show went on as planned.

I remember that I was somewhat disappointed by the program. I had been told that young M. Liszt was a foremost exponent of Beethoven's music. But on this very evening we didn't hear much beside paraphrases on themes from fashionable operas. The well-known violinist Joseph Massart, one of the important teachers at the Conservatoire, was due to join him in the performance of Beethoven's Kreutzer Sonata. He had even begun striking the first chords of the work when someone in the audience started shouting, "*Robert le diable!*" Other members of the audience joined their voices in this outcry and the shouts of "*Robert le diable!*" completely drowned out the sound of the violin. Liszt stood up from his seat at the piano, went to the front of the stage, took a deep bow, and said, "I am always the humble servant of the listener. Would you like to hear the fantasia before the sonata or after it?"

The public responded as one, "*Robert! Robert!*" Liszt, with a nonchalant wave of the hand, sent the honorable professor away and turned his attention to the job at hand: satisfying the audience.

And again I will quote Heinrich Heine:

Indeed here is "the scourge of God" of all the Erard pianos, contort-ed, weeping and bleeding under his hands, in such a manner as it gives an urge to call the Society for the Protection of Animals. Here he is, this handsome youth, unsightly, mysterious, dangerous, and childish; a giant dwarf and hero running wild with the Hungarian sword of honor. Liszt, who through the might of his magic subdues us, whose genius bewitches us. The genial simpleton who through his madness brings turmoil to our senses, and whom we faithfully serve anyway. When we report in the pages of this newspaper on his grandiose success, we sanction the fact that we ourselves comment on this. And whether we add our private applause to the general ovation or refrain from doing so, it's just the same to him, because, after all, our voice is just a lone voice and our expertise in music is not extensive.

The contest held at the salon of Princess Belgiojoso between Liszt and Thalberg was undecided, in the same manner that the contests held between Mozart and Clementi at the Vienna Imperial Palace, over fifty years ago, also resulted in no official winner. "The handsome Sigismond" is what Thalberg's admiring followers called him. And that is also the name his detractors call him in derision. His mother, Baroness von Weglar (who was born into a Jewish family), gave birth to him out of wedlock. She decided that his name would be Thalberg, which is a combination of the two German words *Thal* (valley) and *Berg* (mountain). The idea came to her on hearing what his biological father, Baron von Dietrichstein, said when the baby was born: "Let this child resemble a valley shrouded in serenity, but when the time comes, let him rise to the heights like a mighty mountain."

Heine describes Thalberg as a "perfect gentleman" and is surprised that this fine young man, who could have conquered the world with his handsome countenance and his exquisite manners alone, chose to invest such an enormous effort in the refinement of his pianoforte technique and in competing against his concurrent virtuosos. His lofty extraction shows at once in the way he sits at the piano. In complete disdain of current fashion, he plays his famous thirds, tremolos, and chords with no outward sign of acrobatics. He sits with tight lips, his vest buttoned up to his throat and his back erect and straight like the trunk of a pine tree. According to recent gossip, he acquired this perpendicular sitting position by, during all his training sessions, smoking a long-stemmed Turkish pipe that reached the stand holding the notes before him and allowed no head movement whatsoever. The special trick Thalberg uses to captivate his audience (and very few are those who know its secret), is playing the melody with both his thumbs in the middle range of the piano, while his eight other fingers, four for the bass and four for the descant (the upper register), ran in embellishing arpeggios and wove a supportive frame for the melody. To the stunned listener, this sounds as if three hands take part in the performance. It is my friend Ferdinand Hiller who disclosed this secret to me and showed me how easy it is to imitate. Hiller also showed me a letter from Felix Mendelssohn, in which this very discerning musician draws a comparison between Thalberg and Liszt. Here is what he wrote:

> A fantasy played by Thalberg is a reservoir of marvelous, select, and delicate effects. It is hard to know what is more amazing: the technical difficulties piled up one upon the other or the tiny turns, which, with a perfect charm, accompany them all the way. Everything is deliberate and ingenious, everything shows tremendous knowledge, experience, and control, and is a proof of the finest taste. And on top of this the man has enormous power in his fists, while his fingers are trained and can be light as a feather. This is a very rare occurrence.

> As for Liszt, he is endowed with flexibility and dissimilarity between the fingers and is totally impregnated with a unique musical instinct. I have never met a musician with the feeling of music flowing in him to the tips of the fingers and from there being dispersed to the audience in such a direct manner. In view of this directness and remem-

bering his stupendous technique and masterly dexterity, he would
have left all others far behind were it not for the fact that nature has,
at least until now, deprived him of ideas that are entirely his own.
This shortcoming has permitted other virtuosos to become his equal,
or even to surpass him in the field of original creativity. Still, there
is no doubt in my mind that he and Thalberg, and only they, are the
elite amongst the pianists of our time.

In adding the little disclaimer "until now" to his remark about
the creative powers of Liszt, Mendelssohn not only shows rare
insight, but proves to be a very wise man. I am sure that with the
passing of time and the ripening of his personality, Liszt will find
his way to the trove of creativity; when the ideas are found they
will bring with them the need to withdraw from the career of the
virtuoso, to relinquish the adulation of the public, and to turn
toward new horizons.

As for Thalberg, in the 1860s he decided to follow Heine's
twenty-year-old advice. He abandoned piano playing completely,
bought a vineyard somewhere in Italy, and lived out the last of
his days in pastoral tranquility. His retirement from his former
activities was so complete that in his villa, which was furnished in
the finest taste, there was no place for a piano.

Many of the great virtuosos (and the less-than-great virtuosos
too), whether Parisians or guests, were Jewish or of Jewish descent,
and I knew most of them personally. Of my close friendship with
Stephen Heller and Charles Alkan I have already written in these
memoirs. But I only mentioned perfunctorily my neighbor on the
rue de la Victoire, Henri Herz. The procession of pupils to his

studio started at six in the morning and lasted until midnight. Herz has a fluent style at the piano, but he is shallow and completely devoid of ambition. When Schumann wrote about him that all he wanted was "to entertain the public and to accumulate money," he was absolutely right. Herz is also active in the world of business: he founded a piano factory and is also the owner of a concert hall (also situated on the rue de la Victoire). My heart cries out in sympathy for this harmless musician who has gotten entangled with a conscienceless femme fatale, Thérèse Lachman, better known as La Païva. She broke his heart, robbed him of his money, and utterly destroyed him.

I have already told about my friendship with Camille Saint-Saëns, a great pianist who was never blinded by cheap success. Thanks to him I met Anton Rubinstein, who, during his visits to Paris, was Saint-Saëns's constant companion. When they did not conduct the orchestra at each other's concerts, they sat in the music room on the rue Monsieur le Prince and took pleasure in playing the piano with four hands. Saint-Saëns himself told me this story:

> In the spring of '64 Anton Rubinstein asked me to make arrangements for a concert he would like to give during his next stay in Paris. He was, you must admit, already very well-known as a piano virtuoso, but also wanted to make his mark as a conductor. So he let me know that he would very much like to conduct the first performance of a new work by me, and invited me to play the solo part in it. In other words, he practically asked me to write a new piano concerto. I naturally answered immediately that this was no problem; I only had to make sure of the dates when the orchestra was available and the concert hall free.
>
> To my great dismay, the only possibility to get both an orchestra and a hall was seventeen days away. This was all the time I had to compose and rehearse a new piano concerto!

That morning Fauré had brought to my class at the École Nieder-meyer[23] a short new work of his that he had prepared as an exercise in composition. It was a Tantum ergo in G minor, a beautiful little piece of music stretching over an octave and a half with an accompaniment that in itself was an independent melody. All day long this music haunted me; it played itself over and over again in my mind. It wouldn't let go. It became an obsession. You know how those things sometimes happen…When I got home in the evening I decided to banish the ghost and start work at once on the concerto for Rubinstein. I sat down at the piano and my fingers ran over the keys as if of their own volition, playing a fantasy of broken chords like a run on the organ. I had no command over them. It was a broad tapestry woven around the G minor theme of Fauré's Tantum ergo.

Next morning I went to young Gabriel Fauré and asked his permission to use his theme as the cornerstone for the first movement of my new piano concerto.

The concerto was ready on time and the orchestra members got their parts in due time too. Only I, the soloist, wasn't ready. I think I might have suffered that evening from acute overconfidence and didn't bother to prepare myself properly. In my entire life I've never played so many wrong notes. I blush even today when I recall this incident. I didn't touch the concerto again for four years; then I went back to the Salle Pleyel in 1868 to play it, like the first time with Rubinstein conducting.

---

23 In 1861 Saint-Saëns was appointed piano professor at the École Niedermeyer. As a teacher he put at least as much emphasis on the study of harmony and counterpoint as on that of pianistic technique. Among his pupils were Gigout, Messager, and Fauré. Fauré, who was nineteen at the time (only ten years younger than Saint-Saëns), was his favorite pupil and a close friendship developed between these two sensitive men (J.H.R.).

You know, my publisher stated 1868 as the date of the first performance and totally ignored (probably knowingly) this '64 performance.

Rubinstein was an immense musician, and in his famous concerts, which stretched to unreasonable lengths, he exhibited incredible control of piano literature of all generations. He would not bother with small details; wrong notes did not disturb him in the least because he would stress the broader lines of the music, the inner content. He could draw the most wonderful and delicate whisper from the piano, but he rarely displayed it. Early in life he had learned that the public buys tickets to hear lightning and thunder, not some far-away murmur. By the way, I was recently told that on the tour he made with Wieniawski in America, he stole the show, and this really is no mean achievement.

Bizet carefully avoided displaying his pianistic brilliance in public, because he feared that the stigma of being a virtuoso would harm his career as a composer. Had he been willing to choose the path of lesser resistance, he could have reaped both glory and wealth thanks to his outstanding ability as a pianist, a field in which his prowess surprised whoever heard him. I remember that evening at my brother-in-law Fromental Halévy's, when the guest of honor, Franz Liszt, played one of his *études de concert*. Those compositions are meant to be played solely by the greatest virtuosos. Responding to the compliments showered on him by the audience, Liszt said, "True enough, this étude is indeed an unbelievably difficult piece to play. I know only two people who can measure up to the task of playing it at the prescribed speed: my son-in-law, Hans von Bülow, and myself."

That is when Halévy went to the piano and, as if by chance, played a few chords from the étude. He then turned to Bizet, who was present too, and asked him whether he could remember this passage. Bizet, with his phenomenal memory, sat at the piano and gave a faultless rendition of the sequence. Liszt was stunned. He put the manuscript before Bizet without uttering a word, and Bizet without the slightest hesitation played the étude in full with his usual brio and without the tiniest blemish. Deeply moved, Liszt embraced his young colleague and said, "My friend, I thought that only two people existed who are capable of overcoming the colossal difficulties of this work. I was mistaken; there are three. And to be quite fair I should add that the youngest of them is also the most daring and brilliant."

Bizet was accustomed to being complimented on his piano playing. This sometimes brought him to the verge of bitterness. He said,

> I am aware that I play the piano rather well. But I derive no benefit from it. I am not interested in playing in public recitals and having my creative work branded with the term "music for pianists." The mere thought of a career as a professional pianist is loathsome to me. And this loathing costs me fifteen thousand francs a year. Only rarely do I play at Princess Mathilde's salon, or in a few other places where artists are considered to be friends and not lackeys.

He was so averse of being associated with the flock of piano virtuosos that, in spite of his perfect command of the instrument, he avoided as much as possible composing music for the piano.

I am willing to swear that the rivalry of pianists like "three-handed" Thalberg and Dreyschock "with the two right hands" did not disturb Liszt in the least—not to mention Theodor Döhler, Czerny's pupil, about whom Heine has not yet made up his mind whether to classify him as the last of the second-rate pianists, or the first of the third tier.

But I haven't the slightest doubt that Liszt was greatly bothered by the arrival on the scene of the young Polish artist, Frederic Chopin. Chopin's pianistic world was a world of soft and imperceptible nuances that made the noisy displays of his colleagues sound like much ado about nothing. At a salon party with Chopin playing, Thalberg shouted, "I need noise, all evening I was fed with pianissimos!" And Liszt complained that in this unending quietness the first forte sounded like a peal of thunder and almost threw him from his chair.

Of all the pianists I ever heard, Chopin was the most original. When he arrived in Paris, at the age of twenty, his musical character was almost fully developed and no one could add or subtract anything from it. It is possible that in his early days he had learned something from Hummel, from Weber or from Field, but the basic essence of his style, his personal musical language, is a faithful reflection of his inner self. In shaping it he was pushed by an urge to create a musical idiom whose sensibility would match the sensibility of his spiritual outlook.

Shortly after his arrival here in Paris from his native Poland, he considered getting additional training and he turned to Kalkbrenner for advice. Kalkbrenner proposed to teach him for three years and promised him that after that period he would be able to start a brilliant career as a virtuoso. Chopin had almost made up his mind to accept, but thanks to the intervention of Mendelssohn, who happened to be staying in Paris for a few months at the time, this suicidal plan fell through. He admonished Chopin in no uncertain terms, "What is it exactly that you hope to learn from him? Are you not aware that you are a better pianist than he is? Immensely better! Don't tell me that you are willing to relinquish your uniqueness and become a second Kalkbrenner!"

This seems to have convinced Chopin, who, as a kind of compensation, dedicated his E Minor Piano Concerto to his would-be teacher Kalkbrenner.

Pauline Viardot has had very friendly ties with Chopin, and as a former pupil of Liszt, she is in an ideal position to evaluate the intricate attitude between those two great artists:

> The relationship between Chopin and Liszt was one of love and hate. Chopin was jealous of Liszt's steadfast health and his physical strength. "I would gladly steal from him the manner in which he plays my études," he would say, beaming with deep admiration. Once, during a party at Chopin's home at the Square d'Orléans, Liszt apologized for having broken a string on his friend's piano while playing the Polonaise Militaire. Chopin retorted, "If I had your physical strength I would play this Polonaise in such a way that not one piano string would remain intact." But he flew off the handle at hearing Liszt play his works and add embellishments that Chopin never meant to be there. "Please, play my music as it is written, or don't play it at all." And Liszt answered sheepishly, very unlike his usual self, "You are right, of course. To compositions like yours it is clearly wrong to add even an iota."

> When they played four hands, Chopin would invariably take the accompanying part. He would never let his delicate rendering be drowned out by the thundering chords of his colleague.

Chopin made light of those pianists who strove to strengthen their ring fingers and their little fingers with exhausting practice, and bring their strength to equal that of the other fingers. He used this inequality between the fingers for the integration of chords in a wonderful grading.

The controversial thing in Chopin's pianistic technique was the tempo rubato, a feature he copied into his music straight from Polish folk music. Too many performers tend to forget that these characteristic rhythmical deviations should be kept solely to the melodic line, while the left hand is to keep playing the basic rhythm strictly and accurately. When Chopin was teaching, the metronome on the piano was never idle; he forbade any negligence and excluded any uncontrolled sentimentality. Nevertheless, this rubato playing could bring unfortunate misunderstandings. Once, as he played the F-sharp Minor Mazurka amongst a circle of friends, Meyerbeer, who was there, exclaimed, "This is in 2/4 time!"

"3/4," said Chopin, and his eyes started sparkling.

"2/4," insisted Meyerbeer.

Chopin's pale cheeks turned red and he retorted loudly, "3/4!"

"If you will be so good as to lend me this piece for the ballet in my opera L'africaine, you can come and be convinced that I am right."

"It's in 3/4!" cried out Chopin, and played, counting aloud while banging the rhythm with his foot! He was angered almost beyond control. But nothing helped; Meyerbeer stood his ground. I am afraid that the rancorous Chopin never forgave him.

People said about Chopin that he was a romantic who hated Romanticism. He loathed Liszt's music, made light of Schumann's works, ignored Mendelssohn's and Schubert's works, and even had reservations about Beethoven's music. The only composers he loved with all his heart were Bach, Mozart, and Bellini, and we can find traces of those great artists in his works. The way in which he integrated Bach's polyphony into his own musical language is almost miraculous.

Had I wished to get personally close to Chopin, I could have done so through our mutual friend, Charles Alkan, who lived in the same building, nay, on the same floor as Chopin at the Square d'Orléans and was a close friend of his. I intentionally refrained from forming closer ties because I knew of his negative attitude toward my coreligionists and I preferred to avoid those cold and distant stares that were typical of his gloomy eyes, no less than the fiery inspiration or the dreamy veil.

My thirst for his music, the drunkenness it brought to me, my complete immersion in it never suffered due to even the slightest bitterness I felt about him on a personal level. I didn't let the trace of even the flimsiest cloud spoil the happiness and the sweetness that penetrated to the inner-most part of my soul and made me discover the existence of strata of feelings that without this artist I might never have known.

18

ALKAN

"I no longer feel French—I only feel the burden of old age." This saying of my late friend Charles Alkan depicts quite accurately the way I feel these days myself when my strength decreases and my illusions are shattered. The plight of an old man who has been denied the best remedies against despondency and loneliness: an open-hearted talk with a close friend. For me to have that kind of chat I have to go to Montmartre or to Père Lachaise and drag my feet between the rows of tombs. My old friend Stephen Heller, this noble soul and gentle friend, has been sleeping his last sleep for four years. He departed in that same gloomy year of 1888 when Alkan also met his death. The only difference is that Alkan took his bow in his unusual, eccentric way, when, while fetching a religious text from the top shelf of one of his many bookcases, the whole library of holy scriptures fell on him. Heller, on the other hand, faded out in his usual modest way, like a candle burnt out to nothingness.

They knew and respected each other, the wunderkind from the Jewish quarter of Pest and the child prodigy from the Parisian Jewish quarter. They were so different in almost every sphere of life and character, but they had one thing in common: those two great artists, magnificent pianists, found true happiness only when it could stay confined between the four walls of their room, immersed in composing, in reading, or in reflection.

Young Heller was dragged by his greedy father through Germany and Austria in an unsuccessful attempt to exploit his talent for pecuniary gain. Only after the youth collapsed from frustration and exhaustion did his father release his grip. He went back to Hungary and left his son to recuperate from the nightmare and to shape his own life according to his own inclinations. Heller caught the eye of Schumann, who made him a member of his Davidsbündler under the imaginary name of Jeanquirit. It was as Schumann's messenger that Heller arrived in Paris with the task of delivering the *Kreisleriana* into the hands of Frederic Chopin to whom the work is dedicated. He did not go back to Germany.

"Of all the cities I know," he told me once, "Paris is the city most suited to be lonesome in."

During his first year here he went on fantasizing about a virtuoso's career, but one day he threw the "wonder device," which he had gotten from his teacher Kalkbrenner, through the window, shattered to pieces the silent keyboard he used to train on, and dedicated himself to composition. Thus he condemned himself to living on the wayside. In spite of the fact that powerful patrons such as Berlioz, Fétis, and Hallé spared no effort to bring his name before the public and even though his compositions, so picturesque and poetic, found admirers and even buyers, he forever remained in the shadow of those who were perceived as being greater than him. Because he was entangled in a hopeless love affair with a lady of the nobility, he forewent, like Alkan, the happiness of family life. Indeed, it was a wise choice he made when he decided to live in the city that was "most suited to be lonesome in."

Here is an excerpt from one of the letters he wrote to me in 1875 when I was on one of my frequent trips to my native Bordeaux. Behind his characteristic words, I still can see his gentle face smiling at me, quiet and generous, and my heart bleeds with longing.

...I am still the same man I have always been, if we overlook those small, unavoidable blemishes and the minor physical unpleasantness that Time showers on those under its jurisdiction. My back is a little bit more bent, my hair is white and less abundant, and my eyesight is not as sharp as it was—but what of it? The spirit is awake, the reasoning limpid and firm, and the judgment has become more humanitarian, more inclined to justice and tolerance, while the passions and desires have calmed down and subsided. I do not mean by this that I am now devoid of feelings and sensations or that I do not crave anything anymore; when we get there, it's the end of it all. It's just that I no longer feel miserable or depressed when things do not develop according to my wishes.

I am essentially an artist, thus never insensible to the attractive power of success; I would have liked the world to appreciate me according to my true value—which I quite understand is not of the first magnitude—and respect my memory after I have left the stage. But when this wish does not materialize, and I realize that I am steadily pushed aside into a corner, I am not dejected. I can say that one of my great achievements these last few years is the ability to swallow disappointments and go on to the next step. Blows are always falling from right and left, but there are also expressions of support coming from unexpected places—a hand stretched out here, an unknown voice encouraging and comforting you there...

I would not like to look like our friend Berlioz who, notwithstanding all his success and the heap of honors bestowed on him, poisoned his days with feelings of frustration, bitterness, and discrimination. "You are unable to understand those things," he would tell me when he wanted to moralize me. "You are completely devoid of ambition. Look at what all your talent and all the prestige you have accumulated over the years have brought you: no money, no decoration, and no status. And all this solely because you did nothing to appropriate it."

And I answered, "You are wrong, my friend. I have ambition like every artist, and I am not at all indifferent to the flavor of success. But since success has turned its back on me, I in turn refuse to feel any kind of wretchedness on account of it, and I say to myself that true happiness is not achieved through external things, but from within a person's heart."

I find it difficult to accept the fact that the death of my friend Charles Valentin Alkan has not inspired greater attention in Paris, where he was born, where, like a comet, his career reached its zenith and then collapsed; the city that, to the best of my knowledge, he left only a few times during his lifetime. While someone's parting usually stimulates his contemporaries to dwell on his personality and his achievements, this has not been the case with Alkan. Here, his death under sensational circumstances merely resulted in yet another chapter of negligence and disregard. It was not only the poor attendance at his funeral—only four people—but that the press, which usually magnifies unimportant incidents into fateful events, showed complete indifference toward one of France's most gifted musicians. Only one journalist, Balthasar Claes, reported more extensively and with deep understanding on Alkan's death in *Le Ménestrel* of April 1, 1888:

> Charles Valentin Alkan has just passed away. He had to die in order to remind the world that he had existed. "Alkan?" more than one

reader will ask. "Who is Alkan?" And indeed, this enigmatic personality is almost unknown to our generation. However, Alkan, the
composer of the Études mineures, of the Préludes and of Les quatres âges remains a unique artist. He invented unheard-of forms and
new sonorities for the piano. He stayed true to his personal identity,
almost to the point of extravagance. He has the right to a position
beside Liszt, Chopin, Schumann, and Schubert. We can find some
Hebrew elements in his work—he was a Jew like Heinrich Heine,
and, like him, a strange and whimsical artist. Besides buffoonery
and mockery, his compositions reveal poetry and a strong individual
sentiment. On surveying the life and the achievements of this unusual man, we detect unexpected enigmatic elements. After extraordinary beginnings Alkan's development was interrupted. This break
in his destiny was, for an artist of his caliber, like having been buried
alive. Was this brought about by his very character, his own desire,
his faults, or possibly by an exaggeration of his qualities? Or, can it
be that our French soil is unsuitable for the development of certain
rare artistic plants? I cannot decide. I only feel I have a duty to recall
the name and work of an artist infinitely superior to many of his
more celebrated contemporaries.

Here is what Céleste, Alkan's elder sister, writes in her memoirs:

Morhange is a small town in Alsace where both our parents' forefathers had lived for many generations. And that is the name our
family adopted when Napoléon, in his endeavor to emancipate the
Jews, recommended they change their names and choose a French
patronymic. Charles Valentin has never revealed what caused him
to change his last name to Alkan, his father's first name. This is the
Greek form of the biblical Elkanah (Josephus, Antiquities of the Jews,
Book V: 342). He possibly meant to choose a Hebrew name, because already as a young man he was conscious of the meaning
of traditional Jewish values and excelled in his knowledge of the

holy scriptures. My other brother, Napoléon, who was never on the best of terms with Charles, interprets the change of the family name differently; in his opinion, Charles intended to draw a distinction between himself and his younger brothers, all of them unusually gifted musicians. He meant to show that there were several musicians named Morhange, but only one Charles Valentin Alkan. If this was really his intention, he did not achieve anything by this move; his four brothers quickly followed his example and also changed their names to Alkan. This induced Charles to call himself from then on Charles Valentin Alkan aîné.

My five brothers and I wished to enter the Conservatoire. With this in mind, we trained from an early age in solfeggio, which was at that time considered the basis for any musical education. Before we could even talk properly, we were able to sing children's tunes, street favorites, opera arias, and prayer melodies, with astonishingly accurate solmization. Our efforts were crowned with success; while we were still children we were awarded first prizes in the exacting art of solfeggio. But Charles outshone all of us when he was honored with this distinction when he was only seven years old. His brother Napoléon eventually became doyen of the solfège class at the Conservatoire and was made a member of the Légion d'Honneur, a distinction Charles forever coveted in vain.

Our father, Alkan Morhange, ran a little boarding school on the rue des Blancs-Manteaux in the Marais (the Jewish quarter of Paris) where young children, most of them from good Jewish families, received an elementary education in music and French grammar. My brother Charles, a pupil at the Conservatoire since he was six years old, gave piano lessons in Father's school. At that time he was a gay and charming youngster, good company to his friends by whom he was admired for his outstanding talent. He was at that time already a well-known piano virtuoso, a favorite pupil of the great pedagogue Joseph Zimmermann, and somewhat of a darling of Parisian society.

At the same time I studied in the vocal training class and I felt proud when Charles invited me to participate as a supporting artist at his public performances. We were very close to one other then, and in contrast with years to come, he imparted to me his thoughts, ambitions, and experiences.

At a soirée given by Princess de la Moscova, Charles noticed a handsome young man who had been invited to play the piano immediately after him. Imagine my brother's feelings when, at the scene of his own triumph, he was to witness a virtuosity that relegated him to second place; tears of vexation and sleepless nights where the outward manifestations of his encounter with Franz Liszt. This, for the first time in his life, shook his confidence in his own abilities. This might have been the first warning sign of future violent and recurrent commotions. In the course of time, however, Charles and Liszt became close friends and mutual admirers. In Liszt's own words, "I do not know any pianist whose technique could be compared to that of Alkan."[24]

Again and again I tried in vain to trace the turning point from where the great change took place in his life. Outwardly everything seemed to progress satisfactorily. He became an intimate friend of Frederic Chopin. To the best of my knowledge, Alkan was the only Jew whom Chopin, who was not free from prejudice, counted high on the list of his confidants. Alkan moved to the Place d'Orléans, the most fashionable center of artistic life in Paris. Soon George Sand and Chopin became his next-door neighbors, along with the famous writer Alexandre Dumas, the ballerina Marie Taglioni, the celebrated pianist Friedrich Kalkbrenner, and many other artists lived in close proximity.

---

24 Liszt was never sparing in the dispensation of compliments about his colleagues. He said the same thing about Bizet. He knew perfectly well that this could in no way endanger his unshakeable position at the head of the crowd of virtuosos.

Meanwhile Alkan's concerts drew considerable attention for their "educational" quality. However, his programs tended to leave room for only a modest group of his own shorter pieces amidst an array of rarely performed masterpieces, such as those of Bach and Handel, Couperin and Rameau, Haydn and Mozart, Beethoven and Schubert, Mendelssohn and Schumann.

I remember the sensational occasion when Zimmermann, Chopin, and his pupil Gutman collaborated with Alkan in a performance of the latter's arrangement of Beethoven's Seventh Symphony. When, a few years later, Chopin was asked to participate in a repeat performance, he pleaded insufficient strength to do so.

Liszt's name never appeared on Alkan's programs. Although Alkan dedicated an important composition to Liszt in which he avoided, as a gesture of high esteem, indications of tempi and dynamics, he never played Liszt's music in public. Liszt reciprocated in kind; while very complimentary, when speaking and in writing, about Alkan's work, he never once played his music in a public recital. "You are a great musician, worthy of the highest praises, but your ways are not mine." This statement, though never uttered openly, was evident in the conduct of both men.

Here I must confess that I sometimes find it difficult to respond fully to the compositions of my friend Charles Valentin Alkan. I never took much delight in fireworks, and neither capriciousness nor the bizarre are to my taste. I do, however, like my friend's music when it expresses emotion. This, however, is a rare treat, because Alkan might have thought that his more "romantic" compositions spoke the language of other composers, such as Mendelssohn, Schumann, or Chopin.

Pauline Viardot ranks in my esteem as one of the outstanding artists of our generation. Here are a few words she wrote about my friend:

When, during the early thirties, at the beginning of my career as a singer, I arrived in Paris from Brussels, I was happy to perform with Alkan as a supporting artist. At that time he was a good-looking and pleasant young man. He surprised and charmed his audience with the outbursts of demonic sounds that he extracted from the keyboard. Alkan always impressed me as if he were shrouded in mystery, and rumors about his private life added to my curiosity. I was told that one of his pupils, a Jewish lady of high social standing whose name was a well-guarded secret, gave birth out of wedlock to a son of Alkan's. As the lady was already married, this love affair remained for him a source of deep and constant frustration. This and other violently emotional upheavals that shook the artist at that time might well have contributed to his unexpected disappearance from the concert stage. After his great performance with Chopin in 1835 he vanished from public concerts until his sensational comeback at the Salle Erard in April 1844. During those years of recluse Alkan no doubt matured as a composer, though he gradually became misanthropic to such an extent that it seriously damaged his career as a piano virtuoso.

The identity of Alkan's son is no secret anymore: he became well-known as Élie-Miriam Delaborde, a brilliant pianist who was one of his father's outstanding pupils. He was also a fine painter, a champion swimmer and fencer, and the owner of a couple of monkeys and parrots. He may have inherited his penchant for birds from his father who, in 1859, composed the *Marcia funebre sulla morte d'un Papagallo*. Delaborde's love affair with Mme Bizet became the talk of Paris. Delaborde never made a secret of this liaison. He only became entangled when a deep rift between Bizet and his wife Geneviève became obvious; and it was Delaborde whom Bizet called in his dying hour, in order to ask him to stand by Geneviève. It should also be mentioned that Delaborde was Bizet's partner in that crazy swimming expedition in the ice-cold Seine, a folly that might well have accelerated the composer's death. The announcement of marriage between Delaborde and Bizet's widow that appeared in a French magazine not long after the composer's demise was premature. In the end, Geneviève married the lawyer Emile Straus, while Delaborde, despite his zoo of monkeys and parrots, married Marie Thérèse de Courchant des Sablons.

One more remark about father and son: rumor has it that Delaborde bore a bitter grudge against Alkan for having denied him full legal status. If this had actually been the case, it is difficult to understand why Delaborde gave duet performances with his father on the *pédalier*, and after Alkan's death became the editor, though reluctantly, of his father's most important piano compositions.

I was present when the aged Alkan played *Les quatres âges* at one of his famous, though intimate, Monday and Thursday appearances in a modest room at Maison Erard. Its third part, called "Un heureux ménage," tonally depicts matrimonial bliss, a happiness the composer only knew in his dreams.

August 23, 1848: Alkan to Georges Sand:

I did not wish to bother you again about myself, madame, but I am so worried—I can wait no longer. My rivals—Marmontel, the most unworthy of them all—are gaining ground each day. I see the Conservatoire threatened by the most unbelievable, the most disgraceful nomination in its history. Come to my help, madame, by being willing to make your voice heard to M. Blanc, however distressing the circumstances may be. Otherwise M. Auber, who does not like me, will dishonor the institution, and in returning the friendship of M. Marmontel will give in to him and ruin my candidacy...

Alkan to M. Charles Blanc (director of the Department of Fine Arts):

> Monsieur, my heart bleeds, my face blushes, and I am ashamed to use such means, but there never has been a more bitter battle between justice and injustice. I therefore break my silence as a last resort. The list of pupils on which M. Marmontel bases his candidacy is not correct. M. Marmontel is simply a solfège teacher who was given M. Herta's class during his absence. The pupils who were obliged to follow M. Marmontel's course were forced to seek lessons outside the college, as M. Marmontel's instruction was not up to par. If you rallied the support of leading pianists such as Liszt, Thalberg, and Chopin, or critics like Fétis and Berlioz, I will be elected.

Alkan to the Minister of the Interior:

> *Monsieur le ministre*, if you would sound out the opinion of the public instead of merely that of a small clique, I should be elected. If you bothered to obtain the votes of the most famous musicians in the whole of Europe, I should be elected. If you take care to judge the competition according to three criteria—performance, composition, and teaching—I will be elected.

With deep regret and a feeling of shame I have to give an account of events toward which my friend mobilized all his energy and inner resources. The outcome, however, was most disappointing, and in addition to other misfortunes, contributed, no doubt, to his general decline. It all happened during the summer of 1848 when Paris and its inhabitants had barely recovered from the February revolution. At that time a bitter struggle of succession was in progress within the Conservatoire, a struggle no less bitter than the general political and social upheaval. Joseph Zimmermann, the head of the piano faculty, had to give in to the growing hostility of Auber, the general director of the Conservatoire, and handed in his resignation. Four pianists were short-listed for this important position; my friend Alkan was, by reputation and ability, the most eligible candidate. Emile Prudent and Louis Lacombe, no mean pianists either, where hardly serious competitors against a musician of Alkan's standing. The last one on the list was François Marmontel who, together with me, went to school on the rue des Blancs-Manteaux, and who was given his first piano lesson by the young Charles Valentin himself.

This Marmontel succeeded in ingratiating himself to Auber until he became the most favored candidate. It is hard to understand how an artist of Alkan's caliber could have pursued this appointment with such single-minded eagerness. He was already so famous both as a composer and as a virtuoso that he could well have done without the prestige of an academic appointment. He could have had a more lucrative income by giving private lessons to a few wealthy pupils. However, Alkan once explained to me that he considered a position at the Conservatoire as the first step in the institution realizing an important educational mission that would bring about a change of values in the musical atmosphere as accepted in France. The arbitrary way in which he was prevented from achieving his ultimate goal caused him bitterness and frustration that, in the end, turned him into a lifelong misanthrope.

September 3, 1848: Alkan to George Sand:

In spite of my obvious rights, in spite of your all-powerful support, I have failed. The Republic that I love ardently allows strange blunders to be made. I felt enthusiastically disposed toward educating a whole generation in the vast field of music. However, I have to give way, not to a worthy or even unworthy rival, but to one of the most accomplished nonentities I can think of...

At this point I have to admit that Marmontel, in spite of a rather colorless start, showed himself in the course of time to be a worthy rival, and during several decades of devoted activity, he produced a generation of distinguished pupils, among them outstanding artists such as Bizet and young Debussy. In his book *Les pianistes célèbres*, he goes out of his way to be magnanimous toward Alkan and not to allow unfortunate bygone affairs to alter his admiration for his erstwhile master. Thus he wrote:

Never in my life have I met someone whose artistic personality was more unusual and obscure than that of Alkan. Some enigmatic features added to his remoteness from the public and to an increasing interest in the man and his work. At a certain moment in our careers a most regrettable misunderstanding brought a rift between us without, however, altering our mutual esteem. Then and now, I have the deepest admiration for this great artist, the untiring seeker and powerful creator.

The death of Chopin, less than a year after these events, strengthened Alkan's desire to withdraw from public appearances. On his deathbed Chopin bequeathed his notes on piano methods to Alkan and to their colleague Reber. To his rare visitors my friend used to read with unending delight from these lessons for virtuosos-to-be whose contents corresponded entirely with his own views and principles.

When I asked him to read some of Chopin's notes to me, he eagerly complied:

Use the pedals very sparingly, at least in the beginning, and also later on. [At this point Alkan would burst into laughter.]

The left hand must act like a conductor, regulating and tempering the right hand.

A clean and even staccato eventually brings about a clean and even legato.

Always practice on the best pianos; never be content with a second-class instrument.

Listen to famous singers. They will teach you how to breathe and how to achieve a smooth ending.

Do not practice more than three hours daily.

Do not allow your hands to jump up into the air as if you wanted to chase doves.

Do not play chamber music with amateurs.

Interpret music as you understand it, but never change the score.

At this point I said to him, "Charles, my friend, now that Chopin has passed away, you are the only surviving composer in this country who writes good piano music. You ought to preserve his innovations."

"His innovations?" Alkan responded. "He was no innovator. He just was himself."

"And you?" I told him. "You also are yourself. I have confidence in you, Charles, I trust you."

"Don't count on me," he replied. "You know as well as I do that I am a broken reed—I am at the end, finished…finished."

"I am at the end, finished…finished," he cried, and for twenty-five years he sulked in solitude. Where had he been hiding? His whereabouts were known only to a small circle of close friends. He moved away from the Place d'Orléans and rented two apartments. When a visitor appeared at the door of one of them, the concierge directed him to the other apartment, only to be told that monsieur was not to be found there either. When the visitor inquired when is he expected to return, the curt reply was, "Never."

This is how one day two men came to his door on official business. As usual, they were sent by the concierge to his second apartment. At the second apartment the usual scene repeated itself. Because of his own eccentricity, Alkan was never awarded the much coveted Légion d'honneur that he had felt he was entitled to and that some influential friends had managed to obtain for him. His brother, Napoléon, was decorated in his place.

Alkan did not trust his old housekeeper who was so familiar with her master's strange ways. He used to leave small paper balls under cupboards or under a couch in order to check that the cleaner was not scrimping her work.

He would purchase his provisions himself. You could meet him at Les Halles in his old-fashioned black suit, with his top hat, choosing butter or bargaining over the price of eggs.

Ferdinand Hiller relates with some humor that long hours were devoted to his "Semitic studies," the Gemara and daily Bible verses translated into French. Alkan used to preface his compositions with quotations from the Bible.

Alkan once told me that if he could live his life over again, he would set the entire Bible into music. And I confided that I had no need for a new life; I was already working on this, having put more than a dozen verses from the Song of Songs to music.

Alkan would cast a quizzical eye at various celebrities, such as Wagner, whose music he rejected as "base materialism," or Clara Schumann, whose piano playing he judged in accordance with his personal inclination. His verdict was unequivocal: "Although her admirers overrate her, her performances have given me considerable pleasure—that is, for a woman. For my taste, women never play really well. They either sound like women or they try to sound like men."

When his housekeeper, who had looked after him for fifteen years, left him, his daily routine broke down completely. He complained bitterly,

> Have you ever made up your own bed? This is an intolerable bother. But what can I do? I may have to rent a single room in the Latin Quarter that will serve all my needs—to play the piano, to study, to eat, to sleep, and I may just have to do the chores by myself. Then, at last, I will not have to tolerate a stranger in my abode. I am more and more becoming a misanthrope with nothing worthwhile, good, or useful to do. My situation makes me horribly sad and miserable. Even musical production has lost its attraction for me; for me, it has somehow lost the deep meaning and high achievement I used to find in it.

In spite of all that, he contacted his publisher from time to time and created fine and impressive masterpieces.

I will quote again from his sister Céleste's memoirs:

> During the days of the war, with the siege and the tribulations of 1870–71, my brother suffered badly. Apart from hunger and fear, his patriotism seemed to dwindle away when confronted with his loyalty to friends, foremost Ferdinand Hiller, the director of the con-servatorium in Cologne.

> He confided in me: "For forty-eight days and nights without respite I have been living in the midst of cannonballs. All I have is a shutter and a piano with a hole through them. I have hardly eaten at all. And now? Shall I renounce my friends because they are Prussians? I no longer feel French—I only feel the burden of old age."

> It seems that these experiences strengthened his resolve to play in public again after his self-imposed retirement for almost a quarter of a century. He meticulously devised a program of six concerts of solo and chamber music, devoted to compositions of every school and

period, mostly for the pédalier. This instrument he had, during years of recluse, learned to handle masterly. Charles was of the opinion that this instrument was exceptionally suited for Bach's organ compositions, even more so than the organ itself.

The concerts were to take place at the Salle Erard. The organization was taken over by our brother Gustave, who seems to have inherited our father's business flair.

Here are Pauline Viardot's impressions of this first concert:

The crowd that attended the first performance witnessed an old and bowed Jew mounting the platform, his face wrinkled, with a sly sparkle in his wise eyes, as if to remind his audience of the limited importance he attached to the event. When he began to play, it became obvious that this was the same virtuoso we had known years ago, but only very few of those present were aware of his innermost tension; for the first time in his life he was deeply disturbed by his newly discovered tendency toward stage fright. This, however, did not perceptibly impede his technique, though some mental and emotional rigidity could be noticed. But he still plays with assurance and perfect clarity; his performance was superb, though it sometimes lacked the divine spark…As an immediate response to his nervousness, he decided to begin giving informal recitals twice a week. From then on, acquaintances, music lovers, and their friends could drop in at Erard's, where a small room had been placed at his disposal.

On May 30, 1888, my friend Charles Valentin Alkan was found stretched out lifeless in his apartment. He had, apparently, been crushed to death by an overturned bookcase. Rumor has it that he tried to take a volume of the Talmud from the top shelf, clutching it to his heart while dying.

As Balthasar Claes wrote, "Charles Valentin Alkan has just passed away. 'Alkan?' more than one reader will ask. 'Who is Alkan?' And indeed…"

19

THE TALES OF OFFENBACH

May 18, 1879

Sleep eludes me. What an evening that was! How did they manage to cram some three hundred people into that place at Jacques Offenbach's home on 8, boulevard des Capucines? What a rewarding and emotional performance that was. I think I'll have to call it the pre-premiere of *The Tales of Hoffmann*.

In this incredibly overcrowded room, Offenbach managed to find me; he embraced me warmly, saying, "I really can't tell you how grateful I am, how much I am indebted to you for obtaining this libretto for me."

"It really required little effort," I answered. "What are old friends for if they can't help bridge some gaps and provide the needed connection for an excellent cause?"

When I said "old friends," I really meant it. I remember the three Offenbachs well—the father, Isaac, and the two sons, Judah and Jakob—on their first Friday evening in Paris, in November 1833. They had found provisional shelter under the roof of the cantor of our synagogue, Gimenez. He brought them to the Shabbat service, and all four of them, Gimenez and the three Offenbachs, took turns saying the prayers. It is engraved in my memory as if it were yesterday. What a remarkable and unusual rendering of the service! Judah has in the meantime changed his name to Jules, and Jakob became Jacques. I knew them well from their first days here in France. I became friendly with Jacques Offenbach during those days when he would run up the stairs in the building on the rue de Montholon, where I lived, to go to our neighbor Fromental Halévy for his free-of-charge lessons in musical composition.

As for the thanks Offenbach bestowed on me, I'm sure this deserves a word or two of explanation.

Two years ago, in June '77, I was in Vienna for a few days. At the opera they had staged a wonderful performance of *Carmen*. Eduard Strauss, who was my host, took me to the beautiful old Imperial Opera House. There, in the foyer, before the beginning of the performance, he introduced me to the composer Johannes Brahms and to Eduard Hanslick, the implacable music critic of one of Vienna's leading newspapers. When Strauss told Hanslick that I was Geneviève Bizet's uncle, he warmed up a little bit, and even told me that his friend Brahms was a staunch admirer of *Carmen* and that he had already been to more than fifteen performances of the opera since it had first been performed in Vienna in October '75.

The following afternoon, I was sitting in the lobby of my hotel, enjoying an enormous slice of cake and drinking a cup of the inimitable coffee they make in this city, when both Strauss brothers,

Johann and Eduard, joined me at my table. Johann said he had met with Jacques Offenbach the previous day and that Offenbach would join us presently. Indeed, a few minutes later, Offenbach, who was staying at the same hotel, came down the stairs and joined us. After the Strauss brothers left, Offenbach said to me, "I arranged this meeting with the Strausses because I needed to talk to you. It has been quite a few years since we had a real heart-to-heart talk—actually, since the Jewish community decided that I am persona non grata due to my conversion to the Catholic faith. This is also the reason I chose to meet you in Vienna, so as not to cause you any embarrassment. I think you can help me in a matter that is of the utmost importance to me."

"*You* need help?" I asked, astonished. "With your reputation and your connections I would think that all doors are open to you!"

Offenbach continued,

Before I get down to the business at hand, I think it will do no harm to give you a little background of what my life has been like since I came to Paris. Time and again, I wonder why it was so hard for me to make my name known to the public, to obtain the recognition to which I think I was entitled. My first real success came to me when I was almost forty, when I opened my little theater in that wooden shed on the Champs-Élysées during the Paris Exposition in '55. Until then I had bent under the burden of responsibilities that sapped my strength and eroded my self-confidence. I had a wife and family to look after; the painful gout that doesn't give me a moment of respite had already set in; the frustration emanating from my fear that my gift for musical invention was slowly eroding—all those things had brought me almost to the brink of despair. Why had fate treated me so harshly? Was it because I was a Jew in a gentile world? Or a German amongst Frenchmen? Or a pauper in a wealthy environment? Or was it perhaps because I was that *enfant terrible* pointing my finger and shouting, "Look, the emperor is naked!"?

In the end it was to this remark that I really owed my success. It is to hear that remark, again and again, in one thousand and one variations, that the public crowded my theaters and stood in long lines at the box office to buy tickets. Rossini once called me "the Mozart of the Champs-Elysées," which is a compliment of which I'm not worthy. I think Ludovic Halévy was closer to the mark when he said that I was "the modern Molière of music." And now the wheel has turned again against me; history has changed its course, and the man in the streets sees clothes where there are none; my empire has gone bankrupt.

They say that I was Napoleon III's court jester. Now that the empire has crumbled, in hindsight everyone has suddenly turned into hypothetical heroes who were, at heart, fighters for the Republic a long time ago. Well, well…if they believe it, let them enjoy it. I could not allow myself the luxury of swimming against the current. I had to earn money, lots of money, to sustain my family and pay my debts— and mostly to support my hobbies, playing cards, smoking, lunches at Riche's, a summer villa on the shore, from time to time a cure at a spa or health resort, entertaining guests in a lavish manner, and my love for beautiful women. But to those who talk ill of me and say that I was willing to sell my soul to the devil to achieve this, I say plainly, that is a lie. The truth is that I found a way to honestly earn a comfortable living for all my employees as well as for my own family, while adding my personal contribution to my country and to art. Did those who would throw rotten eggs at me today spurn and avoid visiting, only yesterday, the theaters where I lavishly produced entertainment and fits of giggles in musical satires through which I portrayed the government and its acolytes? I relentlessly attacked corruption, machinations, betrayals, lies, greed, repression, monkey business, hypocrites, grand ceremonials, and dangerous military adventurism. Is that the doing of a "court jester"?

I can't be blamed for the fact that Napoleon III ultimately turned all this against me just by saying, "Who says there is no free speech in

France? Go to Offenbach's theater and watch his operettas. This is blatant proof of my tolerance." He was probably well aware of the fact that people sitting in the theater and bursting into laughter are not in the mood to climb on barricades. Yes, we had a kind of silent agreement—he permitted me to accumulate a fortune by ridiculing him and his regime, and I returned the favor by allowing him to use me as a shield, an alibi, a kind of sponge to absorb popular frustration, bitterness, and dissatisfaction. The truth is that we shared a mutual aversion of one another while needing each other. And the collapse of the Second Empire brought down my realm and heralded the cataclysm of full bankruptcy. And when you go bankrupt in France, there is nowhere to look for mercy, compassion, or understanding. People suddenly discover not only that you are an enemy of the Republic of old times, but that you are a Prussian, a Jew, an antipatriotic zealot undermining the fundaments of the fatherland— all this in addition to being a decadent, a comedian fishing in troubled water, and a composer whose style is out of fashion.

Here Offenbach went silent, his eyes looking at the shining tiled floor, lost in deep contemplation.

"Tell me, Jacques, is your problem money? Do you need a loan or maybe I can help you with a grant of some kind?" I inquired.

Offenbach laughed heartily and said, "No, thank God that side is under control again. Even if they decided to bury me alive in France, there is still a big world outside. From Cairo to Rio de Janeiro, from Lisbon to Valparaiso, and from Stockholm to New York, my tunes are hummed and whistled on every street corner. And my concert tours in the United States of America have more than replenished my empty coffers."

"Speaking of your American trip, how was it?"

"I hope you don't mean the crossing of the Atlantic on that ship the *Canada*. That was a real ordeal, a true nightmare. I was born to live and walk on solid ground, not on the capricious and constant up, down, right, and left of the waves. But in the end this expedition was worthwhile, not only from a financial point of view, but also as a very interesting study in human nature and cultural diversity."

"Would you care to share some of your impressions with me?" I asked.

"Briefly, here are some of the things that really impressed me," Offenbach readily replied. "In the hotels every room has an en suite bathroom. On public transportation, the tramways and the omnibus, there is no conductor. Nevertheless, everyone pays his fare! It is very easy to get Americans to like you. You just have to say thank you in English and you have passed the test and you are the hero of the day. The women's steps are light and graceful, exactly like those of our Parisian women. And every exertion has its reward—it is worthwhile to make an effort to earn $1,000 for the evening.

"And this is a special dish for you, Hippolyte, with your keen interest in religious music. At the Sunday concert of *musica sacra* the program was Gounod's Ave Maria, Schubert's Ave Maria, then there was a string of Offenbach's 'sacred' music: from *La belle Hélène*, 'Dis-moi Vénus,' and from the *Grande-Duchesse* 'Dites-lui qu'on l'a remarqué.' The love letter from *La Périchole* was transformed into 'Prayer' and *Le mariage aux lanternes* contributed the 'Angelus.'"

I signaled to the waiter, showed our empty coffee cups, and ordered a refill. Offenback continued:

Hippolyte, you've talked about doors being open for me. Taking a look at my life in hindsight, I can assure you that this is the thing I missed most of the time: an open door. All my life I had to knock at those closed doors, knock and knock again. I'll never forget the day in November 1833 when I first reached the French border with my father and my brother. All the other travelers who had arrived together with us in the mail coach from Cologne were permitted to resume their trip after a perfunctory look at their papers. But we were kept for hours in a small and smelly room on the pretext of some negligence in the filling out of the forms. We were asked to explain why we carried two violins and one cello, why we needed all those books, half of them written in Hebrew, the other half in German. And how could we explain that our travel permits were issued in Cologne while our residence was given as Deutz?[25]

My father told me later that his father—my grandfather—had taught him that whenever you go to arrange some official business, it is always wise to have some money with you to pass under the table… we had been robbed, but the first door had been opened and we were now in France.

A short time later it was the door to the Conservatoire that stayed locked. Cherubini was furious when we came to ask for admittance; in his heavy Italian accent he shouted, "What do you want from me? This institution is not a shelter for needy children. And it is meant for Frenchman only—foreigners are not wanted here!" And while my father tried to reason with the director and insisted on showing him the recommendation letters he carried for his gifted sons, I opened the cello case and behind Cherubini's back started to play to the best of my ability. Cherubini turned around. He was stunned and speechless for two full minutes. Then he said, "Parbleu, parbleu, parbleu," and sent me out of the room to wrap up the business of my admission with my father. This is how I succeeded in opening an additional door. This same cello opened the door to the orchestra of the Opéra-Comique where I shared the cello stand with Hippolyte Seligman.

This is where I first learned that you can play serious music in a prankish way. We had a lot of fun at a game that Seligman taught

---

25   Deutz is a large quarter of Köln (Cologne) on the right bank of the Rhine.

me—there was a musical phrase we had to play and we shared the playing fifty-fifty: he played one note, I played the next one, he played one note, and I played the next one, and so on.

Now there is another door that needs opening, and this time you are the man who can open it for me. Here is the matter at hand. I think it is time for me to be concerned about posterity. I do not want to leave this world before realizing the dream I have had for many, many years: to write an opera, a real opera, not an overgrown operetta like Orphée or La belle Hélène, but a real opera. And I have already chosen the subject.

I interrupted to say, "Jacques, you don't have to bother about posterity. Believe me, your name will live on for generations. Thanks to those operettas that you seem to make light of so easily, your fame is assured. No opera I can think of will give you more glory than the laurels you have received and will go on receiving by way of those gems you have created as naturally, as easily, as a chicken lays eggs."

Offenbach did not heed my words, and he continued. "In '51 I saw a play by Barbier and Carré at the Odéon. In this play, the central figure was the poet and musician E.T.A. Hoffmann and they intertwined his personality with the characters and action of some of his plays. A fantastic story and very well done. I immediately thought that this could be the material for a successful opera. But at that time I was not as yet inclined—maybe not yet ripe—to tackle such a subject. But the idea never left me. It nagged at me from the back of my mind. So a few months ago, while having to fight against all the trouble and indignities that have come my way since the crumbling of the empire, I resolved to get in touch with Jules Barbier and ask him to supply me with a libretto based on the play—by the way, not before asking Ludo to write it in collaboration with Meilhac. But he politely declined."

"Yes," I said, "it's been…how long? Three, four…no, five years since Carré died. What was Barbier's reaction?"

"It's hard to believe, but just a few months prior to my talking to him, he finished writing the very libretto I was asking for."

"So everything is perfect; what do you need my help for?" I asked.

"Yes, but he has given that libretto to Hector Salomon—you know, the young choir conductor at the Opéra. And they have signed some kind of contract, and Barbier is unwilling to go back on his word. He says it's a matter of professional ethics. I understand this perfectly. But I need that libretto!"

"So what's the problem?" I wondered. "Go to young Salomon and explain yourself. He's a nice and understanding fellow, and I don't think there will be any issue. As you can well imagine, a little compensation will be needed."

"That is not the problem, Hippolyte, my friend," Offenbach replied. "I'm sure you remember that when I married, one of the conditions Herminie's family insisted on before approving this marriage was that I convert to Catholicism. And when I did—I had to comply to open one additional door—the leadership of the Jewish community ostracized me. No member of the community is allowed to have any contact with me. Hector Salomon is a God-fearing, synagogue-going young man. He will not talk to me. Hippolyte, you are a pillar of the Parisian Jewish community. You are respected and wield a lot of influence. Please, ask Hector Salomon, as a personal favor to *you,* to relinquish the rights to *The Tales of Hoffmann* and let me have the libretto."

So, when back in Paris, one of the first things I did was pay a visit to Hector Salomon. I said he was an understanding young man; my judgment was correct.

In July I met Jacques Offenbach at a rehearsal of *Madame Favart* at the Folies-Dramatiques. He was emaciated and pallid, and despite the nice summer weather we were having that year, he wore a big fur coat. We went to the little café on the corner of the rue de Bondy and the boulevard Saint-Martin, and over a small glass of absinthe I handed him the libretto of *Les contes d'Hoffmann.*

"You *did* open that last door…God bless you! The melodies are already running through my head and I am impatient to put them on paper. Now I will add your name to the short list of people who have earned my eternal gratitude—gratitude for helping me to become what I am, to fulfill whatever it is that I have achieved."

"I think," I said, "that if your intention were to write a full-scale opera, you might have turned to Meilhac and to Halévy, your trusted partners from the merry days of *Orphée* and *La belle Hélène.* With their libretto for *Carmen* they have promoted themselves to the highest ranks in that field."

Offenbach lowered his eyes and with infinite sadness said,

When I begged them—yes, I really mean it; I begged them—to help me realize my dearest dream and write for me the libretto for *The Tales of Hoffmann*, they flatly declined. I had no option but to turn to Barbier. And this is where you came in; here you are, bringing this libretto to me. I fervently hope God will give me the strength to finish writing the music, because I plan to put all my soul into this work. And once again, Hippolyte, let me tell you how grateful I am.

But speaking of Henri and Ludo, I cherish the wonderful memories I have from the days of our first real, big success. Let me remind you of a little story you may have forgotten.

A few weeks after the premiere of Orphée aux enfers, the interest the public had first shown in the novelty it created seemed to be waning. I considered shelving it. That is when Jules Janin, the Jupiter of music critics, sent his thunderbolt from Olympus; he wrote in Le Journal des Débats,

> I went a second time to watch the play, and what seemed
> to me at first sight brilliant and entertaining shocks me now.
> In this opera they strangle and exterminate Orpheus and
> Eurydice, so dear to all music lovers; they stone to death
> the dwellers of that antique world dear to all poets and they
> mock and ridicule the splendid, ancient, and sacred myth.

Crémieux, whose name appears solo on the bill as author of the libretto—though actually Ludovic[26] worked in full collaboration with him—answered in Le Figaro that one should not take the honorable critic's admonition too seriously, since the very section he refers to, that part that brought the audience to the paroxysm of laughter, is just a word-for-word quotation from an article written by M. Janin himself about the dancer Émilie Bigottini. Here is this quote verbatim: "Here you breathe a scent of goddess and of nymph, the sweet smell of myrtle and verbena, of nectar and ambrosia. You can hear the cooing of doves, Apollo's songs and Lesbos's lyre. Here are nymphs, here are muses, and the graces are not far away."

For weeks Janin remained the laughingstock of Paris, and the Bouffes-Parisiens was besieged. It was impossible to get a seat even in the remotest corner of the theater— sold out!

Hortense Schneider tried to get tickets for the Prince of Wales. She ran around for a full day in desperation. In the end she managed to get him a seat in the last row of the worst box. Who knows what she had to pay to get that ticket.

Hortense Schneider! This daughter of a poor German immigrant, a tailor, is the woman who gave my operettas that additional dimen-

---

26 As Ludovic Halévy had a prominent civil service job, he wrote most of his early satires under a pseudonym. He had just started work on *Orphée* when he was promoted to secretary general at the Ministry for Algeria; he couldn't compromise his new position and write burlesque plays for the Parisian public, even under a pseudonym. Offenbach had a hard time convincing him to help Crémieux in his work without being acknowledged as co-author (J.H.R.).

sion thanks to her unique personality. She is that rarity, a born actress and singer in one person.

She needed no training of any kind to develop her talent. Quite the contrary, when she expressed the wish to take some lessons to improve her singing, I immediately vetoed the project and threatened to dismiss her if she ever even so much as thought of that again. By the way, she was born in your hometown, Hippolyte, in Bordeaux. She is as much a part of my success as my very dear partners, Ludo and Henri. She moves on the stage like a born queen; her magic obliterates all the women in the neighborhood while whipping the men into a lethargic state of stupor and open-mouthed admiration.

Her dressing room at the theater looks like the altar of some pagan cult where all the who's who in the world get together. Sometimes I think she believes she is a queen, so natural and almost innate is her poise. She did not play, nor even identify herself with the Grand Duchess of Gerolstein; she was the grand duchess. One day, during the Paris Exposition of 1867, she was riding in her coach to the gates of the exhibition. The porter at the gates asked for her ticket or admission pass; she threw a look of contempt at him and said with a haughty voice and a shrug of the shoulders, "Don't you recognize me? I am the Grand Duchess of Gerolstein!"

As for all the wicked gossip about my relationship with Hortense and the nasty rumors about our having—or having had—an affair, I say, categorically, and I hope you believe me, that it is a blatant lie. This would have been contrary to my basic principles. I have always avoided wearing on my fingers the diamonds that are meant to be sold to the public. Only once did I transgress this rule and that was after a long and arduous inner struggle. Zulma Buffar…this gracious, blonde-haired, blue-eyed muse came into my life at a most critical moment, at the time when I needed to replenish the depleted reservoir of my inspiration with youthful energy. She came along and returned to me refreshed spirits, the joy of creativity, and the rejuvenation of the source of my inspiration. I had to terminate this relationship because one of those eternal keepers of public morality thought it was appropriate to inform my wife of this bond.

My beloved Herminie, the mother of my five children, who had supported me faithfully and with so much consideration as I built my career, suddenly turned against me. She refused to understand; with inflexible determination she refused to turn a blind eye to what I considered to be a basic need for the renewal of my creativity. No arguments could persuade her that my love for Zulma in no way harmed or diminished the deep love I bear in my heart for her, the love that I have cultivated during all these years...my one and only wife. Quite on the contrary, my meetings with Zulma only strengthened my ties to Herminie, the true companion of my life since I reached adulthood. But she was unwilling, maybe unable, to understand the need I had, that insatiable need, like the thirst of a man lost in the desert. I was constrained to give in, to break off the beautiful relationship Zulma and I had. The suffering of my wife draws a red line I cannot cross. Zulma accepted the inevitable and stepped out of my life. But her image as the glove maker in La vie parisienne will be carved on my heart for as long as I live. It was her idea to relegate all the parodies based on ancient history and to strike up a satirical song of praise to the life we actually live today.

I'm not going to try to enumerate the three hundred or so people who were there on that memorable evening; I knew at least half of them personally. There were also at least fifty additional people whom I knew by sight or hearsay but with whom I have had no personal connection. Still, I feel a duty to single out some of the guests just to show how Offenbach had been fair and wise in his choice of people

he had invited. Michel Carré's widow had a place of honor next to
Jules Barbier; Henri Meilhac and Ludovic Halévy were there in spite
of their reticence to tackle the plot and write the libretto of *The Tales
of Hoffmann*. So were Gounod, Saint-Saëns, Fauré, Guiraud, Thomas,
Delibes, Massenet, Lalo, and Chabrier. I knew that Alkan and Lecocq
had also been invited; Alkan didn't show up, probably because he so
cherishes his seclusion, and Lecocq was probably going through one
of his fits of jealousy and animosity. All the artists from the Bouffes-
Parisiens—headed by the old Léonce and Hortense Schneider, who
were almost members of the family—showed up; even Zulma Buffar, in
spite of Herminie Offenbach's reservations, was there. I was pleasantly
surprised to see that Hector Salomon had accepted the invitation
and came in spite of all his religious misgivings. He naturally didn't
touch the food or refreshments offered because of the strict rules of
his religion. Léon Carvalho, the director of the Opéra-Comique, and
Franz von Jauner, the director of the Vienna Opera, sat side by side in
the first row. Jauner had already agreed to stage *The Tales of Hoffmann*
in Vienna.

The three singers who sang the main roles were Mme Franck-
Duvernoy (Stella, Olympia, Antonia, and Giulietta), Numa Auguez
sang Hoffmann,[27] and Émile Alexandre Taskin was the overall villain
(Lindorf, Coppélius, Dr. Miracle, and Dappertutto); Edmond
Duvernoy played the piano.

I don't know what the ruling of posterity will be. I only know that I
came home totally conquered by what, in my opinion, is a masterpiece.
So deeply was I moved that it robbed me of my much-needed sleep. It
is hard and foolish to pronounce a definite judgment after only a single

---

27 Offenbach originally intended Hoffmann to be sung by a baritone; this is why
    Auguez sang it that evening. Somewhere along the way he changed his mind
    (J.H.R.).

and truncated hearing of the work—after all, we only had a piano accompaniment. Offenbach told me that he had only just started working on the orchestration.

"There is one last wish I have," he said to me. "To be granted a few additional days so I may be present at the premiere of my last born, the apple of my eye."

Still, my impression is that *The Tales of Hoffmann* is as far from *Orphée* as *Don Giovanni* is from *Die Entführung*; but it is still, and in the best meaning of the term, wholly Offenbach.

What I said to Jacques Offenbach in Vienna is still true: *Orphée, La belle Hélène,* and *La Périchole* have brought him immortality. But I was wrong in trying to dissuade him from trying his hand at a more ambitious task and getting accepted in the big opera house. *The Tales of Hoffmann* only adds another crown, a brilliant crown, to the laurels that posterity will bestow on him.

On the morning of October 5, 1880, Léonce, who was the original Aristée-Pluton in *Orphée*, happened to be strolling on the boulevard des Capucines. As he always used to do when he was in this neighborhood, he rang at Offenbach's door to inquire about his friend's health.

The servant who opened the door informed him that the master of the house had passed away during the night, "very quietly and without waking up."

Léonce, in a true Offenbachian retort, said, "Well, he'll be very surprised when he becomes aware of it!"

20

BIRTHDAY PARTY

August 6, 1897

Yesterday I celebrated my eighty-fifth birthday. I had planned to have a small reunion here, at home, in Versailles, amidst my closest friends and the remainder of my family. But my niece, Geneviève Straus—formerly Mme Bizet, and before that Mlle Halévy—saw it in a different light. And, as usual, she had her way.

Well, I'm home now, here in Versailles after a very tiring but tremendously enjoyable day in Paris. I am home with my faithful servant of thirty years, Jeanette, and with Magali, who has been my guest for the last two months.

Magali Vieyra-Molina is my late sister Nancy-Rachel's great-granddaughter. She is eighteen and studies singing at the Conservatoire. Until three years ago she used to spend two weeks every winter with me while her parents indulged their hobby of skiing. But since her fifteenth birthday, Magali has joined her family on their annual

Chamonix winter vacation. Being aware of my friendly relations with the famous Pauline Viardot, Magali's parents thought I would be able to ask Viardot for some guidance regarding their daughter's career.

Pauline Viardot is the daughter of the great tenor and teacher Manuel Garcia, and sister of the baritone and world-renowned teacher Manuel Garcia Jr. She was also one of the greatest contralto singers of our time, from 1837 when she gave her first concert at the age of sixteen, until her retirement from the stage in 1863. She came back for one more performance in 1870 in Jena, when Johannes Brahms convinced her to sing the solo part in the first public performance of his Alto Rhapsody, op. 53. She was the most influential singing teacher at the Conservatoire until her retirement fourteen years ago.

Magali's parents thought it would be a good idea for her to spend part of her summer vacation with their elderly relative, Uncle Hippo, as they all call me. And, indeed, when I introduced Magali to Viardot, the uncrowned queen of vocal arts made no bones about giving this youngster some excellent advice. She actually insisted on seeing her once a week to give her a lesson. I will not try to describe Magali's elation; this was beyond her wildest dreams.

When I asked Viardot about her fees, she mentioned a ridiculous sum. I laughed and told her that if she would charge me at her normal rate it would certainly not ruin me and if she chose to treat me as a friend she could easily not charge me at all. But what she asked for was absurd. She said to me that this was a matter of principle; in her long experience as a teacher, she has learned that people who did not pay for their lessons would, most of the time, not take their studies too seriously. "I never give lessons free of charge," she insisted. I told her how Offenbach, shortly after his arrival in Paris, a penniless youngster, received free lessons in musical composition from Fromental Halévy. And, I said, Offenbach certainly took full advantage of those lessons. She said that this was the exception that proved the rule.

Then I remembered two previous pupils I had brought to her: Marguerite Romain in '71 and Lina Bernhardt in '73. Both of them could easily have afforded her normal rate. But as a friendly gesture toward me she chose to charge them only a nominal fee. What's more, she invited these two pupils twice a year to a lavish supper that certainly cost her more than she earned from them. Then, jokingly, I pointed out that she, her sister Marie Malibran, and her brother Manuel Garcia had, all three of them, received their musical training free of charge. I was jesting, of course, as it was their famous father who had trained them, but Viardot chose to answer me with complete seriousness. She said,

> That is a different matter. Within the family questions of money should never be raised. If some relative is in need, he should get all the help he can from family. If you have the money to help him, *give* it to him, never lend it to him. Lending money within the family almost always ends in bad feelings and can even lead to a rupture.

This was something for me to chew upon.

Geneviève had decided to celebrate my birthday in style at her place in Paris.

Almost ten years after the death of her husband, Georges Bizet, Geneviève had married again. The groom was the prominent lawyer Émile Straus, a relative of the Rothschild family, and the best man at the wedding was indeed Baron Edmond de Rothschild. The marriage took place on October 7, 1886, at the rue de la Victoire synagogue.

In the spacious house where she lives, she runs a salon that draws the *Nec plus ultra* of the Parisian intellectual elite: writers, artists, scientists, politicians. In regular attendance and kneeling at Geneviève's feet in adoration was a group of youngsters calling themselves "the young geniuses," of which Geneviève's son Jacques Bizet is a prominent member. A youngster with a jet-black mane and golden eyes named Marcel Proust is foremost amongst them. He doesn't stop quoting my niece's witty utterances and showers her with bouquets of flowers and letters bathed in perfume. Herewith is a sample:

> …First I thought that all your love was centered on beautiful things—until I found out that they actually mean nothing to you. Then I thought that your love was directed at human beings. But I quickly had to admit that you actually could not care less. So I came to the inevitable conclusion that the only thing you really love is the style of life that you have adopted, and this is because that style emphasizes your charms: your shrewd wit, your gift for the majestic way you walk amongst people, and not the least your wardrobe. And because you are so bewitching, don't you dare deceive yourself into thinking that your efforts to lessen my love for you have been crowned with success. To prove to you that the contrary is true, I'll send you flowers more beautiful than those I sent in the past, notwithstanding the fact that this will anger you, because you dislike my feeling of admiration that is so deeply immersed in pain.

> The humble servant of your indifferent haughtiness,

> Marcel Proust

For my birthday party Geneviève invited the usual crowd she has at her salon, the sharpest wits in the artistic circles of Paris. She sent her carriage to bring us, Magali and me, to her place at the boulevard Haussmann. Two of her regular guests have recently stopped coming to her salon—the painter Jean-Louis Forain and the novelist Paul Bourget. The reason for this "betrayal" is their adherence to the "other side." Today in France everyone has taken sides in the matter that, these last three years, has divided public opinion into two bitterly opposed factions: those who believe that Captain Alfred Dreyfus is innocent, and those who think he is a traitor. Geneviève's salon is the hub of the Dreyfusards movement, and naturally those among her usual circle who displayed ultranationalist and right-wing, clerical opinions are no longer welcome.

All this reminds me of the very pertinent things Rabbi Zadok Kahn said five years ago. In August 1892, we commemorated—after almost a six-month delay—the thirtieth anniversary of the death of my brother-in-law, the eminent composer Fromental Halévy. A small group of those who respected his memory assembled at the family vault in the Jewish plot at the Montmartre Cemetery. Here is an excerpt from what I wrote in my diary on my coming home that evening:

At the outset we believed that it would be suitable to have representatives of the government, the Institut, the Opéra, and the Conservatoire present. But on second thought we refrained from inviting them. The reason was that the turbid atmosphere already pervading in Paris relating to the death of the young Jewish officer Armand Mayer last June, would have unintentionally turned the commemoration into a political manifestation.

Armand Mayer was a captain in the French army, whose family left Alsace after it was annexed to Germany following the 1870 defeat. Following the publication of an article in Drumont's newspaper *La Libre Parole*, accusing the Jews of serving in the French army of cowardice, Mayer challenged Drumont's partner, the Marquis de Morès, to fight a duel. Armand Mayer was killed in this duel. This incident only added fuel to the ongoing polemics concerning the rights of Jews in our French society.

Still, notwithstanding our wish to avoid any kind of political utterances, we could not refuse Rabbi Zadok Kahn's offer to hold a funeral oration. He is the chief rabbi of Paris and, since 1889, the chief rabbi of France. Though he did not mention the actual events explicitly, he hinted at them obliquely:

We commemorate today the memory of a great Frenchman and a great Jew; a musician who has made a generous contribution to the enrichment of the culture of this country and, at the same time, with his opera *La juive*, he has raised his voice to glorify the valor and the endurance of the Jewish people. A great Frenchman and a great Jew! Who knows better than us that these two entities are the same, because the principles of liberty, equality, and fraternity, which enthralled the heroes of the French Revolution, are also an integral part of the principles guiding Jewish morality. And those trying to deny this, whether they are hot-tempered nationalists or unyielding Jew-haters, are denying the spirit of history.

Barely two years later Captain Alfred Dreyfus, a young artillery officer also of Jewish Alsatian descent, was condemned (on what was obviously trumped-up evidence) to life imprisonment on Devil's Island. Last year new evidence uncovered the truth. But there seems to be a conspiracy in high places aimed at covering the facts, shielding the real culprit, and hindering the progress of justice. This scandal seems to be far from being resolved and in the meantime it has caused such uproar that it endangers the very essence of our democratic republican regime.

All this carries me back to what I wrote following our visit to the Montmartre Cemetery five years ago.

These last few years the list of names engraved on the inner wall of the family mausoleum has grown significantly; among them are the names of the composer's wife (my sister Léonie née Rodrigues) and the composer's brother, the writer and scholar Léon Halévy, one of the earliest of Saint-Simon's supporters.

Léon Halévy's son, Ludovic, has aged tremendously. I made a quick reckoning and found out that the brilliant librettist of *La belle Hélène* and *Carmen* is on the threshold of his sixtieth year. Unlike his usual self, he looked dejected and introspective; he was probably musing at the sight of Esther Halévy's name. She was the wonderful elder daughter of the composer, who is also resting here. Her death in the prime of life, a few weeks prior to their wedding, delivered a cruel blow to him in those far-off, remote days, and only by summoning all of his strength was he able to conquer his grief and resume his life. The young woman whom he finally chose to fill the gap left by our beloved niece, and who is the mother of his two gifted sons, Eli and Daniel, was Louise Berger. Berger's father was an enterprising watchmaker of Neuchatel who emigrated from Switzerland to Paris. He initiated many improvements in the mechanism and design of traditional watches and clocks. The Berger family was, and still is to this day, one of the pillars of the Calvinist congregation of Paris. As Ludovic was the son of a Jewish father and a Catholic mother, he had to find a solution to extricate himself from this entanglement; he adopted the obvious and most reasonable option for him and his family: the absolute negation of religion.

Young Jacques, Geneviève's son from her marriage with Bizet, stood somewhat apart from the crowd, next to his cousin Daniel Halévy, Ludovic's son. They had both just completed their studies at the exclusive Condorcet boarding school, where Mallarmé was their literature teacher. At that time they were in the process, together with their friends Marcel Proust, Henri Barbusse, Léon Blum, and others, of publishing a literary periodical they called *Le Banquet*. In the cemetery, with the voice of the cantor rising with the *El male rachamim* (God full of mercy, a traditional prayer for the dead) as a solemn background, these two handsome youngsters seemed blatantly out of place.

My daughter-in-law and my granddaughter did not come to the ceremony, despite my explicit request. Since the passing away a few months ago of their husband and father, my son Edgar, our relations have become strained and this causes me quite a bit of sorrow and misery.

A publishing house has recently started the publication, one volume at the time, of the French version of the series that includes Graetz's *The History of the Jews*. This has become an important event in the spiritual life of our congregation. I signed up for a subscription to this series for my granddaughter. I wrote to her, "I have no doubt that on reading the different chapters of these monumental treaties, you will feel proud of the heroism and magnanimity our people have shown over the centuries in the face of oppression and persecution at the hands of strangers, mostly stemming from ignorance." I never received a reply to my letter, and I'm afraid that this present, with all its meaningful intentions, is doomed to stand on the bookcase with its pages uncut, let alone read by anyone!

♪ ♪ ♪ ♪ ♪ ♪

On our way out to the cemetery we passed near Offenbach's stately grave. We lowered our gaze to avoid seeing the cross topping the tombstone. With all due respect to the symbol of Christianity, I still ask what this conspicuous display means. When this son of Isaac Levy Eberst Offenbach, the cantor from Cologne, took an unfortunate step in order to be accepted into the bosom of his beloved wife's family, he certainly never dreamt he would have to bear this burden into the next world.

Further down the same path we met Heine's tomb, where the cross is blatantly missing. In his will Heine made a clear provision relating to this matter. We stopped there for a short while and read again the beautiful short poem "Wo?"[28], so sincere, which encircles the poet's name like a funeral wreath.

But allow me to come back to the party. After a light snack—which was, needless to say, of the highest quality—Saint-Saëns sat at the piano and played a toccata by Bach. Then Ludovic Halévy recited a poem he had written especially for the occasion with many hidden hints about my character and my overall activities.

This brought gales of laughter all around.

Our host Geneviève, with her well-known, sharp-witted pen, had concocted a biography of me written in pseudo-biblical style in which she reported on my childhood in Bordeaux, my studies at the Conservatoire and at the University of Paris, and my literary and musical activities along with my successful entrance into the world of finance. She praised the depth of my culture and reviewed the long list of celebrities I had befriended during my life; most of them, I'm sorry to say, departed years ago.

---

28 See chapter seven.

My young friend Albert Cahen played a work he had composed for the occasion: Fantasy for Piano on Themes by Jacob Hippolyte Rodrigues. He was rewarded by thunderous applause. I must admit that amongst the fireworks and the pyrotechnics it was hard to recognize the themes that I supposedly had donated.

The editor Michel Lévy, who has published all my books, listed them all with critical appraisal that was highly flattering. He said,

> In his book *Les trois filles de la Bible*, he made an extensive study concerning the points the three monotheistic religions, Judaism, Christianity and Islam, have in common. The author seems to be convinced that in their actual form these religions can give no answer to the problems of human morality. This is why he tries to sketch the basic rules for a general reform that would help build a modern religion based solely on science and philosophy, admitting no revelations outside the recognized laws of nature. In his exhaustive study concerning Jesus's life and the origins of Christianity—a work much more comprehensive than the works of Renan, Havet, and Peyrat—he draws the conclusion that, in spite of the accepted view among scholars that the veracity of the Gospels is very doubtful and even contradictory in many places, they have built an imaginary personality on the unquestioned acceptance of these dogmatic writings. He goes on to prove that Jesus's teaching was in perfect accordance with the teachings of the different Jewish schools of his time, or as M. Munk put it so well, "The Sermon on the Mount ran through the streets of Jerusalem long before it was uttered." Then he asks the pertinent question: If Jesus's doctrines were so very much identical to Jewish Orthodoxy, why was he put to death?

> M. Rodrigues's explanation is that Jesus's predications were as much political as they were religious and that his condemnation was a political act condoned by the Pharisees as a result of an aborted popular uprising.

I won't bore you any more now by trying to describe the depths of M. Rodrigues's erudition and original thinking. I just wanted to whet your appetite so that tomorrow you all will feel so curious that you will run and buy his books.

After this torrential flow of words, it was time for music to raise its voice. Magali was asked to sing and she was accompanied at the piano by no less a star than Pauline Viardot. I may be forgiven for mentioning here that Mme Viardot has also made a generous contribution to our musical heritage as a composer, and that as a pianist she was at one time a pupil of Liszt and is able to hold her own with any professional performing artist. Magali sang Bizet's "Adieux de l'hôtesse arabe," which is a song based on a poem by Victor Hugo, a song that always moves me very deeply. She continued with "La chanson du pêcheur" (The Fisherman's Song), one of the songs Gabriel Fauré dedicated to Viardot. The words are by Théophile Gautier and in spite of it having been composed during the same period in which Bizet wrote his "Adieux de l'hôtesse arabe," it is so different, so forward-looking and modern, especially in terms of harmonic progressions. Every time I hear it, it leaves me puzzled and with a strange ambivalent feeling of groping for emotional balance while attaining full gratification. This same poem by Théophile Gautier was set to music by Berlioz over twenty-five years ago in his *Nuits d'été*. Comparing both versions, I suddenly realize how much our world has changed in two decades and to what unfathomable depths our musical language has evolved.

The songs were greeted by such enthusiasm and excitement that the two artists were compelled to give an encore. They had been prepared for this eventuality and they performed one of Viardot's favorites, a song by Johannes Brahms, "Von ewiger Liebe" (About Eternal Love). This song was totally unknown here and caused a minor sensation. To my great surprise, in the select group of intellectuals and artists gathered here, the name of Brahms was known only to a very small minority of professional musicians. Viardot was showered with questions about this seemingly tremendously gifted German composer whose style was such a far cry from what was normally expected from German musicians, most of whom are under the overpowering influence of Wagner's followers these days.

I was rather proud to add my personal contribution to Viardot's learned explanations. I recounted how I had met Brahms during my visit to Vienna twenty years earlier. Eduard Strauss had taken me to an excellent performance of *Carmen* at the Imperial Opera House, and there he introduced me to Johannes Brahms, who I suppose was then in his mid-forties. Brahms told me that he was an unconditional and enthusiastic admirer of *Carmen* and that he had been, as of that day, to sixteen performances and planned to go on listening to it. Only then did I tell him that I was the uncle of Geneviève, Bizet's widow, that I had known him well for years, and that I admired the man as well as his music. Brahms seemed very impressed. He avidly asked me about Bizet's other works, and also inquired about his personality. I was rather happy to be able to satisfy his curiosity. Eduard Strauss told me later that Brahms was the spearhead of the "traditional" current in German music and that his musical language was deeply rooted in the heritage of Beethoven.

To my great sorrow, I had to break the news of Brahms's death, earlier this year, to Geneviève's guests. This news had reached my ears only a few weeks ago.

Augusta Holmès then went to the piano and sang, to her own accompaniment, two songs: Bizet's "Le gascon," and her own composition, "La fleur qui va sur l'eau." The lyrics of both songs are by her companion Catulle Mendès, the father of her four children. Her warm contralto, in spite of having lost some of its nimbleness, had certainly gained in depth and richness of color, and the rendering was, as usual with Holmès, masterly. I think she must be fifty years old now, but she has lost nothing of her magnetic personality and of her feminine attractiveness. But obviously I'm talking from the point of view of an eighty-five-year-old philanderer.

Then there came the real surprise of the evening for me: Magali, without my knowledge, had taken from my library one of my little compositions, a setting for an a cappella choir of Psalm 112, and somehow managed to find some printer willing to make a few dozen copies of it. Surreptitiously, she had given everyone present a copy, asking them to hide it until the right moment—and this was the moment! Almost everyone present was to some extent, some with more others with less accuracy, able to read music; suddenly everyone had a copy in his or her hand and we had a wonderful rendering of my Hallelujah.

Hallelujah; ashrei ish yare et Adonai bemitzvotav hafetz meod. (Praise thee, O Lord. Blessed is the man who feareth the Lord.)

Then Catulle Mendès raised his voice and said, "We all want Hippolyte to say a few words. But before that I want to remind everyone present that Uncle Hippo, as I have called him all my life, has been an example to me since my early childhood and has been a friend and mentor ever since. He actually got his first notions of reading, not in French but in Hebrew, together with my late father, in the small synagogue in their hometown of Bordeaux."

I had prepared a written speech, but when faced with all the warmth and friendship surrounding me I spontaneously decided to improvise and say the things that my heart dictated to me on the spot: "My dear Geneviève, my dear friends: I can't tell you how happy you have made me by coming to this wonderful party, showing how much you all love me. You were right, dear Geneviève, when in your entertaining biographical sketch you emphasized my special gift for friendship. In all modesty I proudly claim that in this field, and in this field alone, I'm a true creative artist. And amongst the host of friends I gathered, there have been three prominent ones who have reciprocated friendship and with whom I have built three durable relationships based solely on our mutual appreciation, understanding, and love.

"The first was my friend from our school days on the rue des Blancs-Manteaux, Charles Alkan, a great artist who was struggling hopelessly to get the recognition that was his due.

"Then there was Stephen Heller, a pianist and composer of gigantic potential. His noble heart and introverted personality would not allow him to raise a finger to fight for a place in the sun.

"The third and youngest of them, my beloved Georges Bizet, was overflowing with talent and torn by inner struggles. His immense genius was acknowledged only when it was already too late. By dedicating to me the score of one of his greatest masterpieces, the incidental music to the play *L'Arlésienne*, he filled my heart with indescribable joy and pride.

"And now, my dear friends, one last confession: I had a visionary goal, a hope that would reunite Jews, Christians, and Muslims in the bosom of one humanitarian creed, in peace and brotherhood, in full accordance with the universal laws of wisdom. A few minutes ago Michel Lévy presented a general idea of the immense task I undertook in connection with this belief of mine. But a cruel reality woke me from my dream and slapped me in the face, bringing me down to earth and guiding me back to my original sources. An innocent officer convicted of a crime he did not commit, only because of his Jewish origins, opened my eyes to the fact that the world is not yet ripe for the vision of our prophet Isaiah. So, dear friends, let each of us keep what is his and cultivate his own heritage. And let us pray for an era of justice, wisdom, and truth."

There was no applause when I finished, but each of those present came to me to hug me or shake hands before leaving and dispersing, each to his or her own destination. For me this was an eventful evening, full of emotional reminiscences.

This is where my great-granduncle, Jacob Hippolyte Rodrigues, finished his chronicle.

He died quietly in his sleep, on Shabbat, July 23, 1898, at the age of eighty-six. We buried him three days later in the Jewish plot of the Père Lachaise Cemetery.

Magali Vieyra-Molina

CREDITS

Blom, Eric, ed. *Grove's Dictionary of Music and Musicians*. 5th ed. New York: St. Martin's Press, 1954.

Curtiss, Mina. *Bizet and His World*. New York: Vienna House, Inc., 1974.

Newman, Ernest, ed. *Memoires of Hector Berlioz, from 1803 to 1865*. New York: Dover Publications, Inc., 1966.

Rissin, David. *Offenbach: ou, Le rire en musique*. Paris: Librairie Arthème Fayard, 1980.

Rosenthal, Harold and John Warrack. *The Concise Oxford Dictionary of Opera*. London: Oxford University Press, 1974.

Silbermann, Alphons. *Das imaginäre Tagebuch des Herrn Jacques Offenbach*. Frankfurt: Verlag Ullstein, 1969.

Wikipedia

Various material was copied (with the gracious permission of the relevant authorities) at the Bibliothèque nationale de France and at the archive of the Library of the Conservatoire national de musique de Paris.

The National Library at the Hebrew University of Jerusalem was also an important source for relevant information.

The bulk of chapter eighteen (Alkan) was translated from the Hebrew by **Dr. W.J. Alkan** (Rehovot).

THANKS

To my wife Rica for her relentless support and perceptive criticism. To Sophie Waksman for her initial help in tracking Hippolyte Rodrigues's biographical notes; to Colette Kouchner for her indefatigable sleuthing to make sure that some of the relevant details I used in the text were actually accurate; to David Shenhav, who devoted so many hours of his precious time to read most of the manuscript and who so graciously "unhuged" my hanging participles; to Kathleen Roman for her professionalism and the many useful suggestions from which I shamelessly benefited. And mainly to Hugo N. Gerstl, who, apart from correcting grammar and syntax, read through the manuscript, chapter after chapter, with indefatigable patience, suggesting changes to make the book more attractive and readable.

www.ingramcontent.com/pod-product-compliance
Lightning Source LLC
Chambersburg PA
CBHW052028090426
42739CB00010B/1819